GLOBALIZATION, URBAN PROGRESS, URBAN PROBLEMS, RURAL DISADVANTAGES

This research was financed by the Austrian Science Foundation

Logistical support and housing was provided by INPF/INDER
(National Institute for Physical Planning/
National Institute for Rural Development) Maputo

The production of the manuscript was supported by the
Austrian Ministry of Science

*Dedicated to the demonstrators of Seattle and London
at the end of 1999 and all their supporters around the globe*

Globalization, Urban Progress, Urban Problems, Rural Disadvantages
Evidence from Mozambique

STEFANIE KNAUDER
University of Vienna

LONDON AND NEW YORK

First published 2000 by Ashgate Publishing

Reissued 2018 by Routledge
2 Park Square, Milton Park, Abingdon, Oxon OX14 4RN
711 Third Avenue, New York, NY 10017, USA

Routledge is an imprint of the Taylor & Francis Group, an informa business

Copyright © Stefanie Knauder 2000

All rights reserved. No part of this book may be reprinted or reproduced or utilised in any form or by any electronic, mechanical, or other means, now known or hereafter invented, including photocopying and recording, or in any information storage or retrieval system, without permission in writing from the publishers.

Notice:
Product or corporate names may be trademarks or registered trademarks, and are used only for identification and explanation without intent to infringe.

Publisher's Note
The publisher has gone to great lengths to ensure the quality of this reprint but points out that some imperfections in the original copies may be apparent.

Disclaimer
The publisher has made every effort to trace copyright holders and welcomes correspondence from those they have been unable to contact.

A Library of Congress record exists under LC control number: 00131624

ISBN 13: 978-1-138-73683-2 (hbk)
ISBN 13: 978-1-138-73681-8 (pbk)
ISBN 13: 978-1-315-18569-9 (ebk)

Contents

List of maps and figures	vii
List of tables	ix
Preface and acknowledgements	xii
List of abbreviations and explanation of terms	xv
General information on Mozambique	xvii

PART I: INTRODUCTION AND THEORETICAL BASIS

1	Areas of inquiry and methodology	5
2	Urbanization and globalization	23

PART II: THE TWOFOLD GAP AND THE RURAL – PERI-URBAN – URBAN CHANGES

3	Socio-economic characteristics of the three investigated areas: poverty and relative prosperity	65
4	Poverty and dissatisfaction – job satisfaction	87
5	Migration as a consequence of globalization	95
6	Housing in the two urban worlds and the neglected countryside	107
7	Housing and services as problems	151
8	Female household heads	157
9	Urbanization and the decline of specific social interactions	173
10	Satisfaction and depression in favourable and extreme adverse conditions	193

PART III: GLOBALIZATION AND POVERTY

11   The root causes of Third World poverty in a globalizing world   219

12   Aspects of an alternative development and an alternative globalization   245

Bibliography   269

Appendices   291

List of maps and figures

Map 1:	Mozambique	xvii
Map 2:	The city of Maputo	12
Map 3:	The city of Beira	13
Map 4:	The province of Maputo with control village Massaca 1	17
Map 5:	Overbounded Beira with control village Nhangau	17
Map 6:	The province of Sofala with control village Mutua	18
2.1	The growth of Africa's urban population in relation to the total population	60
3.1	Household income of the lower strata of the cement city of Maputo, the peri-urban areas and entire Maputo	66
3.2	Educational level of household heads by type of area	73
3.3	Participation of the household heads in the labour force	75
3.4	The household size	78
3.5	The age of the household heads	80
4.1	Dissatisfaction with income	88
4.2	Dissatisfaction with the level of education	90
4.3	Job satisfaction	91
5.1	Previous residence by province	101
5.2	Support of and contact with relatives by province	102
6.1	The cement city of Maputo; fully urbanized area	109
6.2	A typical reed house in the peri-urban areas of Maputo with an interview in action	110
6.3	One of the better cement block houses in the peri-urban areas of Maputo	110
6.4	A pau-a-pique house under construction in the peri-urban areas of Beira	111

6.5	A completed pau-a-pique house in the peri-urban areas of Beira	111
6.6	Typical reed houses in the village Massaca 1 with grass roofs	112
6.7	Houses in the village Mutua with the female interviewers of Beira	112
6.8	The age of the houses	115
6.9	Improved traditional latrine with small hygienic slab	124
6.10	The water problem in the peri-urban areas of Beira	125
6.11	School children in a classroom in the peri-urban areas of Maputo	131
6.12	Mutual help and contact with members of the same religion	138
6.13	Kind of shopping facilities used	143
6.14	People awaiting treatment in front of the hospital in Beira	144
8.1	Proportion of age groups of the female household heads compared with the male heads and their wives	165
8.2	The size of the female and male headed households	166
8.3	Educational level of female household heads, male household heads and their wives	167
9.1	The feelings of isolation and loneliness	176
9.2	The frequency of visits by household heads to relatives in the same bairro	179
9.3	The frequency of visiting friends in the same bairro	184
9.4	The frequency of visiting neighbours	186
10.1	Scale from 'very unhappy' to 'very happy'	196
10.2	Scale of being cheerful from 'very rarely' to 'almost every day'	197
10.3	Degree of suffering at this time	198
10.4	Degree of depression on the day of the interview	199
10.5	Overall changes of life since the introduction of PRE	204
10.6	Prospects for the future	209
10.7	The linear structural relations with one independent variable	212
10.8	The linear structural relations with two independent variables	212
11.1	Source areas of slaves and countries of destination	227

List of tables

3.1	Distribution of households with none or some unemployed members	76
3.2	Marital status of household heads	81
5.1	Main reasons for migration of male household heads	96
5.2	Area of birth of household heads by province	99
5.3	Time of rural – urban and rural – rural migration by province	100
6.1	The house walls	113
6.2	Who constructed your house?	116
6.3	Estimated size of the houses	117
6.4	The number of rooms per house	118
6.5	Sanitary facilities	123
6.6	The water supply	124
6.7	Means of transportation to work	126
6.8	School attendance of children between 6 and 14	132
6.9	School attendance of juveniles between 14 and 20	133
6.10	The religion of the household heads	135
6.11	The frequency of going to church	136
6.12	Opinion about the multi-party system	139
6.13	The frequency of visits by the household heads to the barracks	141
6.14	The frequency of watching football of male household heads	142
6.15	The use of health facilities in the first place	145
6.16	The use of health facilities in the second place	145
7.1	Proportion of evaluation of housing and services as problems	151
7.2	Proportions of evaluation of housing and services as a serious problem or a problem, with the differences between the areas	152

8.1	The distribution of the two kinds of household heads by area	159
8.2	The monthly income of the female household heads, the male household heads and their wives	160
8.3	The monthly income of the female and male headed households	161
8.4	Other activities of housewives (multiple response)	163
8.5	Position in the labour force of the female household heads, the male household heads and their wives	168
9.1	Kinds of assistance the household heads give to their relatives who live in the same bairro	181
9.2	Friends of household heads in the same bairro	183
9.3	Assistance household heads give to their friends in the same bairro	185
9.4	Kinds of assistance the household heads give to their neighbours	188
9.5	Main reasons for conflicts	189
10.1	Comparison of combined happiness variables between Maputo and Beira	201
10.2	Time period in which life was or is most difficult	202
10.3	The main problems of the household heads	206
10.4	The most appreciated aspects of life	208
10.5	Correlation matrix for selected single or combined variables	211
11.1	Correlation of the level of urbanization with GDP per capita, HDI and HPI of 1995	221

Tables in appendix 2

Table 1 Demographic characteristics and income of major Third World countries	314
Table 2 Demographic, economic and human development indicators of large developing countries	316
Table 3 Indices of large Third World countries for which not more than one index was missing	319

Additional tables in appendix 3

3.1a	The monthly wage of household heads	320
3.1b	The monthly wage of household heads by province	320
3.1c	The monthly income of households	320
3.1d	The monthly income of households by province	321
3.1e	Comparison of the percentages of the transformed total income of households of the cement city and the peri-urban areas of Maputo of this study with the percentages of the IAF of entire Maputo	321
3.2a	Educational level of household heads	321
3.2b	Educational level of household heads by province	321
3.3a	The participation in the labour force of the household heads	322
3.3b	The participation in the labour force of the household heads by province	322
3.4a	Household size	322
3.4b	Household size by province	323
3.5a	Age of the household heads by province	323
3.6a	Marital status of household heads by province	323
3.7a	Wives of household heads	323
3.7b	Wives of household heads by province	324
4.1	Discontentment with income by province	324
4.2	Dissatisfaction with the level of education by province	324
4.3	Satisfaction with the participation in the labour force by province	324
4.4	Satisfaction with job conditions by province	324
5.1a	Main reasons for migration by province	325
5.1b	Time of arrival in the respective bairro by province	325
10.1a	Scale from 'very unhappy' to 'very happy' by province	325
10.2a	Scale of being cheerful from 'very rarely' to 'almost every day' by province	325
10.3a	Degree of suffering at this time by province	326
10.4a	Degree of depression on the day of the interview by province	326
10.5a	Time periods in which life was or is most difficult by province	326
10.6a	Overall changes of life since the introduction of PRE by province	326
10.7a	Housing in the last three years by province	326

Preface and acknowledgements

In order to carry out a 'relevant' research with Mozambicans in Mozambique, I went there in October 1990 after a long struggle, lasting almost a decade, to find financial support and after acquiring a medium level knowledge of Portuguese. Belonging to the Austrian and European solidarity movement of the 1980s, for which Mozambique was a shiny example in building a new socialist society, it was extremely painful to find by then a very capitalist society with the widening gap between rich and poor, with a high crime rate and a high level of corruption. Both were almost absent in the decade after the political independence of Mozambique in 1975. In addition, the war was still raging in full scale and there was a drought with hundreds of thousands of dead before I left in mid 1992. My previous Africa experience, namely five years in Zambia, where there was no war, no drought and no falling back into capitalism as she – in spite of her state philosophy of humanism – never had really left it behind, did not prepare me for this ocean of sufferings I saw around me and in the daily news. It all affected me deeply. The contradiction could not have been deeper between all this severe human hardship and the academic exercise I was trying to carry out, which lost all its relevance against the background of such massive human tragedy. However, after nine years of slow progress with setbacks, breaks and difficulties, the book materialized, but the question remains: will it bear any fruits in the direction of less human sufferings and more social justice? Will it be at least one of a, say, billion efforts which are probably needed to change the present trend of economic globalization to a globalization with a human face? One can only hope so without ever being able to measure its effects. Constituting an Austrian prerequisite for the attainment of the 'right to teach' (venia) it will go a long way at least in creating awareness of Third World problems among students.

Numerous people contributed to the completion of this research, but three of them have acquired special merits and I feel particularly grateful to them. Firstly, to Professor David Thorns of the University of Canterbury in Christchurch, New Zealand, for his very valuable and encouraging comments during this last year. Secondly, to Professor

Margaret Peil of the University of Birmingham in Britain for many very useful comments on a previous version in 1996. Thirdly, to the economist and statistician Erwin Triebkorn of the Central Statistical Office in Maputo, who supplied me, in spite of his own heavy work load, all along with the newest data of Mozambique, of which the most valuable were those of the first representative sample census of the rural areas of Mozambique of 1996/97. Without his support this research would not even have half the value as my results could have been considered out of date and the rural sample as too small. The census of Mozambique of 1997 was published only after the text of this book was completed. Regarding rural poverty, the book has still sad actuality and my results are, unfortunately, not out of date.

I am grateful for comments also to the Professors Friedhelm Streiffeler of the Freie Universitaet Berlin, Elísio Macamo of the Wissenschaftskolleg in Berlin and Sabine Blaschke of the University of Vienna as well as to Richard Langthaler from OEFSE (the Austrian foundation for development research) and Martina Neuwirth from Jubilee 2000.

The city planner Paul Jenkins, then at the Ministry of Construction and Water in Maputo, who not only gave me comments on the first Portuguese version of the research report in 1993, but also assisted me there in various ways, particularly with the selection of the areas of investigation, deserves my special thanks. Due to his wise guidance, the sample of the peri-urban areas can claim to be representative.

I would also like to thank my two research assistants, Flora Ventura, for her valuable co-operation during my stay in Mozambique and Margrit De Colle for a few, but very efficient months in Austria. Here my thanks go also to my professional typesetter Michael Baiculescu and my professional proof reader Ingrid Susan Janusch. For possible remaining mistakes I bear full responsibility.

In Mozambique I am grateful to the now Minister of Environmental Affairs, Bernardo Pedro Ferraz, then at the environmental section of the INPF/INDER, who was my first contact concerning the planning of the research and after arriving in Mozambique he eased off a number of my initial difficulties. I am also grateful to the two Directors of the INPF/INDER, João L.V. Nhamposse and Felix Mandlate; there also Mário Macamo, Anastásio Namburete, João Simango, Armindo Chauque and Raimondo Nhaka deserve my thanks. In Beira, where I received a very warm welcome, I wish to thank Abdul Taybo Hassane, then in charge of physical planning of the province of Sofala and his diligent assistant Angelo Eugênio.

If I would mention all the people who have assisted me in one way or the other the list would have to be at least three times as long. May all the others receive my cordial 'thank you' without mentioning all the names. Thanks go to all the interviewers, who carried out a cumbersome task with dedication and responsibility. I am very grateful to all those kind and hospitable people who were ready to give the interview – there were hardly any refusals – because without their information this book could not have been written; yet, here the painful contradiction starts again: the majority of them were living in poverty and there they still remain, while another costly book is presented. It can only make sense if its analysis is an eye-opener for some readers and if we all join forces in the struggle for the eradication of poverty.

In this sense I finally want to thank my publishers for their almost endless patience and kindness in spite of my repeated delays in handing in the manuscript.

I also acknowledge with thanks the permission of Oxford University Press to reproduce one table from each of the two volumes edited by Josef Gugler: *The urbanization of the Third World* of 1988 and *Cities in the developing world* of 1997 which constitute the major part of appendix 2 of this book.

Vienna, November 1999   Stefanie Knauder

List of abbreviations and explanation of terms

Action Aid: an international development agency working in 24 – mainly heavily indebted – poor countries.
AIM: Agência de Informação de Moçambique (Mozambican News Agency).
Bairros: neighbourhoods, smaller units than a district, comprising around 200 to 500 families. The term is mainly used for the neighbourhoods in the peri-urban areas (although in a strict administrative sense the first district is also divided into bairros) Bairros is basically the equivalent for squatters, upgraded squatters and Site & Service Schemes.
Bretton Woods Institutions: the IMF (International Monetary Fund) and World Bank, established in 1944 in Bretton Woods.
Cement city: (cidade de cimento) fully urbanized area or urban area of European character in the major cities of Mozambique with predominantly high-rise, concrete buildings. In Maputo and Beira the cement cities constitute the respective first districts (see map 2 and 3).
DNE: Direcção Nacional de Estatística (Central Statistical Office), now called: Instituto Nacional de Estatística (National Institute for Statistics).
Eurodad: European Network on Debt and Development, established in 1990; a network of European NGOs in sixteen European countries with a secretariat in Brussels.
FRELIMO: Frente de Libertação de Moçambique (Mozambican Liberation Front), founded in 1962; was leading the liberation struggle from 1964 to 1975, when Mozambique became politically independent. Since then it was the ruling party until the first multi-party elections in 1994 which were won by Frelimo.
Grupos dinamazadores: political action groups established by Frelimo during the 1974/75 transitional government in neighbourhoods and work-places. They continued to exist in cities as the lowest level of the party and as the lowest level of the administrative structure in the bairros until 1994.
HDI: Human Development Index.

HDR: Human Development Report.
HIPC: Heavily Indebted Poor Countries.
HPI: Human Poverty Index.
IAF: Inquérito às Famílias (inquiry into families), a comprehensive three stage sample census: Maputo 1992/93, provincial capitals 1994, urban and rural areas 1996/97. Each stage consisted of four moduli and lasted one year. IAF was carried out by the DNE, the last stage by the INE.
IDA: International Development Association.
IDC: International Debt Commission.
IFIs: International Financial Institutions.
INDER: Instituto Nacional de Desenvolvimento Rural (National Institute for Rural Development).
INE: Instituto Nacional de Estatistica, the new name for the Central Statistical Office since 1996.
INPF: Instituto Nacional de Planeamento Físico (National Institute for Physical Planning), established in 1983. It was administratively incorporated into INDER in 1991.
MST: Movimento sem terra (movement of the landless) in Brazil.
Non-urban areas (áreas não urbanizadas): basically squatters; they do not have demarcated plots and are spontaneously settled, poor areas. The term has been questioned in recent years.
Peri-urban areas are also called semi-urban areas; these include squatters, upgraded squatters and Site & Service Schemes (see map 2 and 3).
Renamo: Resisténcia Nacional de Moçambique (Mozambican Resistance Movement).
SADC: Southern African Development Community.
SAPs: Structural Adjustment Programmes.
Semi-urban areas (áreas semi-urbanizadas) are mainly upgraded squatters and Site & Service Schemes.
Site & Service Schemes (S&SS): urban areas developed on virgin land. Plot and infrastructure is provided by the city council or other organizations, but people have to build their very low cost houses themselves. Sometimes loans for building materials are available. The term is used in African cities in general.
sSA: sub-Saharan Africa.
Upgraded squatters: plots were demarcated and a basic infrastructure and basic facilities were provided to already existing spontaneous, unplanned settlements. The term is used in African cities in general.

General information on Mozambique

Map 1: Mozambique

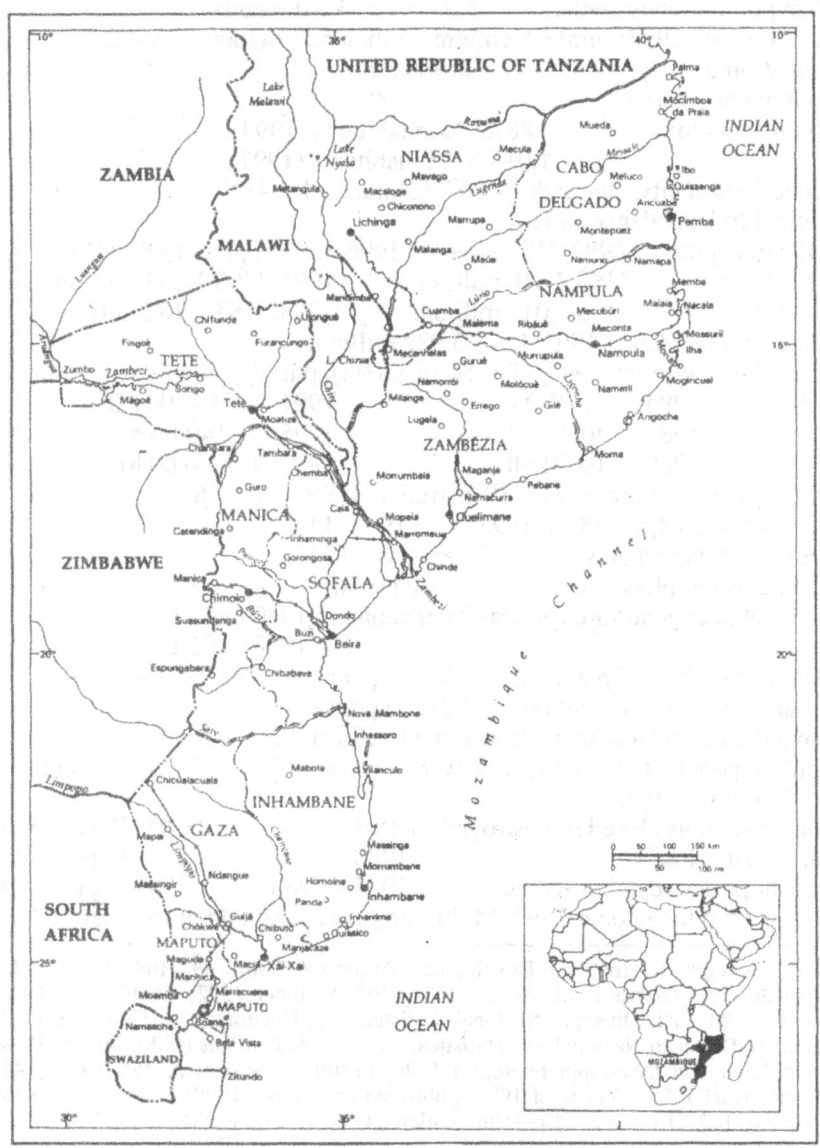

Source: Map No. 3439 United Nations, April 1987

Area: 799.380 km^2;
total population 1997: 16,100,000; 29 per cent urban (1997);
during the war, refugees abroad: 1,725,000,
internally displaced: 3,750,000;
population growth rate: 2.3 per cent;
urban population growth rate: 5.3 per cent (estimated);
fecundity rate 1997: rural 6.8 children; urban 5.2; Maputo city 4.2;
population density: 20.1 per km^2;
economically active: 5,870,000;
capital Maputo: 887,600 inhabitants (1994),
1,015,300 inhabitants (1997),
second largest city, Beira: 307,300 inhabitants (1994).
political Independence in 1975
GDP per capita: 1992: US$ 86,9 1996: US$ 96,4 1998: US$ 131
GDP 1980: US$ 2,810 million 1991: US$ 1,253 million;
1984: US$ 2,012 million; 1998: US$ 2,182 million;
total of foreign debts: 1991: US $ 3,982 million;
Mozambican currency: singular: Metical (Mt), plural Meticais
1 US $ = 1985: 43.18 Mt 1991: 1,434.00 Mt
1986: 40.43 Mt, 1996: 11,140.00 Mt
1989: 710.00 Mt, 1999: 12,500.00 Mt
estimated level of poverty (1989 as well as 1999): 62 – 66 per cent;
infant mortality (per 1000): 1992: 162; 1997: 146;
average life expectancy: 42.3 years (1997);
inhabitants per physician: 50,000 (1990);
government expenditure for health per capita in 1980: 4.00 US$,
in 1988: 0.05 US$
literacy rate 1975: 7 per cent, 1980: 28 per cent, 1997: 40 per cent;
primary school enrolment rate 1991: 63 per cent;
during the war which intensified around 1980 and lasted until 1992
1 million people died, many more were mutilated; 300.000 children were
severly traumatized.
Primary schools closed or destroyed 1983 – 1987: 2,600 (45 per cent),
health posts closed 1982 – 1987: 820 (31 per cent),
rural shops destroyed or looted 1981 – 1988: 3,200 (50 per cent).
Peace accord in October 1992; Multi-party elections held in October 1994.

Sources: Swedish International Development Authority 1988, i, 11; Ripken 1987, 233; Brochmann and Ofstad 1993, 23, 24, 153 – 164; Wellmer 1992; World Bank 1985; Pélissier 1988, 722; Direcção Nacional de Estatística, Documento 2, Fevereiro 1994, 21 and 56; Direcção Nacional de Estatística, Inquérito às Famílias (IAF), Janeiro 1994, xi and 3; Human Development Report 1994; Instituto Nacional de Estatistica, IAF, Relatorio final 1998; Census of 1997: published in October 1999; Summary: in AIM Report No. 167, October 18, 1999; International Organization for Migration 1998.

PART I
INTRODUCTION AND THEORETICAL BASIS

As in any kind of real historical crisis, there exist real choices that can be made. Those who discern them lucidly and act on them with concerted effort are less likely to lose the outcome they prefer than those who put their faith in the unseen historical hand.

Terence K. Hopkins and Immanuel Wallerstein
The age of transition – Trajectory of the world system, 1945 – 2025

Is the world moving inexorably toward one of those tragic moments that will lead future historians to ask, why was nothing done in time?

Ethan B. Kapstein
'Workers and the world economy', *Foreign affairs*

Cities are centres of civilization, generating economic development and social, cultural, spiritual, and scientific advancement which affect the entire human race.

Habitat Agenda 1996

Cities are the key to one of the most important processes of the next century, namely, globalization.

The Forum of Researchers on Human Settlements

Rural areas are places God forgot.

A school teacher of Mukunashi, north-western Zambia

1 Areas of inquiry and methodology

Introduction

The processes of internationalization the predecessors of today's globalization started already within the precolonial times and intensified in the colonial era. However alongside with the processes of internationalization and globalization continues now, as in the previous periods, a process of marginalization of large parts of the developing countries from the benefits of globalization. Although this research tries to take the point of view of the excluded and disadvantaged, advocating social justice and development for all instead of power and wealth for a few, it has, on the other hand, also to acknowledge the positive effects of globalization and the role of the North. Apart from the global aspirations which were inherent also in the communist system, globalization is now, just as in the past and as it will be in the near future, intrinsically related to capitalism; this does not mean that a non-capitalist globalization could not be possible in the far future. It is, however, crucial to raise awareness to the need for change in the global order. Although this research is to a large extent empirical, the presentation and interpretation of the survey results, the analysis of rural and urban poverty as well as the analysis of progress and relative prosperity of some city areas can only be meaningful, if they are seen in the context of globalization and marginalization. Reference will be made to the Southern African region, Africa as a whole and to the Third World in general.

When Mozambique gained her political independence in 1975 after 13 years of liberation struggle, she inherited a twofold gap which in its essential feature is a characteristic of most Third World countries, namely the gap between rural and peri-urban areas and the gap within the cities between the fully urbanized areas, in Mozambique called 'cement city' (cidade cimento), and the semi-urbanized or peri-urban areas, in Maputo called 'reed city' (cidade caniço). What distinguished Mozambique from most of the other developing countries was the resoluteness of the FRELIMO-government to close both gaps. Even if the exodus of the Portuguese had left a serious lack of technical and administrative know-how, the leadership had learned how to mobilize the people during the liberation struggle. After all, a Portuguese army of 30,000 soldiers supported by the NATO was defeated by the Mozambican guerrilla movement (Pinsky 1985). Therefore, it was the intention of the new government to organize the participation of the people to find solutions to the enormous problems in the rural areas as well as in the poorer areas of the cities, solutions developed and carried out by the people. Priority was given to agricultural production. The second main focus was transport and communication and the third objective was the improvement of housing conditions and general living standards (Pinsky 1984).

It was clear that excessive rural-urban migration could be stopped only by improving the quality of life in the countryside, (e.g. education and health care). The leadership was also convinced that a general improvement of living conditions in the rural areas could only be achieved by the construction of communal villages, because only through these would it have been possible to bring the expensive infrastructure which could never reach all the scattered settlements in remote areas. Therefore, in the first few years of independence 1,350 communal villages were constructed for 1.8 million people. They were partly a continuation of those settlements which had already been established during the liberation struggle in the liberated areas, and they were also established in the same localities where the Portuguese used to imprison the Mozambican people in constructions similar to concentration camps, and further they were organized after the big floods in 1976 and 1978. It was planned that by 1990, 60 per cent of all peasants would live in communal villages (Hanlon 1986). In the peri-urban areas of the cities self-help projects were organized (Seavfors 1986). However, notable success in developing communal villages as well as self-help projects was achieved only before 1980. After that, the undeclared war of the then racist South Africa against Mozambique started to destroy large parts of the countryside encompassing increasingly larger areas and caused a considerable decline in Mozambique's flourishing economy. This war, one of the most inhuman and brutal, ever to hit Africa, was to a large extent ignored by the mass media of Europe and the West. Renamo (Resistência Nacional de Moçambique = Mozambican Resistance Movement) and its slaughtering of the civilian population was even unofficially supported by certain right wing circles of Europe and the USA (Austin 1994).

There has been peace in Mozambique since 1992. However, as we will see, the problems are still manifold with the urban – peri-urban and the peri-urban – rural gaps still widening.

Areas of inquiry

The Department of Town and Country Planning of Maputo requested an analysis of the housing problem in the peri-urban areas of Maputo and Beira and an analysis of the process of rural-urban migration. However, in order to grasp the situation of peri-urban dwellers, the disadvantaged 'world' in the cities, it is necessary to compare them with rural dwellers on the one hand and inhabitants of the fully urbanized areas, the privileged urban 'world', on the other. A housing study must include an analysis of socio-economic data as well as infrastructure and social facilities. Even more important than these for a sociologist and psychologist are the people who live in these houses and use the infrastructure and facilities. To what extent do they consider all these as a problem; how do they interact with each other and what is their level of satisfaction and depression. Ignoring the difference between women and men and between female headed and male headed households would deprive the research of an essential aspect. In addition, it is interesting to compare the capital city, Maputo, clearly primate, with the second largest city, Beira.

It can be assumed that the socio-economic and housing situation of the peri-urban dwellers of the two cities is worse than the situation of the inhabitants of the fully urbanized and in many aspects Europeanized areas; because the latter live, so to speak, directly within the economic and political power centre, they benefit to a large extent from globalization, but not in all aspects. Serious problems existed with the 25.000 flats of Maputo as far as maintenance was concerned (Pinsky 1985). In Beira the situation was and is still worse. The comparison between the two 'worlds' in the cities seemed to be worth while also as normally Third World urban sociologists do not distinguish or at least do not compare these two city areas expresis verbis, but deal with urbanization in general or with the poor urban areas only.[1] Recently Castells has made this gap within the cities a specific topic of Latin America (Castells in Schabert 1991), Becker et al. (1994) deal with the differences within the cities of Africa and Hardoy and Satterthwaite (1989) show the gaps within Third World cities in general.

The growth rate of cities in developing countries is three times as high as the growth rate of cities in industrialized countries (Drakakis-Smith 1987). The main growth occurs in the poorer urban areas. This rapid increase of the urban population causes serious problems for the majority of Third World countries and Mozambique is no exception in this regard. In spite of all these problems it can be assumed that the poor urban areas, particularly in their socio-economic aspects, including housing, infrastructure and social facilities are better off than the rural areas. Chief among the reasons of the disadvantages of the latter is their dispersion and another their economic and political weakness. No case study comparing rural – urban inequalities exists for Mozambique, but considering Africa and the Third World in general, the majority of the numerous urban sociologists have established the advantages of the poor urban areas compared to the rural areas (Perlman 1976, Peil 1984, Peil and Sada 1984, Gugler (ed) 1988). In spite of all the research, scattered voices never ceased among sociologists and economists even in recent times, who question the disadvantages of the rural population compared to the urban poor (Jamal and Weeks 1993, Becker et al. 1994, Hardoy and Satterthwaite 1989). Particularly outside the small circle of Third World urban sociologists the belief is still widespread in Europe as well as in Africa amongst scientists and non-scientists either interested or not in development aid that the most disadvantaged part of the population of any developing country lives in the poorer districts of the urban areas. As it is the hope and the intention of the author to reach a wider readership than just urban sociologists, it is necessary to investigate the relationship between these two areas anew and for the first time as far as Mozambique is concerned.

The widespread belief that life in poor city areas in the developing world in general is worse than life in the countryside directly touches the concept of 'over-urbanization' which Gugler (1982, 1988 and 1997 as well as Bradshaw and Noonan 1997) tried to revive. An attempt will be made to refute this concept once again and to show that the improved position of the peri-urban dwellers is at the same time not the cause of the worse position of the rural dwellers.

The analysis of rural-urban migration is essential in the context of this particular area of inquiry. Already in the late 60s and the beginning of the 70s numerous studies investigated this phenomenon (Kuper 1965, Kay 1967, Mabogunje 1968, Jackson (ed) 1969, Janson 1970, among others; for more recent analyses see Elwert and Fett (eds) 1982, Swindell 1995, Parnreiter 1995). Most researchers also dealt with the causes of migration and showed that migrants act economically and rationally when they move to urban areas in spite of the problems they encounter in the urban setting. The magnitude of the gap in Mozambique will be examined in this study.

The process of urbanization is also a process of Europeanization and globalization. Group solidarity is in many aspects substituted by individualism. It can be assumed that, if social integration is measured by the frequency of visiting and mutual assistance of relatives, friends and neighbours only, it decreases with the level of urbanization from the rural via the peri-urban areas to the fully urbanized areas. This thesis has nearly all the classics, but also modern literature as its basis (Wirth 1938, Weber 1958, Simmel 1964, Sjoberg 1955, Pfeil 1972). However, Abu-Lughod (1969) questioned this aspect of the theory of urbanization of the classics (namely that with the process of urbanization impersonal relations increase and personal ones decrease) as valid only for European and North American but not for African cities. Yet, she did not distinguish between the two urban 'worlds'.

Against the background of the widespread belief concerning happy rural life in developing countries it became worthwhile to try to measure the degree of satisfaction and happiness in the poor rural areas and the two urban 'worlds'. It was expected that rural life is not so happy but full of hardship and that, therefore, the rural population would be the most unhappy of the three groups. Already with the first stage of urbanization, when people either move to the peri-urban areas or when they are born there, both can be seen as the first stage or level of urbanization,[2] the degree of happiness increases compared to the rural areas. On the second level of urbanization, by either moving to the privileged part of the city or having been born there, the degree of happiness increases again compared to the peri-urban areas and at the same time, of course, the degree of depression decreases. This thesis is based on the theory of basic human needs and needs in general. Maslow's hierarchy of the fulfilment of human needs apparently still has its validity.[3] In the villages the basic needs of food, clothing and housing are not fulfilled. This lack cannot be substituted by even the most wonderful social integration.

In spite of strong arguments for the highest degree of happiness in the privileged urban areas, not all aspects of life there seem to be privileged and it was therefore still necessary to investigate it. Many people in Europe, as for instance environmentalists and members of green parties, consider city life, particularly living in blocks of flats as unpleasant. Also in Zambia flats above the ground floor where one could not reach the open space immediately were quite disliked by the people and site and service schemes and official low cost houses were preferred (Knauder 1982). Mitchell (1971) observed that in communally-oriented societies even overcrowding is considered less of a problem than living far above the ground. Many questions are still open and the highest degree of happiness in the fully urbanized areas has not been proved so far.

In addition, it would not be sufficient to prove only all the above discussed assumptions concerning the differences between the three areas, but it remains also necessary to look into the magnitude of the two gaps and in particular into the conditions of the three areas as such. To what extent does poverty or even misery exist on the one hand and relative prosperity on the other hand and what are the many facets and effects of poverty? And then there is the crucial question of why people are so poor or relatively well off. Dispersion and lack of economic and political power on the one hand and proximity to a power centre on the other were mentioned as part of the internal causes. But what do they mean in all their complexity? And what are the external and international factors? In what way does globalization and marginalization affect the life of the people not only in Mozambique but also in the Third World in general? The effects of globalization can partly be brought to light through a social survey, but not the underlying phenomenon and mechanisms as such. In order to look into that as well as to find the possible solutions, a wide ranging, interdisciplinary study of literature was necessary.

The method of the survey

The empirical investigation was carried out in three phases:

The first phase:

Fifteen structured interviews were carried out with people in leading positions for planning and urban renewal: Mozambicans and expatriates working in UNDP-projects or as volunteers with various organizations. They were mainly urban planners, architects, and engineers, since social scientists did not have these positions. This phase had three goals: to get more general information about the peri-urban areas and assistance in their selection so that a representative sample could be achieved; to discuss the questionnaire and effective measures for urban renewal. (This last part was later abandoned as the study expanded.) After the construction of the questionnaire, the above mentioned experts as well as social scientists from the Centre for African Studies at the Eduardo Mondlane University were asked for comments.

The second phase: the selection of the bairros and interviewing the authorities in these bairros

The bairros were selected according to their distance from the centre, so that they would be evenly spread across the city, with semi- and non-urban areas proportionally represented as well as the range of standards of housing, facilities and infrastructure. (Nine bairros were selected in Maputo; see map 2– and four bairros were selected in Beira, but only after the survey in Maputo province was completed; see map 3).

After the selection of bairros, and after the permission from the district authorities to carry out the survey, 22 interviews with a structured questionnaire were carried out in Maputo only with two or three people responsible for these bairros. These were normally the secretary and some members of the 'grupos dinamizadores'. This was essential for setting up the main questionnaire. At the same time these visits gave us the opportunity to get acquainted with the authorities of the bairros and vice versa before we arrived with a larger group of interviewers.

The third phase: the survey proper

The representative sample:

The pilot studies A pilot study of 39 interviews was carried out in one of these selected bairros, Polana Caniço A, in order to test the questionnaire and to train the interviewers. Additional training for weak interviewers took place in Maxaquene B.

The research in Sofala was carried out with the same questionnaire as in Maputo. The pilot study in Mananga had mainly the function of training the interviewers there, but also for the principal researcher to get acquainted with the peri-urban areas in Beira.

Sampling After making considerable amendments to the questionnaire and coding almost all questions, 1 per cent of the households in the nine selected bairros in Maputo and the four selected bairros in Beira was

12 *Globalization, urban progress, urban problems, rural disadvantages*

Map 2: The city of Maputo

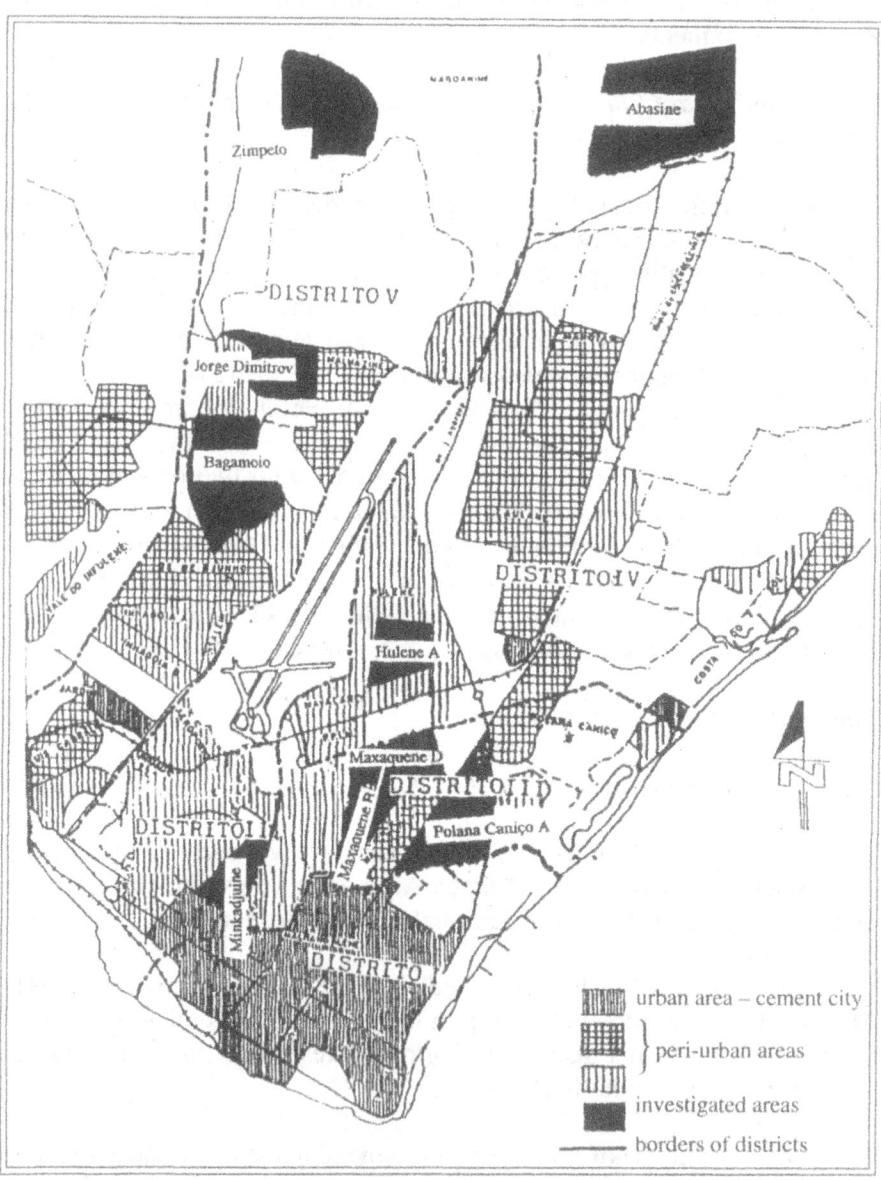

Source: INPF – Instituto Nacional de Planeamento Físico, Maputo

Map 3: The city of Beira

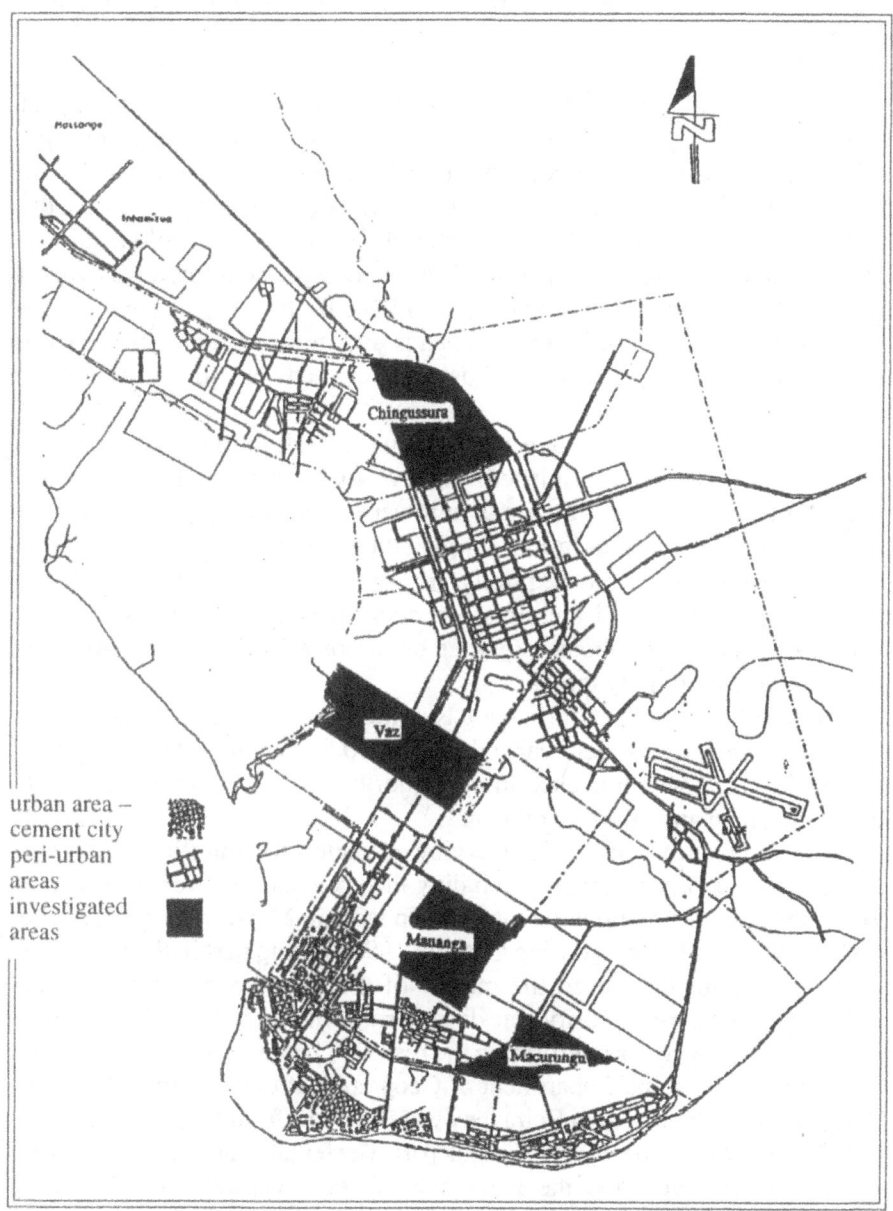

Source: Serviço Provincial de Planeamento Físico de Sofala, Beira

selected from household lists in the Central Statistical Office, choosing every hundredth household, starting each bairro with a different random number.

The interviewing We tried to interview the household head and his first wife in each selected household. However, including the control groups, this was possible only in 48 per cent of the households: in 15 per cent of the households wives were substituted for the male household head as the husband could not be met, in 13 per cent only the male household head was interviewed as the wife could not be met and in 5 per cent there was only a man (single, separated, divorced or widowed). In 13 per cent of the households women were household heads and in 6 per cent women were quasihousehold heads as their husband worked in South Africa or Swaziland.

Three attempts were made to reach the household head and his first wife. After the team had finished, three of the best trained interviewers continued to make further attempts to lower the number of missing cases, but in 13 per cent of the original sample either name or house number was wrong, so we did not find the family. In 11 per cent of the selected households, in spite of several attempts, we could neither meet the household head nor his wife, so about a quarter of the original sample is missing. Refusals were extremely rare.

In the 13 selected peri-urban areas which constitute the representative sample 591 interviews were carried out in 330 households. The sample of household heads which is used in the majority of the tables consists of 30 per cent women and 70 per cent men.

One female and one male interviewer visited the families. The team consisted of six or seven pairs, including the principal researcher, who was part of the team throughout the interview phases in Maputo during July and August 1991 and in Beira during October 1991. Taking part in the interview process, undoubtedly raised the morale of the interviewers and gave the author much more security in discovering interviewer mistakes and valuable experience for interpreting the results. The interviewers in Maputo were students from the Department of Geography at the Eduardo Mondlane University of Maputo and in Beira they were students from a technical school. In both cities staff of the two INPFs took part. The female interviewer normally interviewed the wife and the male interviewer interviewed the husband. However, as the questions are not at all sensitive to sex, they were allowed to shift if this could solve language problems (see below).

Areas of inquiry and methodology 15

The authorities of the bairros were extremely helpful during the interview phase. They distributed petitions to the selected households, signed by the INPF, so that people in formal employment could stay at home on the day of the interview (see appendix 4). However, they could not take away all the hardship from us. Walking two hours in 10 to 20 cm deep sand in the hot, tropical sunshine just for one interview in some peri-urban area was no exception.

The language The interviews were carried out wherever possible in Portuguese or otherwise in local languages: in the province of Maputo in Changana and Ronga and in the province of Sofala in Ndau and Sena. Originally, the questionnaire was translated into Changana. However, it was discovered later, that this was not very useful for the interviewers, who were not used to reading local languages and preferred to translate directly from the Portuguese. Unlike the British, the Portuguese colonizers never bothered about local languages (as they kept the educational level of their colonies at a minimum anyway) so few people can read and write in them. (Mainly the churches promote writing in African languages.) More than half of the interviews in the peri-urban areas were carried out in Portuguese; almost all in the cement cities and even 29 per cent in the villages.

The control groups

The control groups for the fully urbanized areas, the cement cities in Maputo and Beira were chosen from lists of the APIE[4] of run down buildings which were to be rehabilitated by a World Bank programme. In Maputo 35 households (5 per cent) out of 694 households on the list were chosen. The percentage was even higher in Beira. The selection of buildings in bad condition helps to substantiate the assumption concerning the gap between the peri-urban areas and the cement cities in the sense that the differences between the peri-urban areas and the cement cities as significant as they are in this survey, would even be greater if a representative sample of the latter would have been chosen (not only run down buildings).

Three villages were selected as rural control groups. One in the province of Maputo in the district of Boane, Massaca 1 (see map 3; the '1' after the name of the village, which has nothing to do with the English word 'massacre', only distinguishes this village from the neighbouring one:

Massaca 2) was founded in 1981 as a consequence of the war. People were forced to move closer to the district capital in order to receive protection by the Frelimo army. This village was atypical in a threefold sense: firstly, being created recently, it was set up more or less as a model village and was well organized. Secondly, it was only a few kilometres from the district capital Boane and thirdly, it had some industrial employment opportunities nearby (e.g. an orange processing plant). No lists of households could be obtained before the day of interviewing so each interview pair was assigned four families in two sections so that all sections would be represented.

Two villages were selected in the province of Sofala. One, Nhangau, was within the city boundaries of Beira but about 20 km away from the cement city really deep in the bush (see map 4). Because of rapid expansion city boundaries are sometimes well beyond any built up area. It would have been completely inadequate to include this settlement in the peri-urban sample as originally planned because it was so different from all the other areas and had an exclusively rural character. With the exception of the centre it was of a lower standard than Massaca 1, particularly as far as the quality of houses was concerned. In addition it was in a war zone, where people did not dare sleeping in their houses since the last Renamo attack which had occurred almost one year before our interviews took place.

Here we had selected a 1 per cent random sample but, unlike in the peri-urban areas where substitution was not allowed, it was permitted to interview other families as well, since many household heads could not be present as they had to work on the shore (agriculture and fishing) and it would have been too costly to visit the village a second or even a third time.

The third village was selected further away from any provincial or district capital but on the safe Beira corridor, which was protected by Zimbabwean troops from Renamo. The village Mutua is situated about 60 km from Beira. Here we selected only a quarter of the huge village and tried to include families of all sections of this quarter but with female interviewers only as the male interviewers had to remain in Beira in order not to risk forcible recruitment into the army. Mutua was nearest to a typical village (see map 5).

All three villages can be considered privileged, each in its own way. This selection helps to substantiate the results of the assumption, concerning the gap between the peri-urban and rural areas, as the differences between peri-urban and rural areas would be greater than the ones established in this survey, if a representative sample of all villages could have been chosen (not only selecting three privileged ones).

Areas of inquiry and methodology 17

Map 4: The province of Maputo with control village Massaca 1

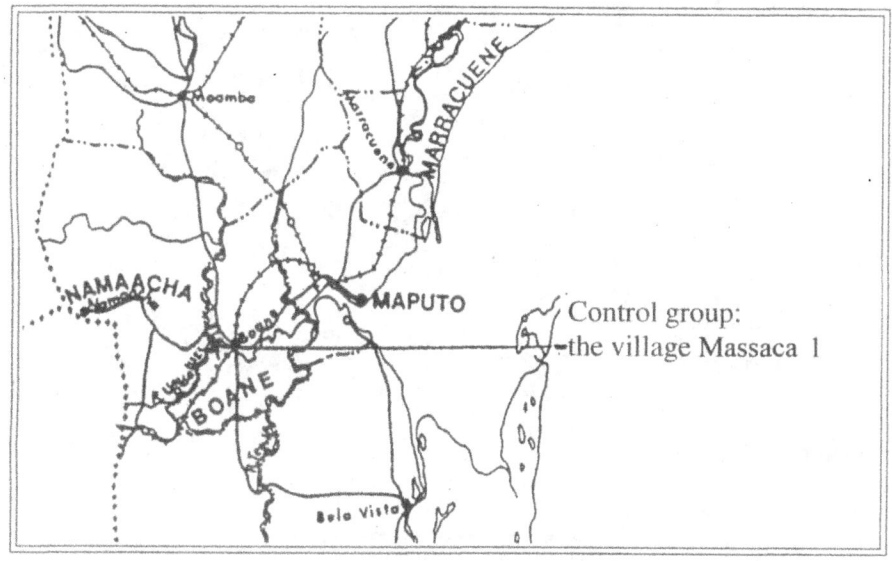

Source: INPF – Instituto Nacional de Planeamento Físico, Maputo

Map 5: Overbounded Beira with control village Nhangau

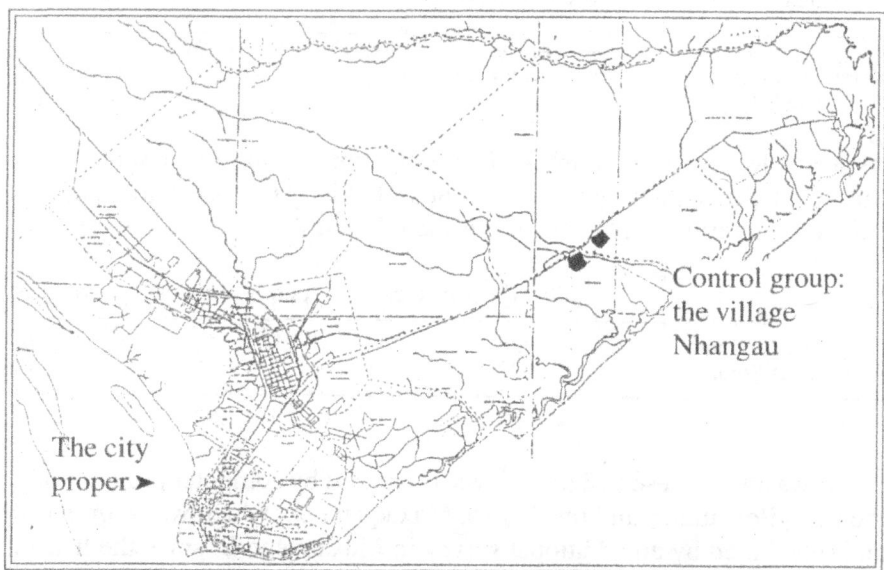

Source: Serviço Provincial de Planeamento Físico de Sofala, Beira

Map 6: The province of Sofala with control village Mutua

Source: Adapted from Map No. 3438, United Nations, April 1987

urban areas	peri-urban areas	villages
///////\	+++++++++++++++++++++++	\\\\\\\
worst areas were selected	representative sample	best areas were selected

As a whole, we had 18 areas of investigation. In the main surveys we carried out 678 interviews in 458 households. The distribution of the number of interviewed households is the following:

	fully urbanized areas	peri-urban areas	villages
Province of Maputo	26	244	30
Province of Sofala	32	86	40
	58	330	70

If we add to these 678 interviews, processed by computer programmes, the two pilot studies and one bairro, Maxaquene A (which was eliminated and substituted by an additional survey in Maxaquene B, since the lists of

Maxaquene A were apparently not up to date and too many missing cases would have been the result) then more than 800 interviews were carried out as a whole.

Processing and presentation

The data were processed first at the Centre for Informatics at the Eduardo Mondlane University of Maputo with a main frame pdp-11 computer. After printing different versions and combinations of frequencies, the ASCII data were transformed to suit a personal computer and then with the SPSS-programme all the cross tabs were created.

After returning to Austria, a factor analysis was carried out with the satisfaction-depression variables, the differences between the areas were measured by the t-test, wherever variables consisted of intervals and a path analysis was made by the LISREL-model with the most important variables of the study.

The results are mainly presented in cross tabs and graphs, showing wherever appropriate the t-test significance, measuring the highly significant, significant or not significant difference between the areas and specific groups or showing a particularly high Chi^2 significance to indicate little or no difference.[5]

For easier reading and in order to avoid too many cross tabs the results are sometimes presented as percentages connected with the greater than '>' and less than '<' sign; e.g. 46<61<82 per cent gave a certain answer or 82>61>46 per cent show a certain characteristic. The first figure always stands for a particular result of the fully urbanized or urban areas, the second for the peri-urban areas and the third for the villages.

Objectives and significance of the study

The results of this research can only be properly interpretated in the light of or in the darkness, respectively, of globalization and marginalization. They reveal the dimensions of poverty in the rural but also in the peri-urban areas, for which all explanations on a national and micro-level would remain very incomplete, would we not consider the underlying world-wide process in which the North wins and the developing world loses. On the other hand, it is an objective of this study to show the process of urbanization also in its *positive* aspects and in the context of globalization.

The significance of the research can in addition be seen in the rather unusual twofold comparison: between urban and peri-urban areas on the one hand, showing the two urban worlds and their deep division and between peri-urban and rural areas on the other hand, an essential frame of reference, which is often neglected in urban studies.

As the United Nations world report on population of 1996 remarks that amazingly concrete and detailed information on the urban poor is still lacking (UNFPA 1996, 6) the core of this study, the first representative, detailed survey of the peri-urban areas of the two largest cities of Mozambique should be useful. There are censuses of the Central Statistical Office, which are of a different nature, had different objectives and did not yet exist in 1991, when this survey started.

For a more international readership, particularly in the North, it would mean a contribution to the widening of the horizons as far as knowledge of the South is concerned, which is unfortunately still widely lacking. For average citizens of Western industrialized countries but also for scientists and even social scientists the enormous problems and the degree of poverty in developing countries, particularly in Mozambique as one of the poorest countries, is hardly imaginable. Even less known are the reasons for the problems. Therefore, an analysis of the root causes of poverty is another essential objective of this research.

However, also human and cultural values of developing nations are widely unknown. Although numerous studies have been carried out there, the number is still diminishing in comparison to the 'flood' of studies in the industrialized nations. Ninety per cent of the money for research is spent in the North and only ten per cent in the South, where ninety per cent of the problems are. Even published reports remain often in certain circles and special libraries while Third World literature can be extremely underrepresented in universities or national libraries. There is no doubt that a lot more Third World research is needed if the problems and the cultural and human values of the South are to become general knowledge of the North, knowledge not as an end in itself but for the creation of a political climate in which changes for the better, for the South and the North, can occur in the direction of a just international economic order, in a positive process of globalization, overcoming the severe disadvantages of the developing world.

In this context the research may contribute to a more critical reconsideration and to substantial amendments to the structural adjustment programmes in the Third World countries in general and Mozambique in particular. It may also contribute in finding a way out of the debt crisis and to a more effective rural development.

It was also one of the objectives of the study to provide data and insights for urban planners, architects, and persons responsible for urban renewal in Mozambique.

Students and maybe also lecturers of sociology and related subjects of the new school of social sciences, about to be created at the Eduardo Mondlane University of Maputo, should be provided with a useful source. Only a few sociological studies of urban Mozambique exist, not to speak of studies comparing the poor urban with the rural areas.

In Austria, which funded this study, it could be useful for the government section dealing with development aid, particularly as Southern Africa is one of the preferential zones of development co-operation and a special country programme for Mozambique has been worked out. Two of the Third World NGOs, the Institute for International Cooperation (IIZ) and the North South Institute are co-operating with Mozambique.

At the Austrian Science Foundation on Development Aid (OEFSE) the rural development of Mozambique is quite well documented (with about 100 sources) but there is hardly any literature on urban problems (with only two sources). An international computerized search for literature on the urban problem of Mozambique did not yield substantially better results: very few articles on specific aspects and no monographs. So the research helps to fill a real gap in the literature.

Notes

1   Although Peil saw two 'worlds' in some cities, she has never made this gap a seperate topic, most likely because in most West African cities this gap does not exist, at least not spatially: 'neighborhoods are economically ... heterogeneous, government offices and facilities are relatively uncentralized and ordinary people have adequate access to them ... (while in many other cities as in Maputo and Beira) ... the center is modeled in a European pattern, with a cluster of government buildings, hotels and department stores; high income residents live in special areas of large, landscaped, and well serviced houses and the mass of the population must contend with long distances and poor transportation to reach government officials or the hospitals, schools, and jobs to which they should have an equal right. In this situation, there are, in effect, two towns rather than one ...' (Peil 1981, 9).

2   In the absence of a more adequate term, the first level of urbanization means the difference between the rural and the peri-urban areas in housing, infrastructure and social facilities, as well as in the socio-economic, social and psychological characteristics of the respective inhabitants. The second level of urbanization means the corresponding differences between the two urban 'worlds'.

3   Maslow found that the fulfillment of human needs normally follows an hierarchical order, particularly in the sense that self-actualization, the top of the hierarchy and an essential source of happiness cannot occur without the fulfillment of basic human needs such as food, clothing, housing, clean water, etc. As second stage in the hierarchy of needs Maslow considers security; security in a physical and psychological sense. Human beings must be secure about the fulfillment of their basic needs also in the future. The third step, according to Maslow, is the need for close loving and social integration and the fourth is self-esteem and being appreciated by others (Maslow 1954).
4   Administração do Parque Imobiliário do Estado, the agency responsible for the administration of state-owned housing and other buildings.
5   A Chi^2 significance as well as a t-test significance of between 0.0000 and 0.0100 means the difference between two or three distributions (in our case 'columns' of percentages) is highly significant, a value of between 0.0100 and 0.0500 means the difference is significant and a value greater than 0.0500 means the difference is statistically not significant. However it still makes a difference whether this value is just beyond the 0.0500 mark or whether it is approaching 1, which would mean absolute equality between two distributions.

2 Urbanization and globalization

The meaning of urbanization and the characterization of urban areas

Urbanization can mean urban growth, the increase of the absolute number of urban dwellers as well as the proportional increase of the urban population in relation to the total population of a country. Increase can occur by 'natural' growth of the urban population (which depends on many factors and is therefore actually not 'natural' but economically and culturally determined) and increase can occur by rural-urban migration. Today 'the natural population growth plays an even larger role, accounting for three fifths of urban growth on average' (Preston in Gugler 1988). This fact is often overlooked by those who try to combat urban growth by restricting rural-urban migration only and not also by birth control in the cities.

Related to the rapid growth of the number of urban inhabitants is, of course, the spatial growth of urban areas. This can transform one kind of an urban system into another: a town into a city, a city into a metropolis or even a giant or global city. The term 'mega city' is applied by the United Nations referring mainly to Third World cities with a metropolitan population of eight million or more while the term 'world city' mainly refers to cities in the First World (Ho 1997). Be it in the industrialized or in the developing world, as soon as a town is transformed into a city it partakes more in the effects of globalization and at the same time facilitates globalization.

Urbanization means the development of unique resources, a particular kind of housing, a particular kind of infrastructure and social facilities, so that this area becomes more distinguished from a rural area. However, it also means adjustment by migrants to urban life. In this research, in the presentation and analysis of the results of the empirical investigation, mainly the last two kinds of urbanization will be discussed, as for instance the change of behaviour, in particular the change of social interaction but also the change of satisfaction, as it can be measured on the rural, the peri-urban, and urban dwellers. This kind of urbanization also includes a change of marriage forms, a change of spending ones leisure time and a change in using social facilities, such as schools, hospitals, clinics,

24 *Globalization, urban progress, urban problems, rural disadvantages*

traditional healers, just to mention a few. With urbanization the major problems and the main likings of the inhabitants change. The prerequisite for all these changes is the above mentioned development of the unique urban resources. This particular housing and infrastructure, these social facilities which transform an area into an urban or at least a peri-urban one will be analyzed in detail in chapter 6. Both of these discussed aspects, the change of the physical environment as well as of the people, the change of their habits and life styles, their feelings, their education, competition and striving for more, all these are also related to rural-urban migration, to the rapid urban growth and to globalization.

But what is actually an urban area, what is a city? 'Everybody knows it, except the experts' (Miner 1967). A satisfactory definition which could be applied at all times and world-wide apparently still does not exist.

> Comparative studies of pre-industrial and industrial towns, of medieval and twentieth-century towns, of capitalist and socialist towns, seem to bring us no nearer to an answer, except to conclude that the definition of 'urban' is culture-based. Nevertheless, it is worth examining the criteria which have been considered important. Even within a single society, drawing a clear boundary between urban and rural places is often difficult. Scholars have given considerable attention to an unambiguous and universal definition of 'urban', but the problem remains (Peil and Sada 1984, 49).

Since we cannot define, we can at least describe a city and enumerate essential characteristics of an urban area. But even to do this is particularly difficult for Third World cities, which today are normally divided into fully urbanized areas (generally richer or rich and better equipped areas) and semi-urbanized or peri-urban areas (generally poorer or very poor areas) for which often the term 'slum' is used inadequately (see p. 44). Areas which may be placed in between fully urbanized and semi-urbanized areas exist in addition as, for instance, low cost housing schemes of relatively high standard. (For a description of official low cost housing areas, Site and Service Schemes and squatters of Zambia see Knauder 1982, pp. 17-22.)

How then can we define or better characterize these divided cities as urban areas, as distinct from rural ones? An attempt should be made here, following a number of sources, older and newer ones. The characterizations and elements applying only for fully urbanized and not for peri-urban areas will be shown in italics.

An urban area is a large agglomeration of buildings inhabited by people settled densely on a limited area of land. The inhabitants of this agglomeration live primarily of trade, commerce and other occupations *rather than agriculture*.[1] Size and density lead to the necessity of a particular kind of infrastructure (higher level of sanitation, transportation, water supply, refuse disposal, etc. than in the rural areas.) Urban areas are places with regular local, regional, *national or international* markets often exerting their *power* and influence over the hinterland. (National and international markets can only be found in fully urbanized areas and only those can exert power over the hinterland.) Also as a consequence of size and density the inhabitants of urban areas show special characteristics, namely social and cultural heterogenity, as well as a greater number and diversification of social contacts, greater social differentiation and stratification as well as a greater mobility than those in rural areas. Urbanism is not only a physical reality but a social one. Cities are an advanced form of human association which enables heterogeneous people to live and work together and to achieve some sense of community. Cities are not only the scene of sophistication in social organization but also the *location of men's and women's greatest achievements in science and culture.* It is not mere coincidence that city life and writing was invented at roughly the same time. *Cities have ever since been the points of contact between cultures and ideas and technical and scientific progress.* (Wirth 1938, Bergel 1955, Sirjamaky 1964, Pfeil 1972, Seymour 1982. For an in-depth discussion of the problems of defining an urban area see Peil and Sada 1984, chapter 2).

However, as already mentioned, not all Third World cities show a clear cut division into poor peri-urban and fully urbanized areas. Apart from the link of official low cost housing areas which exists, for instance, in Zambia, in West African as well as in Chinese cities, the 'fully' urbanized areas are in many aspects intermingled with large areas of poor housing. In Lagos, for instance, Peil observes that, 'most streets have a mixture of buildings, in size, height, age and conditions', and yet she speaks of fully urbanized areas, because she continues:

> The provision of services – roads, water, electricity, telephones, sanitary services – has clearly improved in recent years, making Lagos a more pleasant place to live, except in the newer suburbs (apparently peri-urban areas; remark of the author). New roads in particular make it possible to move around the metropolis at a speed unhoped for twenty years ago (Peil 1991, xx).

The manifold aspects of globalization and its relation to urbanization

Urbanization as facilitating factor and consequence of globalization

Beck differentiates between globalization and globality. One of the main characteristics of globality is, according to him, the fact that many aspects of the present state of the world are irreversible. In particular he mentions the permanent revolution of information and communication technology, the streams of images of the global cultural industry, the post international, poly-centric, global policy with increasing international actors such as the United Nations, global NGOs and movements, the global claim for human rights, even though they are far from being implemented. The global environmental problems, the local transcultural conflicts and the often mentioned increasing density of international trade, financial markets and the increase of TNCs also belong to the state of globality (Beck 1997, 29-30).

On the other hand, Beck sees globalization as a dialectic process between the local and the global which creates transnational social relations and transnational social space, which upgrades local cultures and gives rise to new cultures. The intensification of transnational space, transnational events, problems, conflicts, and even transnational biographies should neither be understood as a linear nor as a total all embracing process but rather as a contingent, dialectic, glocal process (Beck 1997, 150).[2]

Most of these aspects of globalization apply very well also to urbanization. Urbanization upgrades rural cultures in the peri-urban areas even though not all traditional aspects are lost and so a new semi-urban culture is created. This process is repeated on an advanced level, when people move to the fully urbanized areas and become real urbanites. But also the second, and any further, generation of urbanites transform the cities into locations of transnational social relations and transnational social space to an incomparable higher degree as could ever be achieved in the rural areas. However, at the same time this process intensifies not only the rural-urban contradictions but also the contradictions between the global cities of the Triad and the mega-cities of the South.

The United Nations Research Institute for Social Development (UNRISD) lists six key trends of globalization of which the first two are economic dimensions and the third is partly economic and partly political, the fourth is purely political and the last two are multidimensional and multidisciplinary (for the multidisciplinarity of globalization compare Robertson 1998). First, the integration of the global economy (with the marginalization of the developing world – remark by the author), second, the dominance of market forces, third, the transformation of production systems and labour markets, fourth, the spread of liberal democracy, fifth, the speed of technological change, and sixth, the media revolution and consumerism (UNRISD 1995, 22). All these trends can be seen as causes for rapid urbanization in differing degrees but urbanization, on the other hand, is certainly a facilitating factor for globalization. The global society and the global economy are increasingly shaped by processes and decisions originating from global- and mega-cities (but also by capitals of countries which must not necessarily be mega-cities), however, cities in turn are more and more influenced by global dynamics (Feldbauer and Parnreiter 1997). This resulted already from the definition of the fully urbanized areas as locations of the greatest achievements in science and culture, as points of contact between cultures and ideas and technical and scientific progress. Cities served in their early history and do even more so in modern times for the spread of technological change, for the transformation of production systems and labour markets. Consumerism, however, might not be very different in most parts of the Triad (North America, Europe and Japan) in rural and in urban areas but in most parts of the Third World consumerism is absent in rural areas, it exists in the fully urbanized areas and only to a very low degree in the peri-urban areas. The integration of the Third World into the global economy as well as its marginalization mainly functions via the cities and the media revolution primarily takes place in the urban areas.

Urbanization is a consequence of globalization in so far as investment by multinational and transnational companies are mainly, although not only, made in urban areas. In Zambia for example, which is the third largest copper exporting country in the world, copper mines were established by the British South Africa Company in the first half of 20th century. Several cities evolved around the mining sites in the Copper belt and in the 1970s Zambia was already the most urbanized sSA country with almost half of her population living in urban areas.

One of the most important meanings of globalization in the context of this research is the definition by McGrew, who sees globalization as a process

> by which events, decisions and activities in one part of the world can come to have significant consequences for individuals and communities in quite distant parts of the globe. This process results in the forging of a multiplicity of linkages and interconnections between the states and societies which make up the modern world-system (McGrew 1992, 262, quoted in O'Neill 1996).

This modern world-system with its multiplicity of linkages and interconnections between the states functions mainly via the cities; in the case of Mozambique via the fully urbanized areas. Here the decisions are made about the small amount of international trade, investment and production. Although these decisions affect the lives of the peasants directly, they have absolutely no voice in them.

In so far as globalization fosters urbanization, it brings with it real development for the entire country and its economy but particularly for those who manage to become urbanites and even more so for the inhabitants of the fully urbanized areas, as the results of the empirical study vividly show in a manifold way. One can hardly argue that urban development in general takes place on the cost of rural development as countries with a low GNP have also a low urbanization rate (see table 1 and 2 in appendix 2). A higher urbanization rate manifests also higher economic development. Without urban centres technological progress is unthinkable, without airports near the cities developing countries would be even more marginalized and development aid impossible. Without universities in the cities an indigenous leadership could never be established and without central hospitals no progress in health care achieved, just to mention a few simple and obviously positive examples of modernization, urbanization and globalization.

The continued urbanization, the growth of metropolitan areas and mega-cities is more and more seen as inevitable, as an economic necessity, to which no viable alternative has been found, but a parallel development, namely urban diffusion (see chapter 12). Therefore it is necessary to make the metropolitan areas, including their peri-urban areas, economically more efficient. Although urban diffusion, the development of secondary and intermediate towns and cities is just as necessary as rural development, the comparative advantages of metropolises and mega-cities will even grow further in the process of globalization, especially for those urban 'nodal points' which are able to develop into global or world cities, being strongly connected with the international and increasingly global economy (see e.g. Simon 1995, Knox and Taylor 1995 quoted in Schneider and Vorlaufer 1998, 6-7).

In the process of urbanization consumption patterns and life styles of the middle classes of the rich countries have penetrated the affluent urban minorities in the poor countries. On the other hand, urbanites must not necessarily be affluent to show at least some patterns of western life styles. As we will see in the following chapters, a fully urbanized area with its specific infrastructure, social facilities, and housing influences social interaction, leisure time activities, education, health care habits, amongst others, and even well-being. However, not only the urban environment influences the individual, those who manage to move to a fully urbanized area already bring certain prerequisites with them for a global, western life style. This life style has in the majority of aspects not yet reached the rural areas. The rural population and to a large extent also the peri-urban dwellers adhere more to traditions in their social relations and cultural life than do real urbanites.

Globalization, westernization, traditional cultures, and sociological theory

The term globalization is often used in close relation to the modernization theory, which is heavily leaning towards structural functionalism in explaining the 'backwardness' (as modernization theory sees it) of developing countries. The aim for the Third World must be to reach the state of modernity. This can only be achieved by overcoming the characteristics of a traditional society and by moving towards a capitalist one (Behrendt 1968). Hundreds, if not thousands, of authors (Nohlen and Nuscheler 1993, 34) have followed this theory since the 1950s, describing underdevelopment and giving guidelines for development, apparently, with the exception of a few NICs (Newly Industrialized Countries) with little or no success. If globalization is understood only as the world-wide expansion of capitalism – regardless of the fate of the Third World – strongly connected with structural functionalism and the modernization theory, which never succeeded neither in the explanation of the respective ongoing situation nor in the explanation of the prospects of the developing countries, then it would certainly be a negative process.

According to Dibaja adherents of the modernization theory based on structural functionalism

> were not international thinkers, they were in fact nationalists, thinking about the world-system in terms of serving national units. In their attempt to redefine human space in terms of society and man, the issue of bringing back former colonies was met by referring to the functional structure and cultural character of their own societies. ... In his work 'Social System' Parsons (1951) was concerned to keep the model of Western functional society in firm place and to deprive non-western societies of cultural and functional identity (Dibaja 1996).

Also Waters mentions critically the often implied close relation between the concept of globalization and the modernization theory as well as the widespread erroneous belief that the increasing dominance of capitalism is an unavoidable process:

> The concept of globalization is an obvious object for ideological suspicion because, like modernization, a predecessor and related concept, it appears to justify the spread of Western culture and of capitalist society by suggesting that there are forces operating beyond human control that are transforming the world (Waters 1995, 3).

Even if globalization today is firmly tied up with capitalism, the concept as such should not be confined to capitalist and neo-liberal ideology. Globalization could fully unfold all its positive potential only in a post-capitalist era. But already now not all elements of western culture are negative and if positive features of many non-western cultures are combined with it then globalization could have an enormous positive effect. What is urgently needed is a cultural symbiosis between the South and the North or between the South and the East, on the one hand, and the West, on the other hand.

There is no doubt, that globalization just as urbanization is at the same time a process of westernization, not only economically but also culturally, politically, technologically and scientifically. It could hardly be justified to consider this as a negative process only. Where western advancement can contribute to real progress of mankind, it should and must be shared with all peoples. Valuable innovations must be made accessible to all. Of course, where Western culture, economic and political power is forced upon other cultures in an imperialistic respectless way to the disadvantage of the latter, the process is extremely negative.

Sachs in his polemic handbook concerning development aid reproaches western development aid for trying from the beginning to westernize the Third World, without always admitting it openly. According to him, the result is an enormous loss of cultural diversity and the spread of western mono-culture, although traditional cultures would be a real alternative to the growth-oriented industrial society (Sachs 1993, 11-2).

Very similar to rural romanticism, discussed in chapter 1, every now and again one can encounter this traditional romanticism which considers traditional cultures as alternatives for future development. Apart from the fact that the wheel of history can never be turned back, such a projection is, in addition, extremely unrealistic. Exactly those intellectuals who glorify the traditional cultures of the developing world would probably be the last ones ready to leave their privileged position and the 'blessings' of modernization and 'return' to the 'bush' from where we all come from.

In addition, in spite of massive forces of homogenization, which cannot be overlooked and often not justified, the world is still extraordinary rich on cultural diversity, even on traditional cultures. It is one of the positive outcomes of globalization, the media revolution and the advancement of communication that a higher proportion of mankind than ever before can get to know the richness of the world's cultures.

What we need, as mentioned above, is a cultural symbioses or hybridization of cultures, progress with a human face, an alternative development. In such a development not all elements of western culture must be rejected and many elements of traditional cultures could constitute inspiring, useful elements.

In the same way, not all elements of the modernization theory must be rejected. The enumeration of the specific characteristics of 'underdevelopment' correspond with reality. However, an enumeration of characteristics does not make up a theory. Different explanations of the causes of and the solutions to 'underdevelopment' are needed. It is not only although to a certain extent also, the traditional way of life, religious beliefs, the absence of enterpreneurship, etc. which prevent development, but mainly the economic dependency of the 'periphery' (the developing countries) from the 'centre' (the industrialized countries). In the discussion of the root causes of poverty in chapter 11, elements of the dependency theory as well as the world-system theory will come into the forefront again and again. What is needed is a symbiosis of several useful theories in order to arrive at a more meaningful interpretation of the processes of urbanization, globalization, and marginalization as well as their mutual conditioning and to arrive at a concept of change of those negative trends which affect the lives of too large a proportion of mankind fatally.

The economic dimension of globalization, marginalization and competition

Globalization can also be seen as the emergence of a

> tripolar world, (North America, Europe and Japan) rapidly changing North-South relations, growing diversity among the developing countries, poverty and the threat of expulsion for a large proportion of the world's population and in the leading economies, severe problems of unemployment and growing wage and income disparities (Oman 1994, 1; quoted in O'Neill 1996).

There exists not only 'poverty and the *threat* of expulsion for a large proportion of the world's population' but a large proportion is already excluded from progress, living in poverty, not even able to satisfy the basic human needs, particularly in the rural areas of the developing countries, but also to some extent in the peri-urban areas. The different facets of the ugly face of poverty, the manifold, extreme sufferings will be subject of analysis in chapter 3 and chapter 6 to 10.

In so far as the greater part of the developing world is to a large extent excluded from the financial market, world trade and investment, as all these are mainly concentrated in the Triad, North America, Europe and Japan, the term globalization could be questioned and the world economy considered as not really global. However, the situation is worse. The South is not simply marginalized, but was in the decades before 1993 forced to develop the North. Because of heavy indebtedness the capital flow from the South to the North from 1980 to 1990 was US$ 333 billion (Kraener 1994; see also chapter 11). Even though there has been some capital flow from the North to the South since 1993 and at least there are some signs hinting towards a solution of the debt crisis - the majority of the developing countries still suffer severely from repaying debt and interests and from being unable to compete with the centre, the Triad. For the countries lagging behind globalization appears as a monster. The developing countries are ruthlessly pushed out from the set of world producers and converted into chronic dependants.

> It seems that a new era of 'open-door doctrine' has arrived where the weak have to give way for the strong. ... Instead of being national brothers of management, the world market is becoming the only commander in chief (Golansky 1996).

The highest principle of the world market today is economic efficiency. According to this principle industrialized countries are awarded and devloping countries rigorously punished. Countries with a labour productivity above the world's average make profits, those with a labour productivity below that level constantly lose. Unless one is of the opinion that it is the fault of the developing countries when they have a labour productivity far below the world average, the competition is extremely unfair as the poorest countries with a productivity level hundred times below the world average have to compete openly with the industrialized countries who have a productivity of labour many times above the average (Golansky 1996).

Today we are wittnessing sharp inequalities and a growing global economic disintegration. Most of the transactions take place among industrialized countries in terms of trade, capital flows, foreign investment, technology transfers, or activities of transnational enterprises. Most of the poorest and least developed countries, such as Mozambique, are largely by passed by the intensified circuits of trade, capital and investment.

Transnational companies operate under the banner of free trade but this freedom is understood as the freedom of domination, the limits of which are not the freedom of other smaller, weaker companies and countries and so the process of marginalization continues. Fairness in trade has never been recognized (or even agreed upon) nor does there exist a generally accepted definition of what appropriate social stands are. And yet, this would be really important, because globalization is a social process (Fouquin et al. 1995).

Another characteristic of today's globalization is competition.

> The mega-competition that is part and parcel of globalization leads to winner-take-all situations; those who come out on top win big and the losers lose even bigger. ... The way transnational corporations have to operate to compete in the global economy means that it is now routine to have corporations announce new profit increases along with a new wave of layoffs (World Economic Forum 1996).

'Healthy' as well as 'unhealthy' competition can mainly be found in urban areas, although competition is not completely absent in rural areas. To have the largest house with modern, permanent building material, the largest piece of land, the best harvest, etc. are certainly values people are striving for but competition to a much higher degree starts in the urban areas of the Third World. Here one has to compete for jobs and there exists considerable competition on the labour market; one has to compete for enrolment in schools and the educational institutions themselves are highly competitive, particularly the universities.[3] Competition between private companies increases in the urban areas with the process of development and industrialization. Because, even if developing countries are truly marginalized – and in many the situation worsened during the last decades – the development process in general has, in spite of all adverese conditions, not come to a complete standstill.

With a higher degree of urbanization and industrialization the competitive aspects of a society increase – forstering the process of globalization – while at the same time being a consequence of it.

Competition is a prominent feature in this era of globalization not only in urban areas but also on a macro level. Continental political and economic power blocs are emerging. Each bloc is dominated by one or more actors who compete but also co-operate with each other. In each bloc differentiation increases and existing social arrangements come under strain. As mentioned before, much of the world, particularly Africa, is excluded from the advantages of globalization and suffers from additional burdens of 'punishment'. This extremely uneven development has generated crises and in this sense globalization has lead to a world disorder (Krahl 1996).

The new policy of particularly powerful states and the demand by IFIs for deregulation, liberalization of trade and capital movement as well as for privatization, Martin and Schuhmann (1996, 19) call 'turbo-capitalism'. Yet, it is a fallacy to believe that nothing can be done against it and that its breakthrough is anavoidable. Neolibaralism as the new doctrine of salvation needs opposition and alternatives; it must not be allowed to destroy the functioning of the states and democracy.

Beck calls the reduction of globalization to the economic dimension only, 'globalism'. It is the neo-liberal ideology of the supremacy of the world market to the extent that it subpresses or even substitutes political action of the nation states. The exclusively economic dimension of globalization is in addition a linear concept expecting a steady increase of dependency from the world market and reducing the global society to a global market society. Globalism overlooks the multidimensionality of globalization as for instance, the ecological, cultural, political, or civil societal dimension. Globalism deduces its power also from its threats not only from its real power. Neo-liberal globalism is politically highly relevant, inspite of its constant affirmation to act apolitically and purly economically (Beck 1997, 196-9).

According to the neo-liberals, the more freedom is given to companies in investment and employment policies the higher the economic growth rate and welfare for all. The law of supply and demand becomes the most important principle. The expansion of free trade for the sake of free trade is hardly questioned anymore. The higher the production rate and the easier it is to move capital accross borders, the more powerful and uncontrolable the TNCs become. These TNCs which intimidate governments and their electorate alike, already control two thirds of the world's trade. Almost half of this trade is concentrated within their own networks. They are at the centre of the economic process of globalization and speed it up. TNCs have the power to deprive society of material resources, of capital, taxes and jobs. They are, on the other hand, a consequence of accelerated technological inovations and rationalization (in the sense of laying off workers). They foster jobless growth and have so changed the relation between capital and labour fundamentally (Martin and Schuhmann 1996, 157-8).

Kiely (1998) puts the influence of TNCs at least as far as foreign investment and trade are concerned, in a somewhat different perspective. For most TNCs domestic investment is of much higher importance than foreign investment. He quotes Wallace (1996, 24) who found that only 18 of the 100 largest companies of the world kept the majority of their assets abroad. In the year 1993 the manufacturing TNCs sold 75 per cent of their goods domestically in Germany and Japan; in the USA this proportion was 67 per cent. The manufacturing TNCs also held the major part of their assets at home in 1993: 93 per cent in Japan, 73 per cent in the USA and 62 per cent in Britain (Kiely 1998). These proportions are similar to those TNCs specialized in services (Hirst and Thompson 1996, 96).

Global trade shows a similar picture to that of investment and services. The share of trade of the developing world has declined dramatically. Latin America had a share of the world's exports of 12.4 per cent in the 1950s but of merely 3.9 per cent in 1990. Asia's share declined from 17.8 per cent in 1980 to 14 per cent in 1990. Africa had a share of exports of 5.2 per cent in 1950 but of 1.9 per cent only in 1990 (Glyn and Sutcliffe 1992, 79, 90-1; cited by Kiely 1998). All these data show the ongoing process of marginalization of the Third World in general and Africa in particular and do not devaluate the above mentioned power of TNCs and the negative influences they can have in their mother countries and abroad. The far reaching consequences of the forcible integration of the developing world into the capitalist system, on the one hand, but the negative integration into the world trade and the lack of investment, on the other hand, will be shown for Mozambique in the empirical part of this book.

The historical aspect of globalization and the process of urbanization in the pre-colonial and colonial times

Today's particular form of globalization has had several predecessors in the form of earlier periods of internationalization and world systems. Internationalization as well as world systems do not have to comprise the entire world, but a truly global system does. Therefore, there is some justification, to speak of real global, all countries embracing, processes from the middle of this century, reaching an even higher level now at the end of the second milenium. In the second half of the 20th century all the six key trends listed by UNRISD (see above) – be they negative or positive – started to develope fully, communism – as it was implemented then – collapsed, the United Nations and the claim for human rights, and with it women's liberation, gained on importance world-wide and more than ever before. Humankind is starting to 'fly' with two wings (women and men) now, while it was 'flying' with one wing only. China, with one fifth of humankind joined the capitalist system more or less voluntarily. Although the spread of liberal democracy has not yet reached China, it could well be that the media revolution – in particular the internet – could have a substantial effect on China politically. In addition, we have witnessed a world-wide urban revolution in the second half of this century resulting in considerable social change, subject of this book all along.

However, today's global system dates undoubtedly back to the late 15th and the early 16th century. From there onwards, we can speak of a European dominated world economy with a unique social system, which up until to day forms the basis of the modern world-system. This social system could be called a world-system, not because it comprised the entire world (although already then it consisted of a considerable number of nation states) but because it was greater than any legally defined political unit. It was a world-system because the connections between the different parts of the system were primarily economic ones, emphasized in addition by cultural ties and political arrangements and unions (Wallerstein 1986, 27).

The modern world-system emerged in the sixteenth century on the basis of a capitalist mode of production. The mode of production was the most important variable in the origin of capitalism as a predominant form of social organization. Two other key institutions of the system were the world-wide division of labour and the emerging bureaucratic state apparatus in some regions. Many features of today's world and its unsolved serious problems have their origin in the sixteenth century. Already then a centre, a periphery, and a semiperiphery emerged. The centre was con- stituted by the Northern-, North-western, and central states of Europe, while America was the main region of the periphery.[4] The imported goods from conquered regions made it possible for the upper strata in the centre to live beyond their means, they could invest more than they had saved while in the periphery enormous changes in agricultural production led to forced labour in the production of cash crops and even to the import of slaves (Wallerstein 1986, 152).

Certain sectors which formerly belonged to the centre sometimes deteriorated to the semiperiphery particularly as economic institutions, economic rewards, and organization of labour were concerned. What has changed is the geographical distribution. The centre has become tripolar, consisting of the North America, the European Union, and Japan. Recently the semiperiphery has been constituted by the former communist block and some newly industrialized countries (NICs) while the rest of the developing countries still remain in the periphery, to which some of them, sadly enough, belonged already 500 years ago, such as Mexico, Chile, and Peru.

There exists a striking similarity to the world-wide centre, semiperiphery and periphery model within developing countries, also within Mozambique. The centre is clearly constituted by the fully urbanized areas, the peri-urban areas can be seen as semiperiphery, with economic rewards and labour organizations very different from the other two areas, while the rural areas clearly remain the periphery, with many of the characteristics the periphery in general already had in the sixteenth century, such as poverty and monocultures with little opportunity for professional specialization.

Although the differentiation of the labour force and particularly the different kinds of labour force have changed tremendously since the sixteenth century, the world-wide division of labour and the kind of specialization still serve as they did then to maintain this particular mode of production.

With the advancement of the industrial technology in the second half of the nineteenth century and its economic boom, internationalization had reached another, higher stage in the world-system. In some respects the current international economy is less open than the economy from 1870 to 1914 was. Truly transnational companies are relatively rare at present. Most companies are nationally based and trade multinational on the strength of a major national base. Capital mobility is not producing a massive shift of investment and employment from industrialized to developing countries; indeed, with the exception of a small number of NICs, the Third World remains marginalized in both investment and trade (Hirst and Thompson 1996, 3).

Also according to Sachs and Warner (1995) in the period between 1860 and the beginning of the First World War there were low trade barriers and high capital mobility. It was a period with an enormous technological progress particularly in long distance transportation and communications. Capitalist institutions developed and international trade had a strong

North-South dimension. It also promoted capital flows, it stimulated strong growth throughout the world and the rapid spread of industrialization beyond the core of the North Atlantic economies. Sachs and Warner consider this period as one of rapid economic convergence as, according to their view, poor economies grew faster than rich ones largely because of the trade stimulus. So they see many parallels between that era of internationalization and the present era of globalization, particularly as they believe that convergence is also possible today for the countries that join the system and provided they make appropriate policy choices (Sachs and Warner 1995, 61).

Although Bairoch and Kozul-Wright (1996) also see the historical approach useful for understanding the current wave of globalization, they reject the thesis of Sachs and Warner concerning economic convergence at that time and the possibility for week economies today to join the system after having made the appropriate policy choices. Although international production and financial activities were developing rapidly up to 1914, there existed extreme inequalities between the South and the North. International capital flows, like international trade flows, were highly concentrated in the North. Convergence occurred only between a small group of rapidly industrializing economies. All the colonies were prevented from industrializing. Technological change contributed more to economic growth than transnational companies did (Bairoch and Kozul-Wright 1996, 5).

In so far as the majority of the previous colonies, today's developing countries, are still prevented from genuine economic development and substantial industrialization, the parallel is given between the earlier period of internationalization and the present period of globalization. Rapid economic convergence was not possible then and does not occur today as the developing countries are still prevented from joining the system as equal partners and from making the 'appropriate policy choices' as their hands are tied mainly by the structural adjustment programmes to be discussed in chapter 11. 'The world today is not totally new; neither is it simply the same as the previous period of widespread internationalization, often described as a previous era of globalization' (O'Neill 1996).

In this research previous periods of internationalization will be considered as predecessors of today's globalization. Internationalization on a large scale started already in the pre-colonial era and with it a world-wide urbanization. However, long before the pre-colonial times urban centres developed outside Europe on the African and Asian continent. In addition to the often forgotten fact that the first urbanization did not occur in Europe, it is also hardly known that West African and European urbanization had reached more or less the same level by the 17th century.[5] However, in the pre-colonial times, with the big discoveries and the development of mercantilism in Europe the struggle of commercial influence by European merchants and traders started not only in Africa but also on the other continents. And then one of the darkest chapters of history in Europe's relation with Africa started, namely the trade with human beings, the slave trade, which lasted 400 years from the 15th to the end of the 19th century. (In many cases, also in Mozambique, it lasted even deeply into the 20th century.[6]) Through the slave trade Africa lost between 50 and 100 million of its young and able-bodied men, probably one fifth of its population. Along with the slave trade went a massive destruction of the already numerous and flourishing cities. The new towns that were built mainly as ports for slave trade as well as for trade with commodities could not at all make up for the brutal destruction of the indigenous culture and the absolute negation of human dignity for the sake of accumulating wealth and extending power for the industrializing North. (We will return to the problem of the slave trade in chapter 11.)

Only when in colonial times trade with commodities became more profitable than the trade with human beings (slave trade was not abolished mainly for ethical reasons!) and the looting of raw material from the African continent became more and more important for the growing industries in the North, it became necessary for the European merchants and colonial administrators to settle down in Africa which enabled them to exploit more efficiently. In this way settler towns and later cities developed as commercial and administrative centres near mines or huge commercial farms or on sites were railway lines were planned and later built, the only objective of which was to transport raw material to the ports. Ports themselves often constituted the nucleus of a town as was the case with Maputo and Beira.[7]

Already in the 17th century a basis was provided for urbanization in Europe which was on a then unprecedented scale by the industrial revolution. The population of Amsterdam quadrupled from 50,000 in 1600 to 200,000 in 1650 (Kossmann 1970, 366, quoted in Wallerstein 1992, 45) There was rapid urbanization also in the 19th and the beginning of the 20th century. In England, for instance, Manchester quadrupled within 50 years. In 1800 it had an estimated 72,000, in 1850 an estimated 303,000 inhabitants (Seymour 1982). Liverpool almost quintupled in the same time period from 78,000 to 376,000 inhabitants. Birmingham grew from 74,000 to 233,000 and Bradford from

29,000 to 103,000 inhabitants (Kiess 1991, 27). With this rapid urbanization the population living in villages and small settlements declined. In Germany the proportion of the population living in settlements below 2,000 was 63 per cent in 1870, but it declined to 36 per cent in 1925, while the proportion of the population living in cities with more than 100,000 inhabitants increased from 6 to 27 per cent during the same time period (Bolte et al. 1980, 176; Kiess and Bolte quoted in Krammer 1998, 93; rounding by the author). Then as today rapid urbanization went along with a, what was considered for that time, very rapid growth of the world population. While it is estimated at between 200 and 300 million in the year 30 it had reached an estimated 1 billion by 1850 and doubled within 200 years while it was doubling before only within 1,600 years. (Seymour 1982). By the end of the 19th century it became extremely important for the industrializing powers to conquer colonies in most parts of the Third World. In 1895 Cecil Rhodes stated:

> In order to save the 40 million inhabitants of the United Kingdom from a bloody civil war, we colonial statesmen must acquire new lands to settle the surplus population, to provide new markets for the goods produced by them in the factories and mines. The empire, as I have always said, is a bread and butter question. If you want to avoid civil war, you must become imperialists (Lenin, 1979, Original 1917).

Up until now this process of colonization has never come to an end but continues as so-called neo-colonialism and more recently as with that particular world disorder in which considerably more resources flow from the South to the North than vice versa and in which the market barriers in trade, labour and capital cost developing countries ten times more than they receive on aid (Menon 1992).

In the colonial times or second era of globalization peri-urban areas with their special characteristics developed in Africa around the nuclei of new or even old towns with great variations and numerous denotations. The most common equivalents in English for the term 'peri-urban areas' are semi- urban areas or suburbs. To be precise one would have to add 'poor' suburbs as suburbs as such could also mean areas for the upper class near the cities, particularly in industrialized countries. Semi-urban or peri-urban areas include Site and Service Schemes, upgraded squatters and squatters.[8] For squatters again, several expressions exist: spontaneous settlements, unplanned suburbs, shanty towns. In Latin America poor urban areas are called 'favelas' and in French speaking countries 'bidonvilles' is used. Apparently there is no such term in Portuguese so that in Mozambique poor city areas are simply called 'bairros' although this can also mean urban neighbourhood in general, rich or poor.[9]

Too often the most inadequate term 'slum' is used for squatters, upgraded squatters and sometimes even for Site and Service Schemes. Portes (1971) pointed out: steady decay is an essential characteristic of slum areas. Yet squatters, upgraded squatters and Site and Service Schemes are steadily improving in all African countries; this most probably holds true also for the majority of favelas in Latin America, with the exception of some inner city slums. Keeping the most important characteristics 'improving' or 'decaying' in mind, slums can hardly be found in Africa, which does not mean that very poor housing areas with insufficient infrastructure do not exist. The term 'slum' probably mainly designates decaying city areas in some industrialized countries, as for instance the United States and there areas such as Harlem in New York.

Also Hardoy and Satterthwaite do not favour the term 'slum' for the peri-urban areas of Third World cities.

> ...rapid growth of illegal settlements (in the meantime most of them have fortunately become legal – addition by the author) in and around cities can be viewed not as the growth of slums but, in a very real sense, as the development of cities which are more appropriate to the local culture, climate and conditions than the plans produced by the governments of these same cities (Hardoy and Satterthwaite 1989, 8).

The formation of peri-urban areas

Economic success for the Western powers during the second era of internationalization could never have come about would there not have been millions of indigenous people working for them. In East and Southern Africa people were forced to work mainly on plantations and in mines or for the construction of railways in the environs of which cities evolved. Since forcing each and everybody to work would probably have required twice the amount of manpower, the colonial administrators introduced two clever but very repressive methods of indirect force: firstly, a poll and hut tax was introduced, which had to be paid in money, secondly, commercial farming was simply forbidden for indigenous people, who were in addition driven away from fertile land (Sippel 1993; Maize Control Ordinance Act, 1936 and Marketing and Control Ordinance, 1937 in Zambia). Money was unfamiliar to many indigenous people and so they were forced to sell their labour power to the colonialists for starvation wages on commercial farms and mines or as servants in the emerging towns. In the early decades of colonialism only men were allowed to come to towns and these as well as the miners and farm workers had to live in areas separated from the Europeans, with hardly any infrastructure or social facilities where they had to build for themselves tiny huts with local material. These settlements can be considered as the nuclei of today's peri-urban areas. The work force during the colonial period was at first a temporary one partly because the health conditions had deteriorated after one and a half years so that a recovery in the rural areas was necessary partly because the colonial administrators tried to avoid an overcrowding of the cities, which they had experienced in Britain, for instance, and also because they feared revolts of the workers.

However, as shown in the quotation of Cecil Rhodes, colonies were also needed for the export of commodities produced in the West. These new commodities destroyed the flourishing indigenous handicrafts, because they were little by little desired by the indigenous population. So, in addition of being forced to work and live in towns and cities, there came a quasi 'voluntary' reason, namely, earning money in order to buy the newly imported commodities. More and more labour power was needed as the colonial towns and cities developed from merely commercial and administrative centres to 'real' cities with tall buildings illuminated by electricity, with shops and broad tarred streets, with at least some social facilities as schools and health centres (even if accessible for whites only at the beginning), with railway stations, restaurants, and even some small industries. Workers then came 'voluntarily' and in abundance, but during colonial times still regulated and restricted until the different states reached their political independence.

Yet, as urban centres in the Third World were growing during the colonial period and all investment was concentrated on them, the rural areas started to deteriorate, for reasons already mentioned above and because too high a percentage of young and adult able-bodied, intelligent men had been absent for too long from their home area (in Zambia, for instance, almost half of them at any one time (Kay 1967; Heisler, 1974)). Family life, cultural activities and even agricultural production deteriorated. As little by little men took their families with them to town, first illegally, later legally, there was still no housing provided for them, not even a piece of land where they could have built their own tiny traditional houses. They were forced to settle illegally (to squat!) if possible near the place of work. But as these squatters started to mushroom, walking eight kilometres (2 hours) to the place of work was and is for many today, 'normal'.

However, by far not all peri-urban areas came into existence in colonial times but a considerable part of them developed afterwards and are still developing now. As cities grow, particularly peri-urban areas grow and long existing villages are incorporated into the city area.

We have already seen in the characterization of urban areas that peri-urban areas lack many characteristics which fully urbanized areas have. Peri-urban areas although there are remarkable differences amongst them are generally populated by people with low income, who, nevertheless, have to build their houses themselves. As a consequence these houses are often very small, cheap and precarious, although permanent material like cement blocks are on the increase. Insufficient infrastructure, such as transport, sewage disposal, water supply, and sanitary facilities, as well as insufficient social facilities, such as schools and health centres are further characteristics of these poor housing areas. However, life in these areas is not always as desperate and bleak as onlookers from outside might think. There is lots of personal nearness, cheerfulness, mutual assistance and sense of belongingness to and responsibility for the particular community. In Zambia's squatters the police were almost absent (i.e. not needed) (Martin 1975). The peri-urban population could probably be described as half way (or one third of the way) Europeanized or globalized. They have taken on some positive values of European culture, such as formal education and giving certain rights also to the young, not only to the old. They have not yet taken on negative characteristics of European culture such as individualism, egoism, excessive competition, constant hurry, etc. but they have kept positive values of their traditional culture such as group-solidarity, openness, hospitality, friendliness and for them time is not yet an interval that has to be filled with achievements (Knauder 1975). It could be that it is this mixture which makes them so amiable.

> In practice one set of norms is not discarded to pick up another, but individuals adapt and combine them into something which works in the society in which they live. Very few fill the stereotype of marginal 'peasants outside the gates', but few are fully cosmopolitan either. Social life is too complex to fit neatly into a dichotomy (Peil and Sada 1984, 332).

That life in the peri-urban areas is not only desperate and bleak, Perlman shows so vividly when she contrasts the outsiders' perception of a squatter settlement with an insiders' view. It is in addition remarkable that her description of peri-urban areas in Latin America also fits Southern Africa.

> From outside, the typical favela seems to be a filthy, congested human ant heap. Women walk back and forth with huge metal cans of water on their heads or cluster at the communal water supply washing clothes. Man hang around the local bars chatting or playing cards, seemingly with nothing better to do. Naked children play in the dirt and mud. The houses look precarious at best, thrown together out of discarded scraps. Open sewers create a terrible stench, especially on hot still days. Dust and dirt fly everywhere on windy days and mud cascades down past the huts on rainy ones.
> Things look very different from inside, however. Houses are built with a keen eye to comfort and efficiency, given the climate and available materials. Much care is evident in the arrangement of furniture and the neat cleanliness of each room. Houses often boast colourful painted doors and shutters, and flowers or plants on the window sill. Cherished objects are displayed with love and pride. Most men and women rise early and work hard all day. Often these women seen doing laundry are earning their living that way, and many of the men in bars are waiting for the work-shift to begin. Children, although often not in school, appear on the whole to be bright, alert and generally healthy. Their parents ... lay high value on giving them as much education as possible. Also unapparent to the casual observer, there is a remarkable degree of social cohesion and mutual trust and a complex internal social organization, involving numerous clubs and voluntary associations (Perlman 1976, 13).

This simple description could actually be an eye-opener for the reason why, firstly, the expression 'slum' is still so frequently but inadequately used for peri-urban areas and, secondly, why the false belief is still so widespread, namely, that people in the peri-urban areas of Third World cities would be the most disadvantaged rather than those in rural areas because few know squatter areas from within while it is clear that people would not migrate in such large numbers if they could not find improvements for their lives in the cities.

The theory of over-urbanization and its fallacy

The analysis of the results of the empirical investigation clearly shows the advantages of the peri-urban population over the rural population. However, it also shows that in Mozambique even in the peri-urban areas almost half of the population still live below the poverty line in spite of all the advantages. There is common agreement amongst those social scientists concerned with Third World problems that both urban as well as rural poverty is clearly an undesirable state of affairs. However, there is divergence of opinions on what could be the way out of both kinds of poverty.

For the majority of Third World urban sociologists the theory of over-urbanization is outdated. It is, nevertheless, necessary to show its fallacy again because outside this small circle the belief in this theory is extraordinary widespread. In the mass media as well as in private discussions with students, scientists, members of development aid organizations or the common women and men one can often encounters the opinion that a solution to the problem of poverty in the developing countries would be a more healthy economic development which could only come about by lowering the level of urbanization. According to the theory of over-urbanization the rate of urbanization, i.e. the percentage of population living in cities of 100,000 and more inhabitants, must correspond to the level of industrialization, measured by the percentage of the labour force working in non-agricultural activities. Even if already more than half of the entire work force of a country works in non-agricultural occupations, even then, only about 8 per cent of the entire population should be permitted to live in cities of 100,000 and more inhabitants and only if this is the case, one could speak of a 'normal' level of urbanization.

According to this theory Mozambique is over-urbanized because here already 15 per cent of the population live in cities with 100.000 and more inhabitants[10] while only 22 per cent of the entire labour force (37 per cent of the male labour force) work in non-agricultural occupations (DNE Julho 1994, 18).

Now the crucial question arises: would urban and rural poverty, low productivity, unemployment and inflation in Mozambique decline and would the economy grow considerably more rapidly than it does now, (1994: 5.3 per cent; Wellmer 1995) and would the GNP be distributed differently, if the level of urbanization could be reduced to, say, 4 per cent only? Although this question is crucial it can remain only a rhetoric, or better a theoretical one, as it is not possible anymore in democratic societies to drive the urban masses out of the cities back into the rural areas. It is not even possible to stop rural-urban migration drastically as the freedom of choosing ones location of living is part of the constitution not only of Mozambique but of most developing countries. There would remain only two possibilities of lowering the rate of migration, if we would arrive at a common agreement on reasonable grounds that this would boost the economy and lower urban as well as rural poverty.

The first one is hardle applied anywhere at present, but has been used sporadically in the 1970s. It aimed at making the cities unattractive by no longer trying to bring a basic infrastructure to the poor areas (slow down in squatter upgrading) and no longer trying to develop new city areas for the low income people (slow down in Site and Service Schemes) as well as by lowering the minimum wages and by trying to prevent the so-called informal sector from growing. The second possibility would be to intensify rural development which unfortunately is not taken seriously enough neither by the state nor by international aid agencies as will be discussed in chapter 11.

What relevance then can be attributed to the theory of over-urbanization? What was the content of this theory before Sovani, what was Sovani's devastating critique on it and what are the main points of Gugler's arguments against rapid urbanization?

The theory of over-urbanization before Sovani

The viewpoints, which are the main targets of Sovani's attacks, stem mainly from the UN/UNESCO Seminar Report (1957) and from Davis and Golden (1954), were not only widely accepted in 1964 when Sovani's article appeared but are widely accepted even to day, which makes a renewed discussion relevant.

Over-urbanization, as already mentioned, was defined by two indices: firstly, by the percentage of population living in urban areas, in cities of 100.000 inhabitants and above (level of urbanization), a merely spatial index, secondly, by the percentage of labour force (including the labour force of the rural areas) working in non-agricultural occupations, a merely occupational index and an indication for the degree of industrialization. The justification to use these two indices to determine whether a country is over-, under- or normally urbanized was seen in the high correlation between these two indices, namely a correlation coefficient of 0.86 found by Davis and Golden (1954).

The UN/UNESCO Seminar Report (1957) defined Asia as over-urbanized because 8 per cent lived in cities of 100.000 inhabitants and above at that time while the work force in non-agricultural occupations was 33 per cent only. As mentioned earlier, according to the UN/UNESCO point of view already 55 per cent of the labour force have to work in non-agricultural activities so that a level of urbanization of 8 per cent can be justified, because this was, according to the Seminar Report, the case at the end of the 19th century when Germany, Canada, the USA, and France were industrializing.

One cause for over-urbanization in developing countries was seen in the push factor of population pressure in the rural areas and the following consequences were considered: firstly, low productivity and a high level of unemployment in these over-urbanized areas. Secondly, over-urbanized cities were seen as not being able to function as dynamic centres of cultural change as they did and do in industrialized societies, and thirdly, over-urbanization was considered as hampering economic development because of the high demand on infrastructure in the cities requiring investments which could bring about more profitability in other sectors.

Sovani's rejection of the theory of over-urbanization

The problems which Sovani saw in the then existing theory of over-urbanization were not so much the use of the above mentioned two indices but the actual percentages defined by the UN/UNESCO Seminar Report (1957), which would determine an over-urbanized society as well as the correlation coefficient between these two indices found by Davis and Golden (1954).

Sovani calculated this correlation coefficient anew and found a considerable difference between industrialized and developing countries the former showing an r of 0.395 and the later an r of 0.85. This clearly showed that the pace of urbanization in the developing countries is much more closely dependent on the pace of industrialization than in the highly industrialized areas. 'This flies in the face of the entire over-urbanization thesis at least in the way it has been formulated now' (Sovani in Breese 1969, 324). Sovani saw that this correlation coefficient could not be derived for all countries in one lump. In addition, he goes back into history, using Weber (1899) and Kuznets (1957) as sources, and is able to show that the correlation coefficient between these two indices was also 0.84 in 1891 in the USA, Canada and 11 Western countries. These results he rightly considers as proof that this correlation is high in the early stages of industrial development but not in the later stages.

The second problem Sovani sees, as already mentioned, in the given percentages by the UN/UNESCO Seminar Report. Here 8 per cent living in urban areas while 'only' 33 per cent working in non-agricultural occupations was defined as over-urbanization. The point of reference was taken from industrialized countries, where 55 per cent worked in non-agricultural occupations, when 8 per cent were urbanized. Sovani corrects the data of the UN/UNESCO Seminar Report at least for the USA and France. He shows that in the USA only between 35 and 46 per cent of the work force had non-agricultural jobs between 1850 and 1870 and France between 1856 and 1876 this percentage was 48 between 1856 and 1876. In addition, he strongly disagrees that the urbanization process of Germany, France, the USA, and Canada should be seen as model and normal and all other levels of urbanization as abnormal. He gives the impressive example of Switzerland where in 1888 no cities of 100.000 inhabitants and above existed, but 60 per cent of the population worked in non-agricultural occupations. According to Sovani also all the above mentioned countries, *could easily have been called already at that time over-industrialized and under-urbanized* (Sovani in Breese 1969, 326).

To refute the belief that it is mainly the push-factor population pressure which is responsible for driving people to urban areas, Sovani quotes Davis and Golden (1954), who found a negative correlation between population density and migration.

> Davis and Golden also did not find any correlation between the degree of urbanization in a country and the average population density there (Davis and Golden 1954, 10). There is however, they claim, a negative relationship between urbanization and agricultural density defined as the number of males occupied with agriculture, hunting, and forestry per square mile of cultivated land. It can be easily seen that this goes against the whole thesis of rural pressure being the main factor bringing about rapid urbanization (Sovani in Breese 1969, 327 footnote).

Sovani also criticizes the assumption that, because of over-urbanization cities in developing countries could not be called dynamic centres and only urbanization based on industrial development was responsible for the social and cultural changes associated with urbanism or the urban way of life. This view, he rightly points out, neglects that the process of urbanization proceeds differently in different cultures and that different cultures create cities with different social and ecological structures. Sovani believed that an infinite variety of city developments was possible.

And for the dynamic role which particularly 'primate' cities play also in developing countries for their surrounding hinterland, Sovani quotes Hoselitz:

> The primate cities of Asia are the most important centres of cultural change, especially in those fields which vitally affect economic development:

advanced education, new forms of business organization, new administrative practices, and last but not least, new technologies find a fertile soil in them, their intermediate position between East and West, their contact with world markets of commodities and ideas, their land of many traditional bonds make them into eminently suitable vehicles for the introduction of new ideas and new techniques. If economic development is associated with modernization, the mediation of new, 'more modern' forms of social action through the primate cities of Asia is an indispensable part of this process (Hoselitz 1957, 43).

However, it must be noted, that the primate city, as Third World cities in general, cannot be seen as homogeneous as most of them have been divided from colonial times up until now. They are divided into the relatively rich, fully urbanized areas and the poor peri-urban areas though often with links between them and even intermingling of the quality of housing areas. The majority of the elements mentioned by Hoselitz do not, or only to a very limited extent, apply to the poor urban areas: there is little advanced education in the peri-urban areas, hardly any new form of business administration although there are some new forms of political administration. There are few new technologies applied in the peri-urban areas and the role of an intermediate position between East and West – in the case of Africa it would mean between South and North – as well as the contact with world markets of commodities and ideas, even in this era of globalization, is reserved mainly for the fully urbanized areas. However, the land of many traditional bonds, where new ideas and new techniques can at least to some extent be introduced, is certainly the land of the peri-urban areas.

Sovani refutes the argument of the theory of over-urbanization, that rapid urbanization would hamper economic development as the demand for the provision of an economic and social infrastructure in the cities would use up the scarce resources of the developing countries to the disadvantage of the rural areas (compare also Lipton 1977).

> This would be so if the available capital resources in underdeveloped countries would be wholly or mainly devoted to more immediate productive investments. In regard to most of the underdeveloped areas the infrastructure investments are necessary both in urban and rural areas, and a large part of the available capital resources has to go into them anyway. It is only a question of the relative share of the urban and the rural portions of the economy, with respect to the total investment to be devoted to it. ... On the whole, ... the argument regarding the economic burden of rapid urbanization, as hampering economic growth in underdeveloped areas through the misallocation of scarce capital resources, is not impressive (Sovani in Breese 1969, 329).

According to Sovani, it is difficult to prove that the economies of the developing countries would have grown or would grow faster at a lower rate of urbanization. Three decades later, with a lot more statistics available we can, so to speak, 'prove' the opposite: a higher degree of urbanization means not only a higher degree of economic development (and the correlation seems to increase), but also a higher degree of human development and less poverty.

In chapter 11, on the basis of appendix 2, the correlation of the level of urbanization with the GDP per capita for all developing countries with more than 9.5 million people will be shown for 1985, 1993 and 1995. For 1995 also the correlation of the level of urbanization with the Human Development Index (HDI) and the Human Poverty Index (HPI) will be shown.

Additional arguments against the theory of over-urbanization

Gugler has pointed out two additional indirect forms of population pressures, not mentioned by the pervious theory of over-urbanization, which exist firstly, where the rural masses have no access to land because of huge holdings by landlords as is often the case in Latin America, and secondly, where there is lack of resources to open up virgin land (Gugler 1988, 80). Yet, neither these population pressures nor serious rural poverty are sufficiently strong push factors because the poorer the country the lower the level of urbanization.

> In general rural out-migration is fastest in countries whose economic performance allows the best possibilities for accommodating the exodus. This view contrasts with one in which absolute deprivation in rural areas, associated in part with rapid rural natural increase, is seen as the motive force driving multitudes to the city. Poorer countries in general have not only more deprived rural areas, but also more deprived urban ones. The net effect of poverty seems to be to hold population in rural areas (Preston in Gugler 1988, 13).

Already in 1960 the ILO stated:

> Although the push factors of falling incomes and underemployment in agriculture in most of the less developed countries are now very strong, they do not in the absence of strong pull factors, suffice to cause large shifts in manpower between occupations (ILO 1960, 20).

Moreover, not even the most unimaginable cruelty and terror on the rural population, as it was carried out by Renamo in Mozambique, was able to drive the majority of those affected to the relatively safe urban areas but the majority was fleeing to other rural areas or neighbouring countries. The city population of Mozambique during the twelve years of intensified war did not increase to a much higher extent than did other cities of the Third World but 3.8 million people of the then 14.4 million were displaced internally. Only 11 per cent of the interviewed household heads indicated that they moved to the cities because of the war. Pull factors apparently must supplement even the strongest push factors. And that the strongest pull factor is clearly economic advantages has been established by countless authors since Sovani; it was again the result of this empirical investigation: 65 per cent, and if we include the 11 per cent who wanted to continue with their education, – which normally also results in economic improvements then 76 per cent of the peri-urban household heads named economic reasons for their migration.

If in 1957 when the UN/UNESCO Seminar report appeared, all rural-urban migration would have been stopped – as was actually recommended – then most likely development in the Third World would also have come almost to a standstill.

> The large number of migrants going to the towns which some have characterised as over-urbanisation, result in greater demands for housing, water and other amenities than hard-pressed local governments can provide. However, most holders of high-level jobs as well as many of the unemployed are migrants. They provide skills as well as muscle to run the government, the factories, the railways etc. (Peil 1977, 287f).

Another impressive fact which is rarely taken into account is the extremely low percentage of rural population that actually leaves the countryside per year. According to Preston (in Gugler 1988, 12) only 1.4 per cent (or 13.7 per thousand) left the rural areas in 29 developing countries to move to an urban area per year in the time period from 1965 to 1975. This rate was even higher in 20 industrialized countries during the same time period, namely 1.9 per cent (or 18.5 per thousand).

It is in addition difficult to follow the theory of over-urbanization when the process of urbanization of Europe is considered as a model although it occurred in so much poverty, misery, exploitation of, and brutality against the urban masses.

The available documentation – mainly the Blue Books, i.e. the parliamentary inquiries on life styles of the urban poor in the nineteenth century Britain – shows fast urbanization in extremely poor conditions: overcrowded housing in slums, absence of any hygienic services, high mortality, etc. We may even assume that for some decades the urban standard of life remained worse than the rural one. Industrial development was characterized by all kinds of labour for very long working hours at a very low undifferentiated rate of productivity (Mingione in Forbes and Thrift 1987, 31).

Models which formulate, represent, and analyze the past, the present, and the future of American and European cities are not very useful for the Third World. Not only are the function and the structure of the cities very different there, but they are also in a different economic system (Drakakis Smith 1987) namely in the neo-colonial situation, suffering from the process of marginalization, of which rural areas are affected most seriously and even poor urban areas clearly stand for relative progress.

The original theory of over-urbanization as well as Sovani's critique on it both focused exclusively on rural-urban migration as cause for rapid urbanization and did not mention the natural increase of the urban population. This is understandable insofar as in the 1950s modern preventive and curative medical care only started to show some effects. Only in the following decades infant and child mortality decreased and life expectancy increased, while the fertility rate remained stable until recently (Human Development Report, 1990). Today we know that the growth of the city population in the Third World is to 60 per cent due to natural increase and only to 40 per cent to rural-urban migration (Preston in Gugler 1988). In order to keep the city population stable abruptly, no one could be allowed to move to an urban area and in addition a considerable proportion of those living in cities would have to be returned forcibly to rural areas, if birth control is not introduced as drastically as in China.

Gugler's repeated reconsideration of over-urbanization

The article by Gugler, an exponent of Third World urbanization, 'Over-urbanization Reconsidered' which first appeared in the well-known journal 'Economic Development and Cultural Change' in 1982 was reprinted in the volume on the urbanization of the Third World, edited by him in 1988 and a revised edition appeared again in his latest volume of 1997: 'Cities in the Developing World'. This – as well as the contribution of Bradshaw and Noonan in Gugler's last volume – shows that the debate on over-urbanization is not yet over. Gugler's views expressed in this article represent perhaps not so much the views of the majority of Third World urban sociologists but that of wide circles of public and private opinions and even of some development aid agencies: rapid urbanization is negative and keeping people in rural areas is tantamount to a healthy economic development, a view, or better, a policy, which has been followed also by China, yet recently with less rigidity.

The costs for housing even in poor urban areas, costs, which according to Gugler mainly consist of public expenditure, constitute a major component of the damage, which rapid urbanization does to economic development. He points out that rural houses are cheap and people build their houses themselves, without any public support. This is certainly true but the results of this research show that also half of the peri-urban household heads built their houses themselves. and the one third who hire a bricklayer do so within the informal sector without using up public expenditure (see table 6.2).

The rural houses are cheap, *however, the rural population is extremely unhappy with their cheap houses,* with walls consisting of reed, roofs consisting of grass, soil as a floor, and with one or two rooms only. The majority have a strong desire for houses built with permanent, modern material and two or three rooms (see p. 53). Modernization has penetrated almost all rural areas of the Third World to the extent that hardly anybody, not even of the elderly people, exists, not to mention the young, who does not know of better housing and does not basically long for it. In addition, to the data collected in this survey, from five years of experience in Zambia in the late 1970s and early 1980s it becomes very clear that any village family, that manages to built a brick house of two or three rooms is very proud of it and is happy if photos are taken of it by visitors from abroad. Decent housing is a basic human need, even if it is difficult to define what 'decent' housing is and even if housing is the most expensive one of all the basic human needs to be fulfilled. Yet it is completely apparent that rural housing as it exists now in most parts of Africa no longer fulfills this basic human need and that the rural population has a right to develop.

The same applies at least to some parts of the infrastructure and social facilities which Gugler mentions as being cheaper in rural areas (Gugler 1988, 80). He most probably agrees that the rural population would also have a right for better transport, clean drinking water (which is not at all provided for the vast majority of the population in the rural areas; only 20 per cent of the entire population of Mozambique have access to clean drinking water; in the cities this proportion is at least 44 per cent; OEFSE 1995, 11), more and better modern health care facilities, and more and better schools. However, statements about people in rural areas paying less when they hire construction workers, because, firstly, wages are low and secondly, there are no trade unions (Gugler 1988, 81), give rise to the question: could low wages and the non-existence of trade unions be any solution to the problem, any recommendable state of affairs?

Although Gugler admits that the provision of electricity, pipe-borne-water, and health care facilities is cheaper in the poor areas of the cities, he, on the other hand, holds the view that in general the provision of a subsistence minimum is more costly to the urban than to the rural populations. In this statement neither the still smaller percentage of the poor city dwellers in many developing countries compared to the poor rural dwellers nor the problem of dispersion of the rural population is taken into account. The concentration of people around centres in urban areas allows them to have a better infrastructure at lower costs even in countries where more than half of the population live in peri-urban or poor city areas, like, for instance, in Zambia.[11] For all these squatter dwellers rapid urbanization can be seen as a 'blessing' and they are not parasites on the countries economy, but constitute the work force for Zambia's (mainly copper) industries.

In his revised version of 1997 Gugler already omits some of the above discussed aspects and elaborates even more on the distributional dimension of rural-urban migration and the advantages it might bring to the rural population, however, he still mentions among five amenities housing and transport which are, according to him, cheaper or not needed in rural areas (Gugler 1997, 118). It is difficult to understand how one could deprive the rural population of transport which is needed so badly to go to clinics or hospitals or to the nearest town or provincial capital for whatever reason. Fifty-five per cent of the small rural sample of this research consider transport as a serious problem and 32 per cent as a problem.

It is true that some costly services, such as garbage collection and sewage disposal, are not yet needed in rural areas, however, there is already widespread concern how important improved latrines would be (see chapter 6), also in the rural areas, for a better hygiene to combat diseases. The argument that rural people do more for themselves with their own labour as for example, building village roads and irrigation schemes, leads to the question: who works harder, longer working hours and is more productive, the peri-urban or the rural population? Reliable, recent data from Mozambique show that the percentage of under- and unemployed is higher in the rural areas (30 per cent) than in the urban areas (24 per cent)[12] (DNE, Julho 1994, 23-4). If Mozambique would not be an exception and similar data could be established for many other developing countries, this would be another strong argument against the theory of over-urbanization. *Considering this data we would have to speak of an over-ruralization.*

Rural population increases in virtually all developing countries in spite of rural-urban migration, because the natural increase is much higher than the earlier mentioned 1.4 per cent who migrate. However, Gugler's opinion that this natural increase must not mean an increase of the labour force because mainly young and adult men emigrate can also not be supported by statistical data, if Mozambique is no exception. At least in Mozambique the percentage of under- and unemployed men is also higher in rural areas, namely 26 per cent as against 21 per cent in urban areas (32 per cent of the female work-force are under- and unemployed in the rural areas as against 30 per cent in urban areas. DNE, Julho 1994, 24). The rural work force does increase.

However, even if we could speak of an over-ruralization in terms of under- and unemployed it is probably true, although without sufficient empirical evidence, that the rural areas lose the young, the able-bodied, the educated, and the most enterprising men by rural-urban migration. This also means a considerable hindrance for innovation in agriculture and

> a potential loss for agricultural output where uncultivated land is still available where virgin land could be developed and where institutional restraints on the intensification of farming could be overcome (Gugler 1988, 79).

Instead of advocating the persistence of over-ruralization, i.e. just keeping people in the country side and condemning rapid urbanization, it would be more important to advocate in these times of crisis a positive ruralization of the peri-urban areas, namely urban agriculture as a possibility to overcome poverty and malnutrition. Unlike some Asian cities, where the entire population lives from agriculture nearby (Yue 1985), a lot of negative attitudes towards urban cultivators must still be overcome by administrators as well as local and international agencies. Research on urban agriculture is increasing and if its application could be developed fully, it would be another strong argument against the theory of over-urbanization, (see chapter 12).

Also urban people can be motivated to do more for themselves. And if it can be established that rural under- and unemployment is higher than urban under- and unemployment and if we acknowledge the right of the rural population to develop, for a first step, at least to have their basic needs fulfilled, then this would use up considerably more recourses than are now provided for the urban areas and then the level of over-urbanization is not in order. Rapid urbanization is an essential feature of the entire developing world at the turn of the century and it will continue at the beginning of the next millennium and it cannot and should not be stopped. Almost eighty per cent of the population live in towns and cities in the industrialized world, the rural population of the developing world should not be condemned to stay there forever.

> Basic human needs are the same for urban and rural dwellers – adequate means for livelihood, a secure shelter, access to clean water, health care and education, protection against natural disasters and contamination from wastes – as well as basic political and civil rights. ... In choosing to concentrate on the needs of urban inhabitants and the failure of government (and the powerful International Financial Institutions, – see chapter 11; addition in parenthesis by the author) to work with these people to meet their needs, we do not mean to imply that the needs of rural dwellers are less pressing. Indeed, why should the needs of a rural landless labourer forced to migrate to an urban area be any more or less valid before or after they have migrated – or their needs be any more or less valid than a household which has spent its entire life in an urban centre? (Hardoy and Satterthwaite 1989, 6-7).

The extent of urbanization in the Third World today and in the near future

In spite of the relative improvement which the part of the population is able to enjoy that manages to move to the peri-urban or even to the fully urbanized areas as well as those who were born there, rapid urbanization causes, of course, also serious problems for the governments, the city councils, administrators, and city planners. No one can deny that the urban problems in most developing countries are enormous, it is, nevertheless, not justified to consider them in isolation without at least acknowledging that the rural problems are worse.

With the attainment of political independence which took place already in the 19th century in Latin America and in the middle or even second half of this century in Africa, freedom of movement was guaranteed and with it a massive rural-urban migration started which lasts until today. However, as already mentioned, not only because of rural-urban migration, but also due to natural increase the cities of the Third World grew, particularly from the mid 1960s to the mid 1980s (see table 1 in appendix 2). The rate of increase was declining thereafter and is still declining (see table 2 in appendix 2). In spite of the declining rate many Third World – including African – cities might have the three or fourfold size in 2015 compared to 1980. This is actually not an unprecedented extent of growth as such, as it is often regarded. Cities quadrupled within 50 years already in the 16th and in the 19th century as we have mentioned above. The novelty is the proportion of people benefiting from urbanization. At the beginning of this century only one in eight people lived in an urban area (Gugler 1997, xvii) while this proportion is almost half at the end of the century and it looks as if in the 21st century the process of urbanization – as far as its growth rate is concerned – might be completed, with three quarters or even 80 per cent of the population living in urban areas world wide. According to the World Bank (1986a, 240) the trend towards urbanization which we are experiencing today, will continue until the year 2030 or 2035; only then a stationary situation will be reached.

However, Hardoy and Satterthwaite (1989, 249-56) show the unreliability of such long-term forecasts and also give numerous examples of very unrealistic projections made also by the United Nations, which were used by many authors without looking into the specific assumptions on which such projections were based and, therefore, to a certain extent misusing them. Forecasting has improved somehow from the mid 1970s to the mid 1980s, revising downwards the projected population for the year 2000 of the eight largest cities. According to the mid 1980s forecasts Beijing will not have 19 million inhabitants in the year 2000 as projected in 1973-5 but only 11 million. Mexico City will not have 32 but only 26 million, which is still far off reality as the number of inhabitants given for Mexico City in the Human Development Report (HDR) of 1998 for the year 1995 is 16.6 million and even for the year 2015 no more than 19 million are expected to live in Mexico City.

One would expect that population projections would have improved even further from the 1980s to the 1990s. Apparently and unfortunately not in all cases. In the HDR 1998 Maputo is listed with having 2.2 million inhabitants in 1995; it was forecast to have 2.7 million people in the year 2000. Hardoy's and Satterthwaite's critique (1989, 252) did apparently not reach the Population Division of the United Nations, because they argued already then very conclusively that in the census of 1980 Maputo had some

740,000 inhabitants and could, therefore, and also because of economic hardship and war, in no way quadruple within 20 years. In the general information on Mozambique at the beginning of this book the result of the sample census of 1994 is shown. In this year Maputo had 887,600 inhabitants and 1,015,300 inhabitants in 1997. It could be that some figures still float around from the time when Matola, a twin city of Maputo, was incorporated into the administration of the latter, however, even then the figures would be too high as Matola is much smaller than Maputo. Progress was certainly made in the projection method as Dar es Salaam was projected in 1980 to have 4.6 million in the year 2000 (Hardoy and Satterthwaite 1989, 250; underlying assumptions unknown to the author), but is now forecast to have 3.8 million in the year 2015, apparently on the basis of the number of inhabitants in 1995 of 1.7 million. The case is the same for Nairobi; it had less than a million inhabitants in 1980 and was projected to have about 19 million in the year 2025. In 1995 it had 1.8 million and is projected to have 4.2 million in 2015 (HDR 1998).

In 1995, 45 per cent of the world's population were urban (37 per cent in all developing countries, 23 per cent in the least developed countries, 74 per cent in the industrial countries; (HDR 1998, 175). So, one could realistically assume that shortly after the year 2000 for the first time half of the world's population will live in cities or urban areas. This constitutes an enormous progress and is a positive consequence of globalization. Although in the Third World probably about half – in Africa certainly more than half – of the city dwellers will live in peri-urban areas, in relative poverty, they will be, nevertheless, better off than the rural population.

> United Nations projections have been widely used by other institutions to focus governments' attention on city population growth as the problem. But this is misleading. First, enormous numbers of urban centres have not grown rapidly and yet have major problems with regard to poverty and environmental degradation. (Maputo and Beira, the main focus of this study can serve as examples; addition by the author.) Second, most of the really serious problems of poverty, very poor housing conditions and environmental destruction in and around major cities need not have arisen if per capita incomes are higher and more equally distributed, and if city governments had the power, resources and personnel to cope with rapid growth. ... *the issue of how fast or slow a city is growing is of secondary importance* (italics by the author) (Hardoy and Satterthwaite 1989, 253-4).

The majority of the urban population in developing countries still lives in secondary and small urban centres with populations less than 500,000 (Schneider and Vorlaufer 1997, 2; represented in this study by Beira). However, there is a trend towards larger metropolitan areas or mega-cities. Bronger (1996) calls this characteristic process of the 20th century 'megalopolization'. Cities with one million and more inhabitants are considered as metropolises. This category is represented here by Maputo with 1,015,300 inhabitants in 1997. However, it is not only the number of inhabitants that make a city a metropolis, but also its function. It has specific, economic, administrative and cultural functions and the political power of a country is concentrated here, particularly, if the metropolis is at the same time the capital city and in addition a primate city. In the case of Maputo − which is both, capital and primate city − (three times as large as Beira) all these functions are more or less concentrated in the first district, the fully urbanized area or cement city.

Mega-cities are defined by the number of their inhabitants, but − according to Bronger − in addition a density of at least 2,000 inhabitants per km^2 and a monocentric settlement pattern is required (Bronger 1996). The defining characteristic of the number of inhabitants varies. As mentioned earlier, according to Hu (1997), one speaks of a mega-city, when eight million and more people live there, but according to Bonger only 10 million and more make a city a mega-city (Bronger 1996). The UNFPA (1996) defines a mega-city as a city with 5 million and more inhabitants.

If the 10 million mark is adopted for a mega-city, then there was only one such city in 1950, there were 14 in 1994 and it is estimated that there will be 27 mega-cities in the year 2015 (Schneider and Vorlaufer 1997, 4). Only four of them will be in the North − which are actually called 'world cities' or 'global cities' − and 23 mega-cities will be in the Third World. However, in Africa, the least urbanized continent, there will only be two cities with more than 10 million in 2015, Cairo and Lagos. Only 12 per cent of the Third World's urban population will live in mega-cities (UNFPA 1996, 33), which shows the magnitude of urbanization that is going on below the 10 million inhabitants mark. In 1990 only 7 per cent of the total urban population in developing countries were living in eight mega-cities (UNFPA 1996, 33).

The following graph shows the increase of Africa's urbanization from 1920 to 2000.

Figure 2.1 The growth of Africa's urban population in relation to the total population (in millions and per cent)

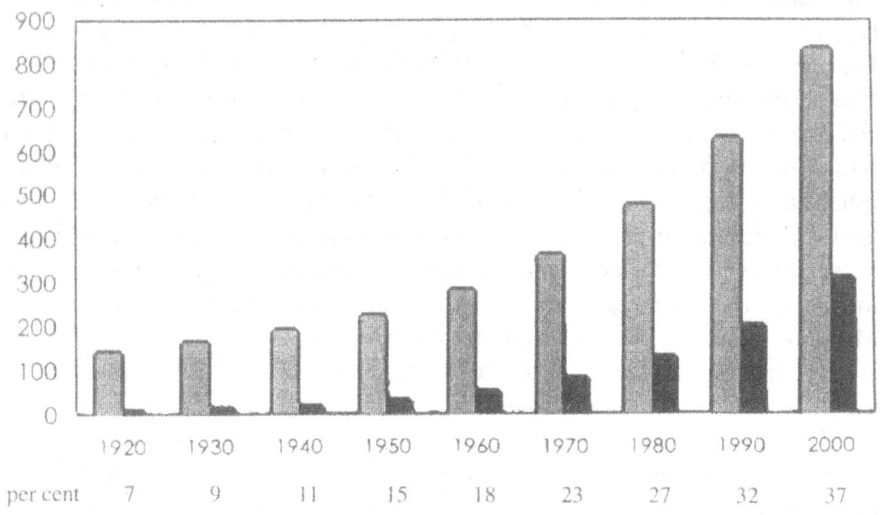

column 1: total of population; column 2: urban population
Source: For 1920 to 1940: UN 1969, 48 and Hance 1970, 16. For 1950 to 2000: UN 1995, 86. Sources and graph adopted from Krammer 1998, 85-7.

Although the figure shows the increase of urbanization impressively, the urbanization rate has to be regarded with caution as it might be less than 37 per cent in the year 2000. The HDR (1998) indicates an urbanization rate for all developing countries in the year 2015 of 49 per cent, but only of 35 per cent for the least developed countries. As the majority of the African countries belong to the least developed, the indicated proportion of 37 per cent urban population, as we are approaching the year 2000, might already be too high.

The biggest challenge for everybody, for ordinary citizens and those in power, is the eradication of rural and urban poverty. Only if we can face this challenge, then the process of urbanization, this profound human transformation, which is comparable to the first profound transformation – the domestication of plants and animals ten thousand years ago that made a sedentary life possible – only then urbanization will constitute real progress; a human progress that started five thousand years ago in the Euphrates and Tigris valleys and it looks as if it could be completed in the next century to give way to another transformation, maybe to the conquering of our surrounding planets, hopefully only after poverty has been eradicated on planet Earth via an alternative development and an alternative globalization.

Notes

1   In a number of African cities more than half of the households of the peri-urban areas grow food on open spaces within the city or in the surrounding rural areas. In Nairobi 65 per cent (Mazingira Institut, 1987; quoted by Streiffeler 1993), in Beira (Mozambique) 66 per cent of the households grow food.
2   Macamo found in the Tsonga ethnicity in Southern Mozambique a very interesting example for the localization of the global. He shows how the global claim of the Protestant ethic brought in by the Swiss Presbyterian missionaries was 'used' or localized by the people there for protection against bad spirits, in which they continued to believe, even though they converted to Christianity (see the section on churches in chapter 6).
3   At the small university of Zambia with only between one and two thousand students at the end of each academic year several students committed suicide because of having failed the exam or even just out of fear of failure.
4   At the end of the 16th century the European world economy comprised of not only Northwestern-, Northern-, central Europe and the christianized Mediterranean regions but also some regions of Latin America, such as New Spain (later Mexico), the Antilles, Terraferma, Peru, Chile, and Brazil. Some islands in the Atlantic Ocean most probably also belonged to it as some enclaves on the Northern coast of Africa. The European world economy included neither the regions in the Indian Ocean, the Far East, the Osmanic Empire nor Russia (Wallerstein 1986, 100).
5   According to archeologists and descriptions of journeys there existed many cities between the 12th and 14th century in Yourubaland in West Africa: Some were estimated to have around 100,000 inhabitants. Islamic historians of the 14th and 15th centuries described the richness of the West Sudanesian cities, particularily those which were residences of kings. Dutch merchants visited the coast of Ghana and were impressed by the cities there in the 17th and 18th centuries (Loth, 1986, 66; see also Rodney, 1973).
6   In the province of Niassa, which is up until now one of the least developed and most thinly populated areas of Mozambique, slave trade intensified in the last one hundred years of trade and lasted well into the 20th century under a different form and name (Macamo, personal communication). As a whole Mozambique might have lost an estimated 1 million people (Newitt 1995 and personal communications). Slave trade destroyed the social structure and prevented agricultural development as people were constantly fleeing.
7   Although Austria never managed to conquer colonies, Maputo was an Austrian foundation under the empress Maria Theresia. This 'colony' lasted only for four years, from 1777 to 1781, when the Portuguese took over the two small forts and a few soldiers. The site between the Iniaca island and the mainland of Mozambique, called Delagoa bay, was discovered and found suitable for a port on a trade route to India and China (Baiculescu, 1995; Original source 1927).
8   Site and Service Schemes are urban areas developed on virgin land. Plot and infrastructure are provided by the City Council or other organizations but the people have to build their very low cost houses themselves. Sometimes building loans are available.

62   *Globalization, urban progress, urban problems, rural disadvantages*

Upgraded squatters are areas where plots were demarcated and a basic infrastructure and basic facilities provided to already existing spontaneous, unplanned settlements.

9   Bairros are neighbourhoods, smaller units than a district, comprising around 200 to 500 families. The term is mainly used for the neighbourhoods in the peri-urban areas (although in a strict administrative sense the first district is also divided into bairros) and is basically the equivalent for squatters, upgraded squatters and Site and Service Schemes.

10

	number of households in 1992 (1)	family size (2)	number of inhabitants calculated by the author
Lichinga	13 628	5.8	79 042
Pemba	14 658	4.7	68 892
Nampula	52 101	5.3	276 135
Quelimane	28 229	5.8	183 728
Tete	18 850	6.0	113 100
Chimoio	17 550	6.8	119 340
Beira	53 919	5.7	307 338
Inhamban	9 907	4.9	48 544
Xai-Xai	14 032	6.6	92 611
Matola	55 317	6.5	359 560
Maputo			867 566 (3)
Total			2,206 767

Total population of Mozambique in 1992:   14, 790 049 (4);
2,206 767 : 147 900 = 14.9 per cent

(1) and (2) listed in: Direção Nacional de Estatística (DNE), Serie: Inquérito às Famílias (IAF), Janeiro 1994, xi and 3
(3) DNE, Serie: Inquérito Demográfico Nacional, Documento 1, Maio 1993, 10
(4) DNE, Serie: Inquérito Demográfico Nacional, Documento 3, Junho 1994, 15

11 In the capital of Zambia, Lusaka, in 1977 already
50 per cent lived in squatters   ⎫
10 per cent in Site and Service Schemes   ⎬ peri-urban area
20 per cent in formal low cost housing areas
20 per cent in high cost housing areas (Knauder 1982, 23).
In the rest of the cities of Zambia the situation was considerably better already in 1974 where frequently only one fifth lived in squatters and half of the urban population in formal low cost housing areas (Ministry of Local Government and Housing, Urban housing stock breakdown by type, Lusaka, 1974).

12 Under-employment is defined as that part of the labour-force (25 per cent in the rural areas and 9 per cent in the urban areas) that works less than 8 hours per day.

PART II
THE TWOFOLD GAP AND THE RURAL – PERI-URBAN – URBAN CHANGES

PART II

3 Socio-economic characteristics of the three investigated areas: poverty and relative prosperity

An attempt was made in the previous chapter to show briefly the history of the peri-urban areas and what distinguishes them from the fully urbanized areas and the countryside. In addition, the interrelation between urbanization and globalization was discussed as well as the positive and negative effects of the latter. The discussion of over-urbanization made it clear that rapid urbanization is never the cause, neither for urban nor for rural poverty. In this chapter, using the results of the empirical investigation, the dimensions of rural and urban poverty as well as relative prosperity in Mozambique should be analyzed. The discussion of other socio-economic characteristics and their differences between the investigated areas will show how social change can be observed from the rural via the peri-urban to the fully urbanized areas, called cement cities in Mozambique.

Income of households

The results concerning the income situation do not have the same degree of reliability – not even in the peri-urban areas – as most other results. Firstly, it is very difficult to assess the total incomes of households in industrialized countries and even more so in developing countries. Secondly, income assessment was not the prime objective of this study. The respective questions were included in the questionnaire only to get some reference as at the time of the survey no recent data on income in Mozambique existed. In the meantime we have the IAF,[1] the results of which can be considered very reliable. Nevertheless, the results of this research will be presented too, because in the IAF there is no separate data on the fully urbanized areas, the cement cities. However, the results of the IAF are of great value insofar as they show that income from employment makes up only for 52 per cent of the total household income in Maputo, 42 per cent in the provincial capitals and 47 per cent of the urban areas in general.[2] According to the IAF income from small trading (selling on the black market, called 'dumba nenge' in Maputo and 'chunga moio' in Beira) accounts for 24 per cent, income from family production for 8 per cent, from remittances for 5 per cent, (mainly from family members working in South Africa), and income from other sources for 11 per cent. The distribution of the kind of household income is very similar in Maputo and Beira (IAF Outubro 1994, 21).

We also tried to find out all productive activities of the wives including urban agriculture as well as the quantity of the remittances, (see questionnaire V19 to 21 and V28 to 35) and after all these lengthy questions we simply asked 'what is the total income of your household per month approximately?' An immediate answer was expected. Therefore it is almost certain that the answers reflect the regular monthly money income mainly of the employed household members since adding all the other bits and pieces would have been too lengthy a process. Taking into account the findings of the IAF, it is justified to double the family income from employment indicated by the household heads in this survey.[3] The new results achieved this way for Maputo only (in order to be able to compare them with the results of the IAF because only the structure of the kind of income is available for Beira) are presented in the following graph.

Figure 3.1 Household income of the lower strata of the cement city of Maputo, the peri-urban areas and entire Maputo[4]

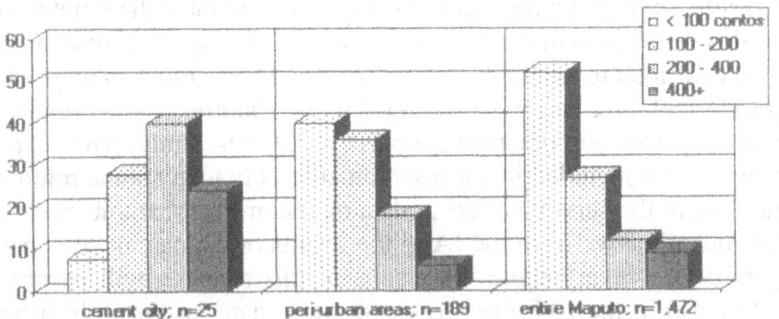

If we put the poverty line at 100 contos family income per month, (no official poverty line exists for the time being in Mozambique, however, according to a lot of oral information it was extremely difficult to live with less than 100 contos per month, approximately US$ 70) we are confronted with the very sad facts, namely that on the basis of the results of the IAF 52 per cent of the entire population of Maputo and on the basis of this research 40 per cent of the population in the peri-urban areas of Maputo live under the poverty line and 8 per cent belong to these very poor, even in the cement city. However, it must be noted that, even in this investigated lower strata of the cement city about two thirds live in relative prosperity, which would increase considerably if a representative sample of the fully urbanized area would have been chosen. At least here, in the fully urbanized areas, where one fifth of the city population lives, the majority can enjoy urban progress.

The population in the peri-urban areas of Beira is still poorer than the one of the peri-urban areas of Maputo, 52 per cent of the households live under the poverty line and in the cement city of Beira 15 per cent are still very poor. (The tables 3.1a to 3.1e in appendix 3 show the monthly wage of household heads as well as the household income and both in the breakdown by province; table 3.1e corresponds with the above shown graph.) Keeping in mind the poverty line of 100 contos per month per household, the tables show that it is not possible for the majority of the families to survive on one wage only. Therefore a big difference exists between the income of the head of a household and the total income of a household.

In view of these facts it is not surprising that more than half of the urban population of Maputo can only acquire half of the biologically necessary food and that one third of the children of Mozambique is undernourished (Ministerio de Comercio 1988).

In 36 per cent of the households of all three areas with husbands and wives, the wives are involved in money earning in addition to housework and child rearing. The percentage is the same in Maputo and Beira. About 20 per cent work most of the day on the family field, about 8 per cent in formal employment, the rest works in the informal sector or as traders or is involved in other activities (chapter 8).

When we asked if apart from husband and wife other family members work we did not distinguish between formal employment, informal sector, trading, agricultural work or others. The following should give an overview over the proportions of families with additional bread winners and the low proportions that receive remittances:

	urban	peri-urban	rural
additional family members work	26	32	13
family members send remittances	7	14	11
relatives send remittances	11	9	6

The income situation is clearly worst in the villages. However, as the sample of this study was very small and particularly on the questions of income the missing cases were high (in the villages of Sofala only 20 per cent replied) we rely on a investigation carried out in five provinces (Direcção Nacional de Estatistica et al. 1990).[5] In large parts of the rural areas of Mozambique people do not really live in a subsistence economy as they cannot sustain themselves but live in absolute poverty and misery. In the study of the 'five provinces' mentioned above, it was found that the poorer part of the population in the rural areas even near the district centres only had 7 contos per household per month:
2 contos came from the production for self-consumption
5 contos from wages
0.2 from selling fruits and animals.

However, for a minimum diet 7 contos per capita would have been necessary in October 1989, which means 5.6 times more per household as the study of the 'five provinces' found an average family size of 5.6 in the rural areas. Even 7 contos per capita (about 40 contos, 24 US $ per household) would not allow to acquire any other goods – apart from food – necessary for a minimum standard of living. Yet,
38 per cent of the households had an average income of only 7 contos per month living at high risk to survive
31 per cent of the households had an average monthly income of 31 contos living at risk; only for another
31 per cent of the families the average income was 88 contos. Only those were able to live without risk for their health (Direcção Nacional de Estatistica, 1990, ix).

Also here, obviously the producer prices or market prices respectively, have been used in the rural areas (the money which peasants receive for their products), to determine their income and with it their level of poverty, a calculation which Jamal and Weeks strongly reject with convincing arguments, particularly where such calculation is compared with consumer prices (the amount of money the people in the urban areas have to pay for food) and this comparison is used to show the rural-urban gap. However, on the other hand, the study of the five provinces specifies the amount of money or the equivalent of products a household needs in order to survive without risk.

Also Tschirley and Weber (1994, 163), who investigated smallholders in the Northern province Nampula, came to the conclusion 'that over half of all households appear to be seriously compromised' not even reaching 80 per cent of the caloric requirements.

This terrible misery existed obviously to a large extend because of the war in Mozambique but most likely not only because of the war. Poverty being worse in the rural areas as compared to the peri-urban areas is a phenomenon of most countries in the Third World. This poverty has many causes, which will be analyzed in chapter 11. Just to mention a few: besides the traditional way of life, it is the dispersion and remoteness of the villages which makes the provision with infrastructure so difficult and expensive and besides the colonial heritage, it is also a policy of neglecting rural areas of most modern governments of the South and the powerful international institutions of the North which excludes mainly rural areas from the benefits of globalization, keeps them politically weak with a low level of education and lets rural development programmes fail. In Zambia, for example, where there never was a war in recent history 79 per cent were considered as poor and very poor in rural areas in 1980 but 'only' 26 per cent in the peri-urban areas (squatters, upgraded squatters, Site and Service Schemes and low cost housing areas, ILO/JASPA 1981, xxiii). Crehan (1981), who explored the penetration of capital in the North-Western provinces of Zambia, hits the point when she concludes her paper with an outcry of a village-teacher: 'rural areas are places which God forgot'.

Apart from the existing rural-urban gap in virtually all developing countries (and in the majority of them one would have to add the peri-urban – urban gap), the distribution of lower and higher level wage jobs in general, is, according to Wallerstein (1996, 233), becoming somewhat more even world-wide similar to the fifteenth and eighteenth centuries. However, according to him, the gap between those wages at survival level and those above is widening. This would again correspond with the rural-urban gap on the one hand, (whereby rural wages and incomes are more often below survival level than peri-urban incomes, as we have seen) and the North-South gap on the other hand. This wage gap between the North, the triad, which consitutes the centre or core and the South, which constitutes the periphery, will be seen increasingly as a class phenomenon in all countries and for the first time the periphery has sufficient destructive weapons (as the recent atomic tests of India and Pakistan show) to be a real threat for the industrialized countries, the core (Wallerstein 1996, 234).

The have-nots will rise against the haves whether the haves like it or not. Is it not therefore spiritually and morally more rewarding to correct injustices willingly before one is forced to lose unwanted privileges through superior force? (Kaunda 1974, 19-20).

Again we can ask the question, as we put it on the front page: is the world moving toward one of those tragic moments that will lead future historians to ask, why nothing was done in time? (Kapstein 1996).

The analysis of the extreme negative aspects of the socio-economic characteristics, particularly in the rural areas of Mozambique but also in the peri-urban areas, may contribute to the awareness how serious the situation is. The root causes for this inhuman poverty alongside a world of affluence in the North will be analyzed in more detail in chapter 12.

However, the ugly face of poverty does not only appear in extremely low income – although this is the main problem – low income has also many concomitants as will be shown in the following paragraphs and then in the chapters on housing and depressions.

The colonial past has in most Third World countries particularly in Africa aggravated rural poverty but it is not the only reason for the disadvantages of the rural population compared to the urban one. China, for instance, has hardly ever been a colony but the city population is privileged compared to the rural one even though enormous efforts are made to close the gap. The ratio of personal consumption was estimated at 2.5 : 1 in 1981 but lowered to 2.1 : 1 in 1982 (Gugler 1988, 35). However, it is questionable, whether the ratio will become 1 : 1 in the near future as the rural population is still disadvantaged compared to the urban one also in industrialized countries.

Jamal and Weeks (1993) argue that the rural-urban gap has disappeared in sSA in the last two decades and that in some cases the rural areas are already even better off. We do not agree, neither to the assumption that the gap has disappeared nor that rural areas have overtaken poor urban areas, but a narrowing of the gap has undoubtedly occurred, although in a tragic way. The rural areas have not been developed up to the level of the peri-urban areas, but the peri-urban areas have sunk back to the level of rural poverty. This is mainly due to the structural adjustment programmes. All along in this book, the seriousness of urban poverty will be discussed, however, evidence of the even more disastrous rural poverty is equally strong.

Socio-economic characteristics 71

Alongside a very valuable review of data in which Jamal and Weeks discovered fatal errors made by high-ranking experts, such as Turner (1966) who did not discover that in many national surveys producer prices in the rural areas were compared with consumer prices in the cities, the analysis of Jamal and Weeks shows shortcomings as well. They admit that their definition of rural-urban inequality is quite restricted.

> We shall direct our critique to the standard of living of farmers and wage earner households as measured by monetary income and the imputes value of non-market consumption, that is, we shall be primarily interested in the trend in the rural-urban gap in terms of household welfare and the implications of that for household behaviour (Jamal and Weeks 1993, 3).

Only sometimes the authors deal with other aspects of the rural-urban gap such as social services. Household welfare and household behaviour is also not really dealt with explicitly as the authors state themselves that their 'argument does not address itself specifically to the broad issue of the quality of life in town and countryside'. So income remains their main variable for comparison. Even if rural and urban income were equal, which is not convincing in spite of all their data, there would still be a great difference in housing, infrastructure and social facilities left to be analyzed for Mozambique in chapter 6, which this time is hopefully also for Jamal and Weeks and their followers not just an 'empirical manifestation' and not just 'dubious measures of urban and rural welfare access to social services (and) infrastructure' (Jamal and Weeks 1993, 2-3).

It also can not be justified to compare peasant production, on the one hand, and urban wages, on the other hand, to determine the non-existing rural-urban gap. Only about half of the household heads were found to be peasants in the rural areas of Mozambique (see figure 3.3 and footnote 7 of chapter 3).

> ... a large proportion of the rural population is engaged, full-time or part-time, in non-farm activities such as manufacturing, repair, construction, retail and wholesale trade, restauranting, transport, personal services, and salaried employment in teaching health services, and public administration. Surveys from four Asian and three African countries report that non-farm income generated by rural households ranged from 14 to 45 per cent, averaging 35 per cent (Gugler citing Tomich, Kilby, and Johnston 1995, in Gugler (ed) 1997).

The number of wage earners in the urban areas is exceptionally high in Mozambique but they are generally shrinking in Africa. In Sierra Leone,

Tanzania, and Zambia, for instance, wage employees now constitute on average only 16 per cent of the urban labour force (UNRISD 1995, 45). Of course, Jamal and Weeks do acknowledge the growing informal sector, but when comparing, they mainly speak of agricultural production and wages.

Even Jamal and Weeks' contribution to the structural adjustment problem and the awakening of the awareness for urban poverty is highly valuable, the questioning of any rural-urban differences (which are admitted anyway again and again) is problematic. Sometimes their assumptions are based on shaky grounds. As Mozambique did not belong to their sample countries, Zambia should serve as an example. For Zambia they postulate 'that the average farmer produced at least sufficient calories for the family'; in addition they assumed 'that food comprised 75 per cent of rural family income' (Jamal and Weeks 1993, 78). Both these assumptions are questionable. According to an NFNC/FAO survey of 1970-72 three quarters of the children in remote rural areas showed some degree of malnutrition. Of course, this statistic can be doubted again, but maybe the multiple deprivation in the countryside just can not be denied:

> remoteness, lack of surplus to sell, lack of markets, problems of supplying and maintaining services for health, education, roads and water, shortage of goods and their high prices – would be serious on its own. Together they compound each other (ILO/JASPA 1981, 26).

One of the great merits of Jamal and Weeks was the re-examination of the magnitude of the rural-urban gap at least as far as income was and is concerned. This gap was by far overestimated in many countries. In Zambia, for instance, Jamal and Weeks calculate an income gap of 1:1.9, which was previously widely accepted as a gap of to 1:4.9 or at least 1:3.5, depending on the source (Jamal and Weeks 1993, 78-9). A gap of 1:1.9 is shown by the newest data of a sample census in Mozambique, the third stage of IAF, carried out by the Central Statistical Office, where statisticians obviously already used the proper calculations. In 1996/97 urban households (although the cement cities included) had an average income of 799 contos which are about 72 US Dollars, but rural households (although obviously including commercial farmers) had an average income of 418 contos, about 38 US Dollars. This means that poverty in Mozambique has increased even after the war, since prices have also increased due to SAPs and already at the time of interviewing in mid 1991 the poverty line was around 70 US Dollars. Jamal and Weeks point out again and again that the main contradiction is not the rural-urban one but the intra-rural and intra-urban inequalities. In this research the commercial farmers and other wealthy people in the countryside could not be included, they are only hinted at a few times when presenting the results of the third stage of the sample census of the IAF, but the intra-urban gap has truly been made a subject of discussion even though the real urban elite was also not included.

The level of formal education of the household heads

The educational level of the population in a given area depends amongst other factors on income and on infrastructures. These are inferior in the peri-urban areas to those even in the worst parts of the cement cities – also the level of education is worse yet, it is still much higher than in the villages because, again, there the level of income and the level of infrastructure are lowest.

Figure 3.2 Educational level of household heads by type of area

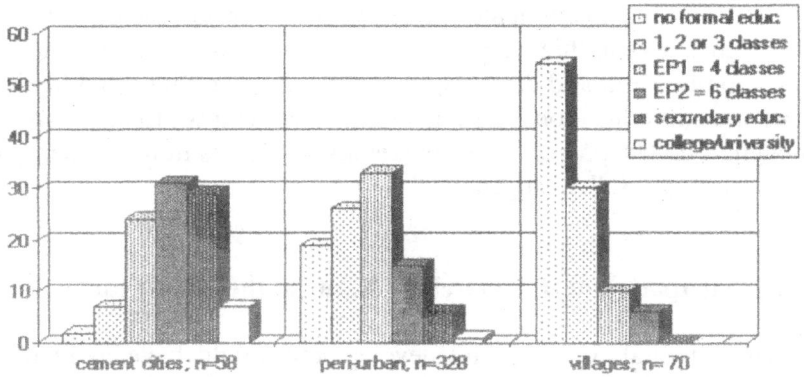

The differences in the level of education of household heads between the three areas are considerable. However, it is difficult to define which gap is wider: the one between the two urban areas or the one between peri-urban and rural areas. If we took illiteracy of household heads as a criteria, then the peri-urban – rural gap would be wider but it is not wider in all the other categories than the gap between peri-urban areas and cement cities:

  2   < 20   < 54   per cent do not have any formal education
  7   < 26   < 30   per cent have completed 1st, 2nd or 3rd class
 24   < 33   > 10   per cent reached the first level of primary school
                                (EP1=4 classes)
 22   > 15   > 6   per cent completed primary school (EP2 =6 classes)

In the distribution of the educational level in the fully urbanized areas we can observe urban progress as the proportion of household heads with secondary school education and even college or university level is considerable. The problems start in the peri-urban areas and are worst in the villages. Secondary schools are very rare and ill equipped in the peri-urban and completely absent in the rural areas. This is most likely not the only reason why such a low proportion of household heads with secondary school education can be found in the peri-urban areas because if somebody has reached secondary school level, it is much easier to find employment and housing in the cement cities. Not only in developing countries but world-wide in this era of globalization, training on the job gains importance besides the level of formal education. Here we can observe the same pattern, namely of the fully urbanized areas being privileged, the peri-urban areas taking on a middle position and the rural areas being neglected.

57 per cent in the cement cities
32 per cent in the peri-urban areas
12 per cent in the villages have had on-the-job training.

A considerable higher percentage of household heads has no formal education in Beira and the villages of the Sofala province and in all other categories the educational level is lower except that we found, surprisingly enough, a higher proportion of university graduates in the cement city of Beira (see table 3.2b in appendix 3).

The participation of the household heads in the labour force

Urban and rural progress and development would have to include the possibility to participate in the labour force either in paid employment or having the opportunity and the means to pursue urban agriculture and in the rural areas it would have to include in addition land rights and the possibility to produce enough food for consumption and sale. Unfortunately, Mozambique will still have a long way to go to reach this goal, while the problems of unemployment are growing even in the industrialized countries.

The mode of participation of household heads in the labour force in the cities is employment with the government. The rates are almost the same in the cement cities and the peri-urban areas: 40 and 38 per cent respectively. In the villages however only 5 per cent work for the government; naturally the mode here is agricultural work (44 per cent). Also in the study of the 'five provinces' 46 per cent peasants were found,[6] which again supports the findings of the small control group of this research essentially.

Figure 3.3 Participation of the household heads in the labour force

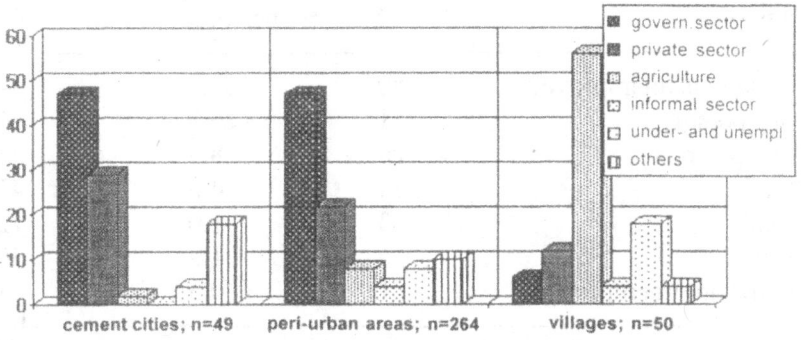

The private sector employs a quarter of the household heads of the cement cities and 18 per cent of the household heads of the peri-urban areas. Here 7 per cent work mainly in the fields. Most likely these are the female household heads engaged in urban agriculture. Only 3 per cent work in the informal sector.[7] Another 3 per cent are unemployed but 5 per cent work only occasionally. Only 1 per cent each work for a co-operative, as domestic workers or as business men; 3 per cent are already retired (see table 3.3a and 3.3b in appendix 3).

Naturally, there is a higher rate of unemployed other family members than household heads. The latter were asked: 'How many of your sons, daughters or relatives over 14 years, who live with you, do not have employment and do not go to school?' The replies in the peri-urban areas are shown in the following table.

Table 3.1 Distribution of households with none or some unemployed members

type of answer	households f	per cent	unemployed f
nobody is unemployed	180	57.5	—
one person	81	25.9	81
two persons	28	8.9	56
three	14	4.5	42
four	3	1.0	12
five	6	1.9	30
seven are unemployed	1	0.3	7
	313	100	228[8]

We can conclude that there are about 22 per cent unemployed in the peri-urban areas. The Central Statistical Office (CCR July 1994, 23f) found 21 per cent of the male labour force and 30 per cent of the female labour force under- or unemployed in the entire urban areas of Mozambique. These results can be considered as an additional support for the representative sample in the peri-urban areas of this study. It was already mentioned in the last chapter that under- and unemployment in general are higher in the rural areas of Mozambique than in the urban areas (26 per cent of the male labour force and 32 per cent of the female labour force; CCR, Julho 1994, 23f). This is, unfortunately, also true for the household heads. The percentage of under- and unemployed household heads increases from 4 per cent in the cement cities via 8 per cent in the peri-urban areas to even 18 per cent in the villages. It is self-evident that being under- or unemployed is a much more serious problem for a household head and his dependants than unemployment for another family member.

The proportions concerning the participation in the labour force of the household heads correspond somehow between Maputo and Beira (see table 3.3b in appendix 3). In the villages of Sofala a considerably higher proportion stated that they were housewives and not working mainly in the field. However, women in the countryside normally do both: they work in the fields and work in the house. If we take this into account, then also the two distributions of the villages of the two provinces correspond.

Considering the fact that unemployment is high also in Europe (in Spain, for instance, 20 per cent), the unemployment rate of Mozambique does not constitute the main problem although it is serious enough everywhere. What aggravates the problem here and in many other developing countries is the absence of unemployment insurance. Yet, the main problems remain to be extremely low wages and extremely low productivity in the rural areas.

Even though only household heads have been investigated in this study, from the results of the IAF one can conclude that Mozambique is an exception as far as the informal sector is concerned. In other African countries it is estimated that between half and almost three quarters of the work force are engaged in the informal sector: 70 per cent in Mali, 75 per cent in Burkina Faso and Sierra Leone, 48 per cent in the Ivory Coast, and 58 per cent in Niger (Altmann 1991, 7; ILO 1995, 22). However, also this exeptional status does not seem to solve Mozambique's severe problem of poverty. This is a strong argument against the attempts of the development policy to formalize the informal sector in other countries or even to eliminate it by discrimination or persecution which has not been successful anyway (Stacher 1997b, 152).

In the face of the severe problems of unemployment in most developing countries, of low productivity and low income, the contrast could not be bigger when we consider that a discourse has started in the industrial countries about the end of work and the era of full automatization or that, according to Martin and Schuhmann (1996), 20 per cent of the work force would be sufficient in the next century to run the world economy.

If wage labour would diminish drastically and give way to fully automatic production, it must not necessarily be a catastrophe or not even a crisis, because it would also open up great chances of freedom. If really 20 per cent of today's work force could run the world's economy in the next century, it must not necessarily be a 20:80 society, but each person's working years or any other unit (working weeks, working days) could be reduced to one fifth. Already Marx saw the shortening of the working day as a fundamental prerequisite for real freedom, which begins when labour performed out of need and external purpose ceases to exist (Fromm in Bottomore 1964, xvii). In Marx's view such a state of affairs could, of course, only come about after capitalism has been overthrown by the working class. However, in to day's view of the future possibilities of fully automatic production, 'real freedom' would come about by technological and scientific progress and even by the questionable successes of capitalism. On the other hand, a just distribution of very little work and much wealth could no longer be called capitalism. Exactly this is the real resistance by the powerful TNC that jobs should become concentrated in the hands of fewer and fewer people, who have to work overtime in order to save costs and maximize profits.

On the other hand, even if material (and in these times) communicative production could be managed by a small fraction of the work force, these must not necessarily bring about more chances for freedom. There remains the necessity of the psychological 'reproduction' of humankind. Ringel found that the vast majority of the children in Austria are neurotic and disturbed in their personality development and formation, the result being tormented, humiliated and broken people whose joy of life has extinguished (Ringel 1984, 9-11). If Austria is no exception then - apart from all the structural changes – an enormous amount of psychological and psycho-therapeutic work will be necessary to 'create' a healthy society world-wide.

The household size, age and marital status of household heads

Although the mode of the number of members per household is 5 – 7 persons in all three areas[9] there is a statistically highly significant difference between the peri-urban areas and the villages concerning the household size with a t-test significance of 0.000 while the difference between peri-urban and fully urbanized areas is only almost significant, with a t-test significance of 0.056.

Figure 3.4 The household size

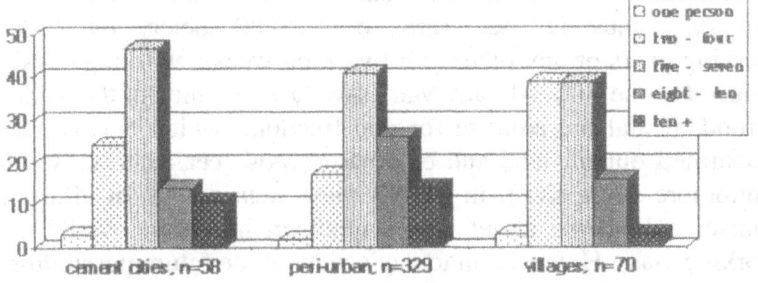

The graph also shows that the size of households in the villages has a second mode with 2 – 4 persons whereas in the peri-urban areas the percentage rate closest to the mode lies by 8 – 10 persons per household. One very likely explanation for this result is emigration from the villages to the urban areas, even more so as the villages for this research were chosen close to the urban areas. In many cases the younger ones emigrate, the old and the children are left behind. The results of the small rural control group show again a surprising and striking similarity to the results of the study of the 'five provinces'.[10] The 2 per cent of the households of the representative sample in the peri-urban areas of Maputo with one person only, receive support from the findings of the IAF (1991,50).[11]

While the smaller average family size in the rural areas is obviously due to emigration, which is also one form of social change, the smaller families in the fully urbanized areas are most likely due to another form of social change, namely a change of attitudes towards large families, a process of modernization. It is interesting to note that both of these different changes have economic factors as underlying causes. The main reasons for emigration are economic. People are struggling to survive or to improve their lives. The decision to have less children and therefore smaller families, is a very complex decision, but also to a large part economically determined as a strive for a higher standard of living. Although in the cement cities another factor could be crucial for the smaller household size compared to the peri-urban areas, namely, that Western egoism and individualism have substituted group solidarity and relatives are less often welcome. Thirteen per cent of the households in the peri-urban areas consist of more than 10 persons and 1 per cent has 20 or more members. This is certainly to a large extent due to the acceptance of relatives in the household, but also to the housing shortage for young families, who have therefore to remain in the family of origin.

The household size of the provinces of Maputo and Sofala corresponds to a large extent. It only seems that it is somewhat smaller in the peri-urban areas of Beira as well as in the villages of Sofala than in the peri-urban areas of Maputo and the village Massaca 1 (see table 3.4b in appendix 3).

The age of the household heads

The majority of the household heads are aged between 30 and 50 years. In this respect there is no difference between the three areas of investigation nor is there any difference between Maputo and Beira (see table 3.5a in appendix 3).

Figure 3.5 The age of the household heads

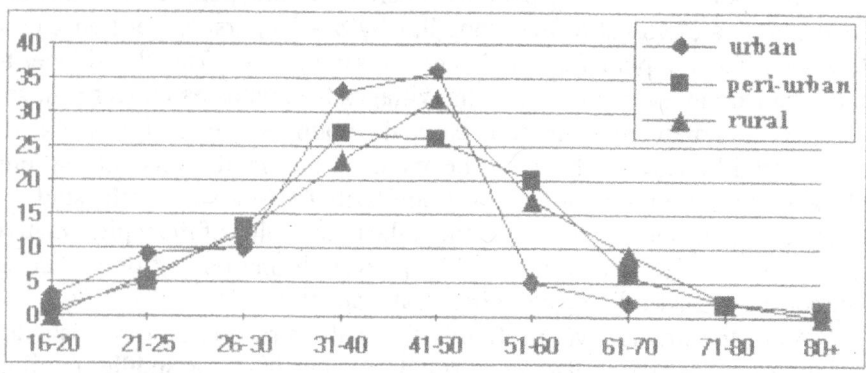

Apart from the finding that the majority of household heads belongs to the two age categories between 30 and 50 years, there is a statistically significant difference between the fully urbanized and the peri-urban areas, with a t-test value of 0.026, but there is no statistical difference between the latter and the rural areas, the t-test value being 0.679. Household heads in the fully urbanized areas are younger: the mean age is between 33 and 43, while the mean age in the other two areas is beween 38 and 48. This is surprising as one would expect the opposite, namely that traditionally in the villages and in the peri-urban areas both sexes get married at an earlier age than in the more modernized cement cities and become young household heads. This does not seem to be the case. Apparently the higher percentage of singles who are at the same time household heads in the fully urbanized areas are young singles. The other explanation could be that young couples can afford to get independent from their parents earlier and move to their own flat while in the other two areas married couples still have to stay with their parents.

Marital status of household heads

In Africa three kinds of marriages can be distinguished: firstly, formal marriages, which mean that a couple got married at the registrar's or in church or both, regardless whether a lobolo (bride price) had been paid or not; secondly, traditional marriages, which mean that the husband has paid the lobolo, but that the couple is not registered and thirdly, informal marriages, which mean that the couple lives together without registration, without payment of the lobolo and without the blessings of the church.

Table 3.2 Marital status of household heads

	urban	peri-urban	rural
single	10	4	3
married formally	53	17	7
married traditionally	14	50	67
married informally	16	15	9
separated	3	3	3
divorced	2	2	3
widow/er	2	10	9
n	(58)	(327)	(67)

Formal marriage increases with the first stage of urbanization, which means the difference between village life and life in the peri-urban areas, but it increases drastically with the second stage of urbanization, which means the difference between life in the peri-urban areas and the cement cities. In the same way as formal marriages increase, traditional marriages decrease from the villages via the peri-urban areas to the fully urbanized areas. The peri-urban areas are clearly areas of transition on the path of social change and modernization between the rural areas and the cement cities. However, it must be noted that, here as in many other cases, the difference between the peri-urban and the rural areas is considerably smaller than the difference between the peri-urban and the fully urbanized areas. We could cautiously speak of a ruralization of the cities in regard to the peri-urban areas.

Formal marriages are already declining in some industrialized countries and are substituted by informal marriages. As informal marriages have been a long established pattern in Africa (Caldwell 1977), they do not increase drastically in the first stage of urbanization and the percentage even remains the same between peri-urban and fully urbanized areas.

There are three main differences between Maputo and Beira (see table 3.6a in appendix 3). Firstly, a much higher percentage of household heads in the cement city of Maputo stated that they are single than in the cement city of Beira, which could be an indication of a more advanced degree of modernization of the capital city in comparison to the much smaller city Beira. In Western cities the percentage of singles is also on the increase.

Secondly, the percentage of formally married is much higher in the cement city of Beira than in Maputo, which could be due to widespread Catholicism in Beira. Thirdly, a much lower percentage is married traditionally in the peri-urban areas of Maputo than in the peri-urban areas of Beira, which could equally be seen as an indication of a higher degree of modernizatiin of the capital even in its peri-urban areas as compared to the peri-urban areas of a provincial capital. Therefore, we can also observe social change from the provincial capital to the primate city.

Number of wives

The proportion of polygamous families in Africa is often overestimated. If all areas of investigation are considered, then 10 per cent of the household heads have two wives. We found only one man with three wives (0,5 per cent) and another one with five wives, but the vast majority has one wife only. Although the difference between the areas is statistically not significant (Chi^2=.2098) We can still say that the habit of being married to two wives is decreasing from the villages via the peri-urban areas to the cement cities: $6 < 11 < 13$ per cent are married to two wives, the difference between the villages and the peri-urban areas again being much smaller than the difference between the latter and the cement cities.

If one could agree that monogamy means progress over polygamy, particularly for the women, as well as the disappearance of paying lobolo, then both stages of urbanization constitute real progress. According to Caldwell, as mentioned above, informal marriages were common alongside with traditional marriages in Africa, but they have become common only in the last few decades in Europe. Could it be that globalization at least in this aspect (apart from music and dance, for instance) is finally occurring the other way round: the West is learning from Africa and would have to learn a lot more – especially about essential values, if a non-capitalist humane process of globalization should take place.

Summary

The benefits of globalization in the form of relative prosperity in the fully urbanized areas could be shown clearly on the basis of empirical data. Here, income and education are relatively high compared to the peri-urban and rural areas, few household heads are under- and unemployed and the forms of marriage reveal global trends. Although there is progress in the cement cities of Maputo and Beira, they remain Third World cities, suffering from global exclusion, so, in spite of all positive aspects, the problems are still manifold. Additional problems will be shown in later chapters.

In the peri-urban areas it depends on one's point of view whether problems outweigh progress or vice versa. From the urban point of view, problems might prevail, looking from the countryside, real progress can be observed. In some socio-economic conditions the distance of the latter is wider to the rural and in some to the urban areas and often it is very difficult to determine which gap is wider, the rural-peri-urban or the peri-urban-urban gap, for instance, regarding the income situation and the level of education of household heads. However, the peri-urban areas are closer to the rural areas than are the two urban areas to each other as far as the age of household heads and particularly the marital status are concerned. The frequency of traditional marriages and polygamy decreases more drastically from the peri-urban to the fully urbanized areas than from the villages to the peri-urban areas and the increase in frequency of formal marriages is also considerably higher between the peri-urban and fully urbanized than between the other two areas. These aspects of social change seem to occur with a higher intensity in the second stage of urbanization namely in the change from a peri-urban to a fully urbanized society. All these should not detract from the fact that there is considerable social change even within the rural areas. One example was shown in this chapter, namely the fact that through modernization more than half of the household heads are no longer peasants.

Considerable differences in marital status could also be observed between Maputo and Beira indicating that the capital and primate city seems to be more modernized than the provincial capital. The participation in the labour force corresponds between the two cities but the level of education is lower and the income situation worse in Beira.

Notes

1. Direcção Nacional de Estatistica (Central Statistical Office), Inquérito às Famílias (IAF Inquiry of families, in future quoted as the IAF); This survey investigated 1,214 households in Maputo comprising 8.542 persons (nearly 1 per cent of the population) and had only 2 per cent of missing cases. Each household was visited three times during one week and a lengthy questionnaire left with the family to fill in, amongst many other subjects, expenditure and income every day. The procedure was repeated four times during one year (four 'moduli'). Besides Maputo all provincial capitals were investigated. Including all cities and the finalizing of the documents the survey lasted from 1991 to 1994.

   Meanwhile, in 1999 the final report of the third stage of the IAF carried out in 1996/97 including all urban, but now, for the first time, also all rural areas is available. As a whole 8,274 households were investigated, of which 2,516 were urban and 5,758 were rural, encomprising 671 villages.

2. Structure of monthly family income according to type of income

TYPE OF INCOME	PERCENTAGES OF MAPUTO CITY	ALL PROVINCIAL CAPITALS
Income from employment	51.6	41.5
Income from family production	7.7	23.0
Income from trading	24.0	18.8
Income from occasional work	0.4	1.5
Income from property	0.7	1.0
Remittances	4.6	1.2
Other income	11.0	13.0
TOTAL INCOME	100	100

   Source: Inquérito às famílias, Relatorio sobre os resultados finais das capitais provinciais, Outubro 1994, 19.

   Family production, trading and occasional work was subsumed under self-employment in the third stage of the IAF which found – very similar to the sample census of the provincial capitals – also 43 per cent of the family income deriving from self-employment, obviously mainly in the informal sector (unpublished material of IAF, 1998).

3. The income categories were doubled as follows: all categories < 50 contos were considered as < 100, 50 – 100 as 100 – 200, 100 – 200 was considered as 200 – 400 contos.

4. 1 conto = 1.000 Meticais (singular: Metical = Mt is the Mozambican currency). The official exchange rate during the time of interviewing, mid 1991, was 1 US$ = 1.434 Mt. However exchanging on the black market was already very common then, where the US Dollar traded for 2 contos or more.

   The official monthly minimum wage for workers was 32.175.00 Mt (= about 20 US$), for agricultural workers 24.310.00 Mt (= about 15 US$). Noticias (daily newspaper) January 30, 1991.

5. Direcção Nacional de Estatistica (DNE) e Ministerio do Comercio: Departamento de Segurança Alimentar (DSA) *Estudo sobre as condiçoes actuais de produção e consumo de alimentos em cinco provincias*, Maputo 1990. This study was carried out in 24 districts of five provinces. In total 1,166 families were interviewed; it will be referred to as the study of the 'five provinces'.

Socio-economic characteristics 85

6 Direcção Nacional de Estatistica (DNE) e Ministerio do Comercio: Departamento de Segurança Alimentar (DSA) *Estudo sobre as condiçoes actuais de produção e consumo de alimentos em cinco provincias*, Maputo 1990. In this study
    45.6 per cent peasants
    26.3 per cent officials
    3.4 per cent traders
    21.2 per cent other
    3.5 per cent unemployed were found (compare table 3.3a in appendix 3).

7 In the urban areas of Zambia in 1979 between 14 and 23 per cent of household heads worked in the informal sector and between 3 and 8 per cent were unemployed in Lusaka (ILO/JASPA 1981, xxi) while in a study of Nici Nelson in Mathare Valley in Nairobi 80 per cent of the male household heads and 90 per cent of the female household heads worked in the informal sector (Nelson in Gugler 1988). Maybe this increase from 3 per cent via about 20 per cent to 80 per cent reflects the differences from a, at one time socialist society, via a mixed economy to a purely capitalist one.

8 Since the average number of persons per household is 6.7, the replies to this question covered 2,097 persons; about 50 per cent are less than 14 years old (IAF 1991, 6) which makes 1,048 adults; 3 per cent (31 persons) are retired which leaves us with 1,017 adults as 100 per cent; 228 unemployed of 1,017 adults is 22.4 per cent.

9 The IAF found an average household size of 6.7 persons in Maputo (IAF 1991, 6).

10 The following family sizes were found:
    2 to 4 persons - 40 per cent
    5 to 7 persons - 40 per cent
    8 and more   20 per cent

11 This investigation did not distinguish between peri-urban and fully urbanized areas, but found in 4 per cent of the households of entire Maputo one person only. The slight difference can well be due to the standard deviation.

4 Poverty and dissatisfaction – job satisfaction

After the attempt of analyzing the root causes of rural and urban poverty, it is now interesting to see to what extent people indicate their subjective suffering under poverty or what are some of the bright aspects in spite of poverty. For the time being, we only look into dissatisfaction with income and education, leaving the problems with housing, infrastructure and social facilities and particularly the degree of depression as such for later chapters. However, the satisfaction with the participation in the labour force should also be analyzed here.

Dissatisfaction with income

Although we have seen that rural poverty is much worse than peri-urban poverty, two thirds are dissatisfied with their income in the latter areas, but only one third in the villages. This could on one hand be a hint towards the phenomenon of relative deprivation. Relative deprivation occurs if people see needs fulfilled for other people which are not fulfilled for themselves but which they want to be fulfilled (Harvey 1973). This concept will be discussed more fully in chapter 8. It should only be mentioned here that the feelings of relative deprivation obviously occur more frequently in the peri-urban areas as the people there are constantly confronted with the inhabitants of the fully urbanized areas of which they know very well, that their income is much higher. The villagers also know about the higher income in the fully urbanized as well as in the peri-urban areas but only visit these areas once in a while. (Two fifths of the household heads of the peri-urban areas go to the cement city almost every day but only one quarter of the household heads of the rural areas visit Maputo or Beira twice per month and about one third once per month.)

88 *Globalization, urban progress, urban problems, rural disadvantages*

Figure 4.1 Dissatisfaction with income

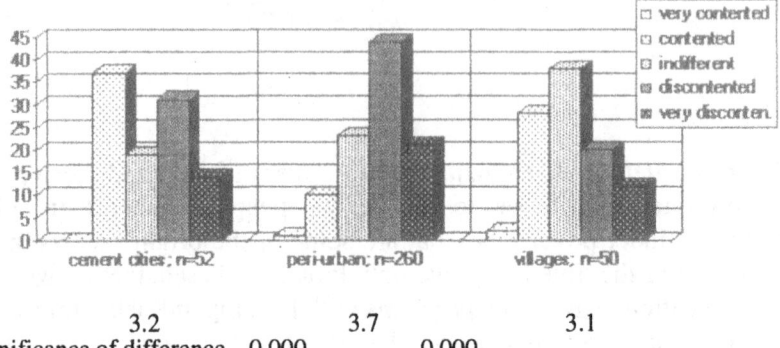

mean:	3.2	3.7	3.1
t-test significance of difference	0.000	0.000	

However, the validity of the theory of relative deprivation might diminish essentially if we look at the two fifths of the indifferent in the villages. A large proportion did not know their monthly income in money terms and having very little or no money, was not the major problem for them and does not constitute the major part of their poverty, but food shortage, the war situation and housing (see table 10.3). Almost a third is even satisfied with their income in the rural areas, obviously those who do not live at risk and do not feel relatively deprived.

That more than two fifths are dissatisfied in the disadvantaged parts of the fully urbanized areas, where only 8 per cent live under the poverty line, is also not surprising. Also they are constantly confronted with those whose living standard is much higher than theirs.

Considering the means of the three distributions it appears as if the poor villagers would be not more dissatisfied with their income than the much better off household heads of the cement cities. However, as mentioned before, the high percentage of indifferent and the different meaning of income in money terms do not allow such an interpretation.

In the cement city of Beira the percentage of the contended is higher than in Maputo, while in the peri-urban areas the proportion of very discontented household heads is greater in Beira than in Maputo, which is not surprising as the household income in those areas of Beira is even lower than in Maputo. The main difference between the villages of the province of Sofala and those of Maputo is the much higher proportion of the indifferent in the former (48 per cent as against 28 per cent), indicating that income in money terms meant even less to the villagers in Sofala than to the villagers in the province of Maputo. Here, where one fifth is formally employed, almost half of all household heads are satisfied with their income, while this proportion makes up only for one fifth in the villages of Sofala, where only 10 per cent are formally employed (table 7a in the appendix).

There is no statistical difference between women and men as far as contentment with the household income is concerned. The proportion of contended with household income is even slightly higher amongst women (21 per cent) than amongst men (18 per cent).

Dissatisfaction with the level of education

One concomitant of poverty is lack of formal education and with it social insecurity. In the chapter of social facilities the schools and school attendance in the investigated areas will be analyzed further.

People in most developing countries and so also in Mozambique are longing for more education. The majority of the household heads in all areas belongs to the two categories of the very discontented and the people discontented with their level of education: $58 < 66 < 74$ per cent. The peri-urban areas occupy the middle position but not as far as the proportion of satisfied is concerned. Here we find no difference between the peri-urban and the rural areas: $32 > 22 = 22$ per cent are either satisfied or even very satisfied with their level of education. The rest is indifferent. The satisfaction or dissatisfaction respectively does to some extent correspond with the real level of education as amongst the least educated, the villagers, the percentage of discontented is highest, it is lower in the peri-urban areas, and lowest in the fully urbanized areas, where people have the highest educational level. However, it does not correspond, as we have seen already, in the categories of the contented. A comparison of the means and the not significant difference between the rural and the peri-urban areas again seems to support the theory of relative deprivation as in the actual level of education the gap between the last mentioned two areas is just as great as the gap between the two urban areas. The household heads in the peri-urban areas apparently are much more dissatisfied with their lower level of education than the villagers as the former can see the advantages of the higher educated inhabitants of the fully urbanized areas almost every day.

90 *Globalization, urban progress, urban problems, rural disadvantages*

Figure 4.2 Dissatisfaction with the level of education

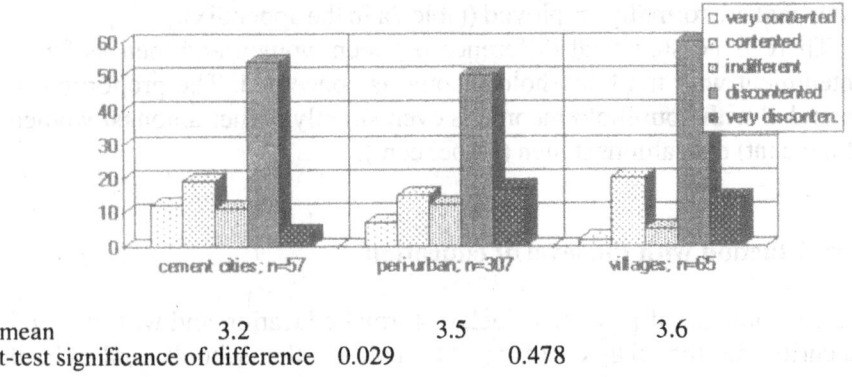

mean   3.2   3.5   3.6
t-test significance of difference 0.029   0.478

The level of satisfaction does not correspond with the actual level of education if the two provinces are considered separately (see table 4.2b in appendix 3). We found a higher educational level in Maputo and the village of the province of Maputo, however, the proportion of very discontented is greater in Maputo and the province of Maputo than in Beira and the province of Sofala. Although there are almost twice as many household heads without formal education in the peri-urban areas of Beira the proportion of contented is, nevertheless, twice as high, an interpretation of which is very difficult. It could well be that in a smaller city the feelings of relative deprivation have not yet developed in all aspects. – There is absolutely no difference regarding the level of satisfaction with education between women and men.

Satisfaction with the participation in the labour force or job situation respectively

The majority of household heads is discontented with income and education, but as far as satisfaction with one's position in the labour force or job situation respectively is concerned, we find just the opposite results. A large majority belongs to the categories of the very satisfied or at least the satisfied with their position in the labour force: 88 > 70 < 78 per cent. In this case the peri-urban areas do not take on a middle position: a smaller percentage of household heads is satisfied with their job than is the case in the rural areas. The household heads of the fully urbanized areas are closest to the level of satisfaction with occupation in industrialized countries. Just to take Austria as an example: in the social survey of 1993 also 88 per cent of the males and 91 per cent of the females belonged to the categories of the very satisfied or the satisfied with their occupation (Austrian Social Survey 1993). This once more illustrates urban progress and the process of globalization. Only if we would consider the very contented separately, the peri-urban areas would be in middle position again: 48 > 25 > 19 per cent are very contented. However, the proportion of contented grows in the opposite direction: 40 < 46 < 59 per cent are contented with their position in the labour force. In this case the combination of these two categories apparently reflects the real situation better.

Figure 4.3 Job satisfaction

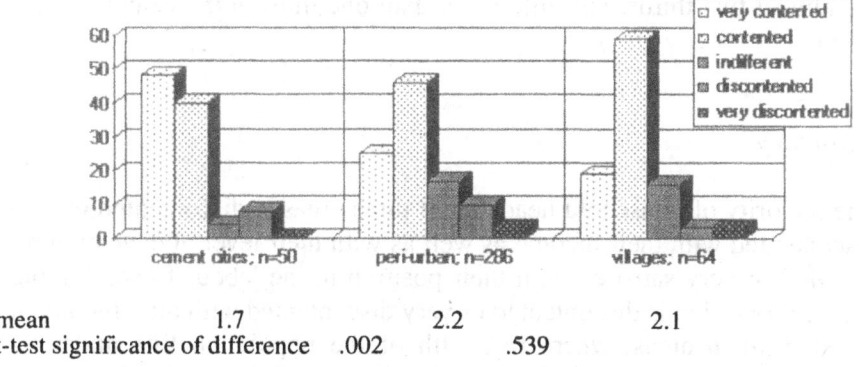

mean 1.7 2.2 2.1
t-test significance of difference .002 .539

Finding 8 per cent more contented or very contented household heads in the villages than in the peri-urban areas is interesting. Apparently, in spite of all the hardship the peasants like to be peasants and those with other occupations like their occupations in the rural areas. Here the theory of relative deprivation could again serve as an additional explanation. However, the 18 per cent more satisfied or very satisfied household heads in the fully urbanized areas do correspond with reality because it is certain that those in the fully urbanized areas do have better professions than the household heads in the peri-urban areas. The difference is again significant between the last mentioned two areas but it is not significant between peri-urban and rural areas.

A higher proportion of household heads of the Maputo province were very discontented in all areas with their level of education and now a higher proportion of household heads of the Maputo province is very contented with their profession or occupation in all areas than in the province of Sofala, which could mean that they really do have better jobs, which they like very much, but at the same time feel that they would, nevertheless, need a lot more education (table 9b in the appendix). In the cement city of Maputo even a majority (58 per cent) of household heads is very satisfied with their job. However, if we combine the very satisfied with the satisfied, then we find a striking similarity between the two cities and provinces particularly in the peri-urban areas.

Also the vast majority in all areas is either satisfied or very satisfied with their job conditions, meaning the atmosphere on the working place, the colleagues at work, the boss, transport to and from work and other benefits.

And again the very contented we can find more frequently in all areas in the province of Maputo than in Sofala; in the cement city of Maputo these are almost two thirds, but little more than one third in the cement city of Beira.

Summary

The majority of household heads in all three areas is discontented or very discontented with their income as well as with their level of education but satisfied or very satisfied with their position in the labour force. A much higher proportion is discontented or very discontented with their income in the peri-urban areas, where two fifth of the population live under the poverty line, than in the rural areas, where two thirds live under the poverty line. Relative deprivation in the peri-urban areas, where people are constantly confronted with the better-off inhabitants of the cement cities, could be made responsible for these results, if there would not be a high proportion of indifferent in the rural areas for whom income in money terms obviously does not mean much. However, relative deprivation could be seen as one of the reasons, why only about an equal proportion of the household heads of the rural areas compared to the peri-urban areas are dissatisfied with their education, while the real educational level is much lower in the country side. On the other hand, one could say, the 'ceiling' of such a high level of dissatisfied is almost reached and therefore the difference between the last two areas cannot be much higher.

In spite of their poverty the majority of the household heads of all three areas are satisfied or very satisfied with their participation in the labour force. Here again there is little difference between the peri-urban and rural areas, but as in the case of income and education, there is a significant difference between the two urban areas. The gap concerning dissatisfaction or satisfaction respectively with education and participation in the labour force is much wider between fully urbanized and peri-urban areas than between the latter and the rural areas.

In one aspect the data shows the process of urbanization as a process of Europeanization or, in this sense also of globalization, as the level of satisfaction with one's position in the labour force is in the fully urbanized areas only very similar to the level of satisfaction in industrialized countries, as Austria might not be an exception in this regard, generalization could be permitted.

The household heads of the peri-urban areas of Beira are more discontented with the family income than those in Maputo as their actual income is also lower. Their level of education is also lower but they are less dissatisfied with it than the household heads in the same areas in Maputo. It could be that relative deprivation has not yet taken roots in all aspects in a smaller city. The high level of satisfaction with one's job situation is very similar between Maputo and Beira and their is no difference in this regard between women and men.

5 Migration as a consequence of globalization

The rate of rural-urban migration is already declining in most developing countries but not yet in Africa. The causes for migration cannot only be seen in the rural-urban income and living standard differentials. Rural areas have been negatively affected by the division of labour in the world system since colonial times but even more so in the last few decades. On the other hand this world-wide division of labour has stimulated migration by creating connections between cities and countryside. Market forces have penetrated the local economies and weakened them by mechanising agriculture, concentrating land, and competing with an overwhelming power with industrial products against handicraft. Rural areas became more and more marginalized, the hinterland, the periphery. But this same process tied the rural areas more and more to the national and international urban centres. The ever deeper but very uneven 'integration' of the countryside into the national division of labour created an effective potential for migration (Feldbauer and Parnreiter 1997).

The main reasons for migration

The brief presentation of the socio-economic data in chapter 3 showed the enormous disadvantages of the rural areas in comparison to the peri-urban areas, but also the disadvantages of the latter in comparison to the fully urbanized areas.

Already in the 1960s and 1970s, when research on rural-urban migration boomed, it was clear to the majority of authors, as it is today (but is questioned now and again by some) that migrants act economically and rationally when they migrate from rural to urban areas.

> Most rural-urban migrants correctly assess that they are improving their life chances. A paradox arises between the rationality of the individual and small group decisions to migrate and the irrationality of the migratory movement when

considered at the level of the national economy. This micro/macro paradox is resolved when the migratory movement is seen as a mechanism that allows some of the disadvantaged rural population to partake in a small measure of resources disproportionately concentrated in urban areas. In absence of effective policies to redistribute productive resources and/or income across the rural- urban divide, rural-urban migration can be argued to contribute to economic development, defined to include the distributional aspect (Gugler 1982).

This policy of 'redistributing productive recourses and income' would not have been absent in Mozambique. Agricultural development and the setting up of communal villages had priority immediately after independence and later the priority was given to the support of the so-called 'family sector' in the rural areas and all along of co-operatives. However, the undeclared war by the then racist South Africa and later the introduction of the structural adjustment programmes has negated the major part of all these efforts.

Therefore, it is understandable that people keep migrating also in Mozambique, just as in most developing countries. They do it mainly for economic reasons. Seventy six per cent of the peri-urban household heads gave such reasons. To continue one's education actually also means the search for better living conditions. Normally, this has as a consequence an improvement of economic conditions as well.

Table 5.1 Main reasons for migration of male household heads

	urban	peri-urban	rural
employment	23	51	33
education	20	11	2
better living conditions	14	14	7
joining family members	9	8	5
war	9	11	40
droughts/floods	—	—	5
other reasons	26	5	9
n	(35)	(237)	(43)

These results correspond with the findings of Peil in Lagos, although there the emphasis was on the opportunity of being self-employed in the formal or informal sector which is still rare in Maputo. 'Enterpreneurship, large or small, is seen as the prime opportunity for getting ahead – the main reason for coming to Lagos in the first place' (Peil 1991).

Also Schneider and Vorlaufer found an overwhelming majority moving – out of economic reasons – to secondary cities in Kenya (84 per cent), Thai-land (76 per cent) and the Philippines (60 per cent); 3 per cent, 10 per cent and 27 per cent (in the above mentioned order) migrated for educational reasons. In order to join family members 12-13 per cent migrated in all three cities (Schneider and Vorlaufer 1997, 243).

In the table above only male household heads were considered. For more than one third of the wives in Maputo and almost half in Beira marriage was the main reason for migrating. Joining family members and 'other reasons' remained below 10 per cent with the exception of the cement cities, whose inhabitants had obviously more complex reasons for migration as were foreseen in the pre-coded questionnaire. – There exists a striking similarity between the two cities and provinces (see table 5.1a in appendix 3).

Only 11 per cent emigrated because of the war which had been going on for the last 16 years before the time of the survey. So we can conclude that the growth of the cities in Mozambique is only to a lesser extent due to the war and was frequently overestimated. All cities in Third World countries do grow at an incredible speed even without any war, as discussed in chapter 2.

If city growth has to be slowed down then comprehensive and rigorous programmes of birth control in the cities themselves, which would have women's education and emancipation as their prerequisite, would be much more effective than curbing rural-urban migration, as natural increase of the city populations accounts for three fifth of the growth.

The data from the villages indicate that the main reason for migration from one rural area to another was the war. The majority of the persons who had to flee from the attacks of Renamo did not move to the cities, but to other rural areas. This is an essential result. Speaking of the attractiveness of cities and their enormous growth, we have to take into consideration that even during a war and although the people knew very well that there were hardly ever attacks in the cities, the majority of them still preferred to flee to another rural area. Apparently we have to take into consideration two tendencies of the rural population: the tendency to migrate to urban areas but also the much more widespread tendency to remain in the rural areas, even under extreme difficult conditions, as the Mozambican rural population had to go through during thirty years of war.

Areas of birth of household heads and the time of migration

According to Peil, migration from rural to urban areas is in the majority of cases a direct one and step migration, where people move first to a small town then to a larger one and finally to a city, is relatively unimportant, especially concerning migration to central cities. (Peil 1981, 42). This also seems to be the result of this investigation when we compare the area of birth with the previous residence (see table 5.2 and table 5.4).

In Mozambique there exist 68 very small towns, called 'vilas' (Jenkins 1993). It is difficult to define them within the concepts of 'urban' or 'rural'. On the one hand, we could consider life in a small town at least as urbanized as it is in the peri-urban areas, on the other hand, vilas are frequently considered as belonging to the rural areas in the general understanding in Mozambique. So if we follow this understanding, then 77 per cent of the household heads of the peri-urban areas of Maputo and 79 per cent of those of Beira migrated at one time from the rural areas. Less than a quarter of the household heads of these areas in Maputo and a fifth in Beira never migrated from the rural areas and only those could be called second generation urbanites or at least second generation semi-urbanites as they do not live in a fully urbanized area. At least we can consider them as those who do not know rural life from a first-hand experience. However, if we include vilas into semi-urbanized areas, then about half of the peri-urban household heads have never lived as real peasants. (As the differences in this chapter, particularly as far as the control groups are concerned, are considerable between Maputo and Beira and the villages in the respective provinces, the following tables will be presented not only by area but also by province.)

Table 5.2 Area of birth of household heads by province

	urban		peri-urban		rural	
	M	B	M	B	M	S
village	39	16	50	51	67	83
small town (vila)	8	29	27	28	27	3
other city	23	29	8	2	7	5
other bairro	31	23	13	10	—	5
this bairro	—	3	3	9	—	5
n	(26)	(31)	(241)	(82)	(30)	(40)

M=Maputo city or province of Maputo; B=Beira; S=Sofala province

In the fully urbanized areas of Maputo as well as in those of Beira more than half of the household heads are second generation urbanites and less than half were born in rural areas, if vilas are included into rural areas.

Seven per cent of the household heads of the village in the Maputo province, Massaca 1, and 5 per cent in the villages of the province of Sofala were born in a city but now live in a village. This kind of migration happens, but it is rare. A quarter of the household heads of Massaca 1 were born in a small town and now live in this village as it is a new creation and has been set up because of the war. People had to move closer to the district capital Boane, so that they could be protected from the attacks of Renamo.

The urban and peri-urban household heads of Maputo were born in the following provinces:
- 31 per cent in the province of Maputo
- 39 per cent in the province of Gaza
- 23 per cent in Inhambane and
- 7 per cent in other provinces (see map in the introduction).

There is little economic opportunity in Gaza and the soil is not fertile which explains the influx from that province to the capital of Mozambique, the primate city.

The urban and peri-urban household heads of Beira were born in the following provinces
- 49 per cent in the province of Sofala,
- 13 per cent in Inhambane and
- 38 per cent in other provinces.

Here the influx from the surrounding hinterland of Beira is also understandable as there is no other city in Sofala near the size of Beira.

Time of migration

Corresponding to the above defined second generation semi-urbanites, only a quarter of the household heads of the peri-urban areas of Maputo and even less than one fifth of those in Beira stated that they had never migrated from the rural areas.

If we add the last two categories of table 6, then we can see that the vast majority of the household heads of the cement cities (Maputo: 79 per cent, Beira: 67 per cent) as well as in the peri-urban areas (Maputo: 68 per cent, Beira: 76 per cent) have not migrated from the rural areas or have done so before independence.

Table 5.3   Time of rural – urban and rural – rural migration by province

	urban		peri-urban		rural	
	M	B	M	B	M	S
less than 6 months ago	—	—	1	—	—	3
approx. 6 months ago	—	4	—	—	—	—
approx. one year ago	4	—	2	—	—	—
approx. one and a half years ago	—	—	—	—	20	—
2 years ago	—	—	4	—	5	—
3 – 5 years ago	—	—	6	2	25	15
6 – 10 years ago	—	17	5	9	20	21
11 – 16 years ago	17	13	13	13	10	56
17 and more years ago	33	50	43	59	15	44
never emigrated	46	17	25	17	5	12
n	(24)	(24)	(218)	(75)	(20)	(34)

Three per cent of the peri-urban household heads of Maputo migrated from the rural areas during the previous year of the time of survey in mid 1991. As the urban growth rate of Mozambique was 5.3 annually and natural increase accounts for three fifths on average (Preston in Gugler 1992), and not only household heads have migrated but also family members and relatives, the 3 per cent might be slightly too high, but only a small error which still lies within the standard deviation and can be seen as astonishing correspondence and shows the accuracy of the survey. In the peri-urban areas of Beira no household head migrated within the last year but it is, nevertheless, possible that family members or relatives came. Four per cent of the household heads in the respective fully urbanized areas do not mean a big growth of the city population as the cement cities house only about 20 per cent of all the inhabitants of the respective city.

Previous residence and contact with relatives

Only 4 per cent of the household heads of the fully urbanized area of Maputo, but almost a third of the household heads of that area of Beira, lived in the rural areas before their arrival in the bairro they live in now, if we again consider the small towns as rural areas. One third of the peri-urban household heads of Maputo, but almost half of the peri-urban household heads of Beira, seem to have moved there directly from the countryside. This can be seen as another indication that Maputo is more urbanized than Beira as urbanization is also a process of adjustment from rural to urban life. It could well be that none of the household heads was born in the cement cities, as these areas were reserved for whites only before independence.

Figure 5.1 Previous residence by province

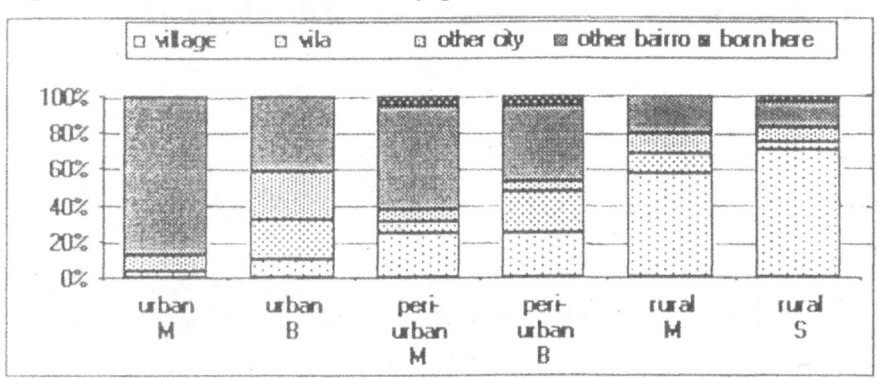

The movement between the peri-urban bairros seems intensive: more than half of the household heads in Maputo and two fifths in Beira lived in another bairro, before arriving in their present bairro, while few lived in another city, except the cement city of Beira, where this proportion makes up for a quarter. Moving from one 'bairro' to another in the villages obviously means moving from one section to another as Massaca 1 and Mutua are very large villages.

There is a great difference between all areas regarding mutual contact and assistance of household heads to relatives in rural or urban areas respectively. A correspondence exists only insofar as the proportion of those who give support to relatives is surprisingly low in all areas and that it is even absent in the cement city of Maputo. As far as frequent contacts with relatives in rural areas are concerned, the proportion of household heads of the peri-urban areas of Maputo is twice as high as the proportion of household heads of the peri-urban areas of Beira. The reasons could be, on one hand, the much more intensive warfare in the province of Sofala, where Renamo had its headquarters, on the other hand, most might not be able to afford the costs of transport as the household income in the peri-urban area of Beira is even lower than that of Maputo. However, in spite of the war situation, the household heads of the cement cities of Beira give assistance to relatives in the hinterland, most probably to those in the safe Beira corridor and they are able to pay for the transport. An explanation why none of the household heads of the cement city of Maputo assists relatives in the hinterland is difficult. Could it be that a higher degree of urbanization makes people more individualistic or even selfish? More research would be necessary to substantiate such an interpretation.

Figure 5.2 Support of and contact with relatives by province

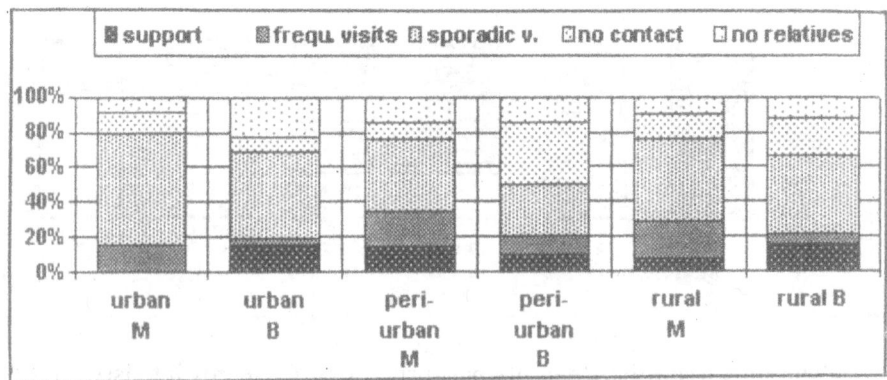

Migration as a consequence of globalization 103

The fact that more than three times as many household heads in the peri-urban areas of Beira have no contact with relatives in the rural areas as the household heads in the peri-urban areas of Maputo might be equally due to the different intensity of war in the two provinces. Almost two thirds of the household heads of the cement city of Maputo and half of the household heads of the cement city of Beira visit their relatives in the rural areas at least sometimes.

In spite of the substantial differences between the two provinces it should be justified to make an exception here and present the results for the two provinces combined, for easier perception and overall analysis:

support   8 < 13 > 11 ⎫
frequent visits 10 < 18 > 12 ⎬ 75 > 69 < 74 per cent do have contact
sporadic visits 58 > 38 < 51 ⎭
no contact   10 < 17 > 15
no relatives   15 > 14 > 11

In this case the peri-urban areas never take on a middle position: the percentages are either higher, lower or almost equal to one or both other areas. However, a higher percentage supports and a higher percentage visits relatives frequently in rural areas which is not at all surprising, when less urbanized people have more contacts to rural areas. This support and frequent visit is not outweighed by the 17 per cent of the household heads of the peri-urban areas who do not have contact with relatives in the rural areas as compared to 10 per cent only who do not have this contact in the cement cities; an almost equal percentage does not have relatives in the rural areas. As a whole, about three quarters of the household heads of the cement cities do have at least some contact with relatives in villages and an equal percentage of village household heads do have at least some contact with relatives in town. This respective percentage is somewhat lower in the peri-urban areas but the percentage of the more intensive contact and even of assistance is higher here.

Of the household heads living in the villages approximately half visit their relatives in the cities or in town. The rate of frequent visits is significantly higher in Massaca 1 (21 per cent) where there is a bus service to Maputo and the district capital Boane is near. However, only 5 per cent of the household heads of the villages in Sofala province visit their relatives frequently in the cities. The zone around Nhangau was a war stricken area, in which the families did – for more than a year already – not sleep in their homes but stayed overnight at the beach where they were protected by FRELIMO soldiers. In this region there was no regular public transport into Beira. In Mutua it is possible to travel but only with very expensive, sometimes unlicensed, private mini-buses. Thus, it is possible that many household heads could not afford it. In both provinces 11 per cent of the village household heads have no relatives in the cities and 15 per cent have no contact with them.

Summary

Mainly direct migration from rural to urban areas, as it has been established for other developing countries, apparently occurs also in Mozambique. Three quarters of the peri-urban household heads were born in the rural areas, but before arriving in the present bairro half lived already in the same city, only in another bairro. One quarter came directly from the rural areas. As only one quarter of the peri-urban household heads was born in a city, only this quarter can be called second generation urbanites as they never lived in a village. However, as the peri-urban areas are areas of transition, contributing in some aspects to a certain amount of ruralization of the cities, it is more adequate to speak of one quarter of second generation semi-urbanites.

Less than half of the household heads of the fully urbanized areas were born in villages, therefore the majority are second generation urbanites and therefore these areas are truly urban not only because of their physical appearance, their infrastructure, and their social facilities but also as far as their inhabitants are concerned as the process of urbanization is also a process involving time for the migrants adjustment to urban life. Under these aspects the household heads of the cement city of Maputo – and their way of life does not remain without effect on their families – can also be considered as more urbanized than those in the cement city of Beira, as a lower proportion came directly from the rural areas to the city.

Apart from those who never migrated as they were born in a city, almost half of the household heads of both kinds of urban areas migrated before independence. Apparently the boom of migration after independence, when restrictions were loosened, consisted of wives joining their husbands with their children and relatives. Few came within the last year and even the proportion of people who came within the last five years is low. Although these are household heads, it is still an indication that excessive migration because of the war was usually overestimated.

Assisting relatives or visiting them frequently in the rural or urban areas respectively is not high on the agenda in all three areas, but a higher percentage of household heads in the peri-urban areas do support and visit more frequently kin than in the fully urbanized areas. This could be interpreted as declining links to rural relatives with a higher degree of urbanization.

The majority of household heads migrated for economic reasons, whereby migration as such and urbanization as such cannot be seen as a negative process, but measures are needed to overcome rural as well as urban poverty. Here the North has an enormous amount of responsibility.

One essential result is the high proportion of villagers who fled from one rural area to another because of the war. One could argue that the rural control group for this investigation was very small, but we also know from the almost two million displaced internally because of the war at that time, that only a small percentage came to the cities. Two tendencies of the rural population have to be taken into consideration, the tendency to migrate, but also the tendency, hardly discussed in the literature, to remain in the rural areas even under extreme adverse conditions.

6 Housing in the two urban worlds and the neglected countryside

The concept of habitation means more than just a house, a shelter against climatic factors, a place of intimacy, for resting during the night and for preparation of meals. It also means the existence of a local infrastructure like water supply, sanitation and transport as well as social facilities like schools and medical centres. All these factors together are indicators for the quality of a habitation. This quality again is determined by economic and cultural factors. The peri-urban areas constitute a link – not only in Mozambique but in the majority of the developing countries – between a traditional and a modern culture. Both of these types of cultures have their own value. Unfortunately, large parts of the traditional African culture of housing were destroyed by European aggression during the times of slavery and colonialism and also in recent times by neo-colonialism, the penetration of capital also in the rural areas and the negative effects of globalization. In the investigated villages we did not find an intact culture of African traditional housing, only remains of it.

In the same way run down buildings in the cement city, which were chosen as the other control group, do only in part represent modern housing. Nevertheless, it was possible to study the big differences between these three areas.

The built environment in particular housing, infrastructure and social facilities are consequences as well as causes of social change. The consequences of social change can be observed when the proportion of houses with permanent material is on the increase, when sanitation, water supply, roads etc. have improved. However, one can also observe a negative change to some extent, a certain loss of the richness of traditional vernacular architecture and planning (Yachan 1990). Vernacular housing was built in harmony with the community, with nature and religion, but one did not ask primarily about the housing needs of the individual. When more and more specialization evolved, particularly in the scientific and technological revolution, systematic efforts were made world-wide to understand human requirements better (Studer 1993). In this way housing was a very significant consequence of social change, a considerable step historically. This chapter will show the present spatial coexistence of the various historical forms of housing. In the (run-down but still) modern buildings of the cement cities of Maputo and Beira we will encounter the global trend of specialists building houses for other people, while in the rural and peri-urban areas people mainly build their houses themselves. However, also here global trends do have their – although quite weak – effects on the change of building material and infrastructure. The more remote the area the weaker the effects.

Housing and the built environment are undoubtedly also a cause of social change as it becomes apparent in an extraordinary manifold way throughout the analysis of the results of this empirical investigation and as it already has been shown in the previous chapters.

In the following very technical and detailed presentation of the different variables of housing one should not forget that all these houses are also homes. Whether they are rural, peri-urban or urban homes, they are among the most central physical settings of human life.

One should also remember, how many millions of people have lost their homes during the war in Mozambique. In such times of upheaval and loss the physical, social and psychological importance of homes becomes apparent and the centrality of residences is brought to the forefront. Human well-being, individual, family and cultural viability are not possible without residences and dwellings, in other words, without homes (Altmann 1993).

A multiplicity of meanings can be attributed to housing.

> Rapoport (1980) pointed out that housing has been approached as a product, as a commodity, as a process, as a place (including such concepts as the expression of identity, self-worth and status of the inhabitants), as territory, as private domain, as a 'behaviour setting' (a unit of analysis in ecological psychology), or as the response to a set of purely functional requirements (as a locus of activities) (quoted by Francescato 1993).

According to Francescato, it is most probably this multiplicity of meanings that has to be blamed for the neglect of a definition of housing until recently. (For a profound discourse on the meaning and use of housing see Arias ed 1993.)

In the following very 'sober' presentation of the survey results these brief theoretical reflections should be kept in mind to give a framework and the proper meaning to the numerous percentages and tables.

Figure 6.1 The cement city of Maputo; fully urbanized area

Figure 6.2 A typical reed house in the peri-urban areas of Maputo with an interview in action

Figure 6.3 One of the better cement block houses in the peri-urban areas of Maputo

Figure 6.4 A pau-a-pique house under construction in the peri-urban areas of Beira

Figure 6.5 A completed pau-a-pique house in the peri-urban areas of Beira

112 *Globalization, urban progress, urban problems, rural disadvantages*

Figure 6.6 Typical reed houses in the village Massaca 1 with grass roofs

Figure 6.7 Houses in the village Mutua with the female interviewers of Beira

The house[1]

All of the houses in the villages belong to the head of the household, whereas in the cement cities only houses belonging to APIE[2] were selected for the control group. In the peri-urban areas of Maputo only 10 per cent and in Beira 20 per cent belong to APIE. In both peri-urban areas the vast majority of houses are property of the household heads. In Beira for one fifth of the houses a rent is paid to a private owner. It was illegal for owners to collect rents in Mozambique but obviously not everybody adhered to this rule, particularly in Beira were FRELIMO was not as popular as in Maputo.

Building material

Two fifths of the walls of the houses in the peri-urban areas of Maputo are built of a bamboo-like reed, called caniço, and more than a third are constructed of concrete blocks; the rest has corrugated iron sheets or sun dried bricks/adobe as walls.

Table 6.1 The house walls

	urban		peri-urban		villages		IAF 671
	M	B	M	B	M	S	villages
reed/grass	—	—	41	5	87	78	71
corrugated iron	—	—	12	3	3	2	—
pau-a-pique	—	—	—	51	3	—	—
bricks/sun-dried bricks	42	26	11	2	3	17	23
concrete blocks	58	74	36	39	3	2	2
n	(26)	(31)	(242)	(85)	(30)	(41)	(5,758)

The percentage of the houses the walls of which exist of concrete blocks or sun-dried bricks exactly correspond to the results of the IAF, however, houses the walls of which consist of corrugated iron are slightly under-represented in this study.[3]

As already less than half of the houses are built of reed (caniço) the concept of 'cidade de caniço' (reed city) has seized to be adequate. In earlier times the peri-urban areas of Maputo, were and are still today, often called 'cidade de caniço' to distinguish these areas from the 'cidade de cimento' (cement city).

In the peri-urban areas of Beira half of the houses are built with the 'pau-a-pique' method, a wooden structure filled with stones and mud.[4] The majority of the houses in the villages of both provinces are made of grass or reed.

Although the latest sample census IAF of 1996/97 found only 71 per cent of the houses in the rural areas with walls consisting of grass or reed, the results are, nevertheless, close to those of the villages in the Sofala province as the IAF also show 3 per cent of the houses with cement blocks as walls in the entire rural areas, however 22 per cent (not only 17 per cent) with sun dried bricks. This is, nevertheless, a real surprise, when a tiny sample of 41 households can almost stand comparison with a sample of 5,758 households. However, Massaca 1 does not correspond too well with the highly reliable data of the IAF as it turned out to be atypical all along.

Two fifths of the peri-urban houses had cement or adobe floors compared to half in Massaca 1 and a quarter in the villages of Sofala; the rest of the floors still consist of soil only. The third stage of the IAF found 68 per cent soil floors in the villages.

The roofs of about three quarters of the houses in both peri-urban areas consist of corrugated iron sheets but increasingly fibre cement sheeting is used: 14 per cent in Maputo and in Beira 21 per cent. Most of the houses in the villages use grass for their roofs but there is increasing use of corrugated iron; in Massaca 1 more than a quarter of the houses are covered with this material. In entire Mozambique the IAF found 84 per cent of the rural houses with grass roofs, 7 per cent with corrugated iron and 1 per cent with fibre cement. Eight per cent used other material. Only 0.5 per cent (it could well be that these were the commercial farmers) had tiled roofs.

The building material of the flats and houses of the cement cities is, of course, similar to any European city. They have been built by the colonizers and for themselves only. So, also in this aspect, the gap between these and the peri-urban areas is huge.

The age of the houses

The proportion of houses which are between 7 and 16 years old is larger in the peri-urban areas of Beira than of Maputo, there are also more houses in Beira which are even older than 16 years. It is not surprising that the houses in the peri-urban areas of Beira are older as houses are constructed traditionally in the pau-a-pique technique, which leads to durable constructions, as we have seen already, whereas in Maputo traditionally reed was the preferred material.

Figure 6.8   The age of the houses

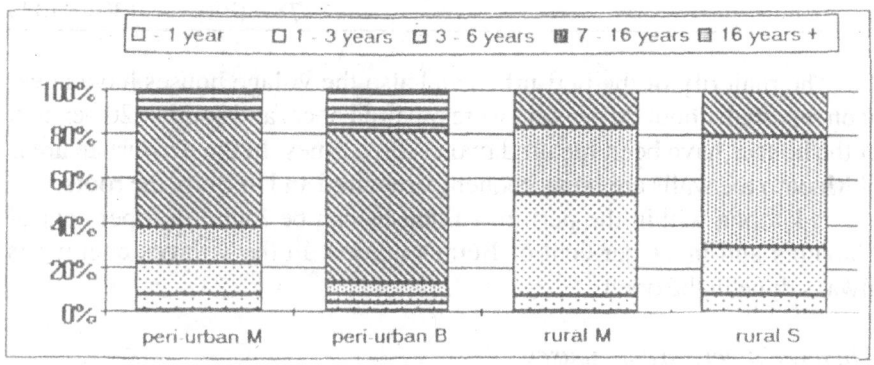

As Massaca 1 is a new foundation, the mode of the age of houses is 1 – 3 years, in Nhangau and Mutua the mode is 3 – 6 years. In these two villages surprisingly the pau-a-pique technique is not used, which could be due to the lack of wood and/or clay.

Construction and repair

Approximately one third of the houses in the peri-urban areas of Maputo and Beira were built by the head of the household himself or herself, 13 per cent and 9 per cent respectively with the help of relatives. It is, however, surprising that only in 2 per cent of the cases neighbours had helped with the construction of the houses and this had happened only in the peri-urban areas of Maputo. It seems that this kind of neighbourly assistance also does not exist in the villages.

Table 6.2 Who constructed your house?

	peri-urban M	peri-urban B	villages M	villages S
myself	32	37	87	71
help from relatives	13	9	3	12
help from neighbours	2	—	—	—
bricklayer	34	18	7	12
others	11	24	3	5
not applicable/don't know	8	12	—	—
n	(237)	(78)	(30)	(41)

The majority of the peri-urban and also the village houses have never been repaired; about 20 per cent were repaired once, and another 20 per cent of the houses have been repaired two or three times. In the peri-urban areas of Maputo the walls are most frequently repaired and in Beira the roofs.

A kitchen within the peri-urban houses can be found in 8 per cent of Maputo's and in 11 per cent of Beira's houses. In the villages cooking is always done in the open.

Windows of peri-urban houses

	Maputo	Beira
no windows	35 per cent	5 per cent
windows but without glass	43 per cent	77 per cent
windows with glass	22 per cent	18 per cent

In the villages the majority of the houses have, of course, no windows, only 20 per cent in both provinces have windows without glass. In Massaca 1 one per cent of the houses have windows with glass.

The estimated size of the houses

The size of the houses was only estimated by the interviewers together with the interviewee. Therefore, these results should be treated with caution. On the other hand, judging from the relative correspondence between Maputo and Beira, although completely different interviewer teams were working in the two cities and from the impression of the size of the houses of the author, there is reason to believe that the estimates come close to reality.

Table 6.3   Estimated size of the houses

	urban		peri-urban		villages	
	M	B	M	B	M	S
less than 10m^2	—	—	6	8	27	69
10 to approx. 25m^2	4	13	44	34	69	23
25 to approx. 70m^2	77	71	41	52	4	5
more than 70m^2	19	16	9	6	—	3
n	(26)	(24)	(231)	(77)	(26)	(39)

In addition to having grass walls, grass roofs, soil floors and no windows, rural poverty is shown particularly in the villages of Sofala in the smallness of the house. As we will see below, overcrowding is much worse in the rural than in the peri-urban and urban areas. Not only in the construction material, but also in the size of the house, the urban – peri-urban gap becomes visible once more.

The number of rooms

The houses in the peri-urban areas of Beira have more rooms than the ones in Maputo, which is due to the more sophisticated pau-a-pique construction method and, resulting from it, the higher durability. If someone builds a house of which he knows it will last for about two decades, he will probably build it larger than one of which he knows it will last less than one decade. The other reason could be that there is still more space available in the peri-urban areas of Beira.

118 *Globalization, urban progress, urban problems, rural disadvantages*

Table 6.4   The number of rooms per house

	IAF results of entire Beira urban *and* peri-urban	urban M	urban B	peri-urban M	peri-urban B	IAF 671 villages
1.....	9	—	—	20	7	20
2	24	19	3	34	23	34
3	31	58	32	17	29	23
4	28	11	36	20	30	17
5 +	8	12	29	9	11	6
n	(597)	(26)	(31)	(236)	(84)	(5,758)

The mode in Beira is four rooms followed by three and two. In peri-urban Maputo the mode with respect to the number of rooms is two, followed by four and three. One fifth of the peri-urban houses in Maputo have one room only, whilst this is the case only for 7 per cent in Beira.[5] The number of rooms per house does not correlate to the household size (r = 0.0741), which means large families can have small, medium or big houses as there is just no correlation.

The results of the second stage of the IAF for Beira correspond well with this research as shown in table 6.4, however, the number of rooms in the villages deviate considerably therefore only the results of the third stage of the IAF are shown.

Comparison of the present house with the previous one and the most preferred house

The interviewees were asked to state whether they consider their present house better, equal or worse than the one they lived in before. The house before could have been an old house in the same place or any other house where the household heads had lived before.
The present house is better than the one before, stated   73 > 60 > 30 per cent.
The present house is the same as the one before, said 13 < 18 < 20 per cent
The present house is worse than the one before, said   14 < 22 < 41 per cent.

This evaluation shows once again the middle position of the peri-urban areas between villages and the cities. It also shows that even in the peri-urban areas and in spite of the serious economic problems in Mozambique and – as was also shown – even with the very low salaries the standard of the house has improved for 60 per cent. This is one of the main reasons why the concept 'slum' does not apply to most cities in Africa because 'slum' signifies essentially a deteriorating city area while the peri-urban areas in Mozambique, one of the poorest countries in the world are improving. The villages, however, are once more the most disadvantaged, they are excluded from any benefits of a global economy as for two fifth the present house is worse than the last one. Even in the run down blocks of flats which have been chosen as control group, the people considered their present home to be better than the one before. As we have seen in table 5.2, the majority of the household heads in the cement cities had lived already in another bairro before they moved here which most of the time might have meant a bairro in the peri-urban areas.

For about a third of the household heads in all three areas the most preferred house type would be a three-roomed house. One fifth in the peri-urban and the fully urbanized areas would prefer a house with four rooms. The code 'this house is good' was chosen by $35 > 16 > 11$ per cent, which shows that only few are satisfied with their small, poor village house. Two thirds of the village household heads would prefer a mason house.

Liked and disliked aspects of the house and necessary improvements

Of those aspects of the house which the household heads of the villages did not like, the mode is the smallness of the house (37 per cent) followed by 'it is made of grass' (22 per cent). In the cement cities, where the majority of the houses have three rooms and where nobody has a house with one room only, 32 per cent say, 'the house is too small'. This clearly shows how needs, once fulfilled, steadily increase thereafter. For 19 per cent of the household heads of the peri-urban areas the house is too small. Here 11 per cent do not like it because the walls exist of caniço, 8 per cent do not like it because the rain enters through the roof, 16 per cent because it is not finished, 16 per cent because it is already too old, 3 per cent because it is about to collapse, and 18 per cent do not like other aspects of their house.

In spite of all the complaints, if asked differently, namely, 'which aspects of your house do you like most?', a surprisingly high proportion chose the code, 'I like all of it': $65 > 43 > 39$ per cent. This could be understood in the sense: I still like it, even though, it is too small, made out of grass or caniço and even though, it needs to be repaired. The proportion of those household heads who chose the code 'I like everything, because it is the product of my own efforts' is highest in the villages: $4 < 26 < 45$.

Liking one's own house, even though one would prefer a better one, must not necessarily be a contradiction.

Of two fifths of the peri-urban houses the walls should be improved, but 'other aspects' were mentioned with the same frequency, which meant in many cases: 'finishing the house' or 'building a new one'. About a seventh of the peri-urban houses need roof repair.

Of the village houses, about one third need improvements of the walls, but more than two fifths of the household heads mentioned 'other aspects'. One fifth of the roofs need to be repaired.

In the cement cities, were the criteria to be chosen for this control group was, living in a run down building, the majority chose the code, 'other aspects' of improvements (64 per cent) and this meant in many cases: 'we want to build our own house'. In a research conducted by the APIE in Maputo in the buildings that are going to be renovated with the financial help of the World Bank, 694 households were investigated and 63 per cent said that they would like to build their own house, only 35 per cent want to come back to the building after the renovations (Universidade Eduardo Mondlane 1989).

In all three areas 55 < 81 > 72 per cent are not going to be able to carry out necessary improvements or to build a new house in the near future, the main reason being, of course, lack of financial resources, only 24 > 15 < 19 per cent stated that they will be able to do so.

The different kinds of illumination and the fuel for cooking

The most commonly used light in the peri-urban areas are petroleum lamps, used by about three quarters of the households. There 18 per cent already have electricity (24 per cent in Maputo and 4 per cent in Beira), while in the rural areas electircity is apparently restricted to commercial farmers only with 0.9 per cent of the households that use electricity. One hundred per cent of the families in the cement cities have electricity. In the villages 38 per cent use a petroleum lamp for lighting, 53 per cent use fire wood and 3 per cent have no light at all (IAF 1998). (We found 4 per cent without any light, 32 per cent using a petroleum lamp, and 64 per cent using fire wood.)

About half of the families in the peri-urban areas and almost all households in the rural areas use fire wood for cooking but only 3 per cent in the cement cities do so. Charcoal is a frequent substitute for wood in the peri-urban areas, used by 36 per cent. In the cement cities 35 per cent use gas and 50 per cent use electricity for cooking.

Using firewood as the principal form of fuel is a serious problem, well known not only in Mozambique but in the whole of Africa. In a circumference of about 30 km or more of Maputo, forests do not exist anymore. Private households of Mozambique use 15 million m³ fire wood, which means 10.000 ha of forest are destroyed every year (OEFSE 1995, 14). However, unfortunately no alternative source of fuel has been developed so far. Therefore, the planning and implementation of agro-forestry schemes in the peri-urban areas and their surroundings would be particularly important for finding a way out of the ecological dilemma of fuel provision.

Summary

Apart from hunger, rural poverty shows its particularly ugly face in poor housing, which is perpetuated also by the process of globalization – amongst other factors. Housing, a basic human need, is the most difficult and the most expensive one to fulfill. In areas without sufficient food supply one cannot expect 'decent' housing.

It seems that concerning the quality of the house as such, the rural – peri-urban gap is just as wide as the peri-urban – urban gap. The majority of the village houses have grass walls, grass roofs, and soil floors. They are very small and normally have one room only without any window and they have to be renewed about every six to ten years. No satisfactory explanation has been found yet, why the majority of the rural houses have one room only, although there is ample space and the building material is provided by nature.

Compared to the poor village houses the peri-urban houses are of a much higher quality, the walls of already more than half of them consist of permanent material, particularly in Beira, the floors consist of cement, and corrugated iron is mainly used for roofs. Their size is between ten and seventy m² and the majority has two to four rooms with windows, most of the time without glass, though. They last sixteen or more years. Only about ten per cent have a kitchen inside.

Because of the pau-a-pique building method, the peri-urban houses of Beira are of a higher standard than those of Maputo. They are not only more durable, their walls need repair less often but they are also larger than in Maputo, the mode being between twenty-five and seventy m² and they have a much greater number of rooms, almost a third having four rooms and almost another third having three rooms while the mode in Maputo is clearly two rooms.

Nevertheless, not even in Beira one could speak of a satisfactory housing situation in the peri-urban areas and by far less in Maputo. These areas are still, in spite of considerable advantages and positive changes, compared to the village houses undoubtedly poor housing areas and therefore the gap between them and the blocks of flats in the cement cities, which are in most aspects of European standard, is enormous.

In the subjective judgement of the household heads concerning the comparison of their present house with the previous one, the rural – peri-urban gap is wider than the peri-urban – urban gap, which shows once more the deteriorating situation in the villages but also the improvements people experience when they move to the cities or during their stay in the cities.

The infrastructure

As mentioned above, the infrastructure is part of the housing situation. It is not possible to survive without water and, in addition, the water must be clean. People need sanitary facilities, transport and – as a basis for transport – roads in good conditions. In the cities refuse disposal is essential and everywhere an informational infrastructure, such as radios, is crucial for development.

The sanitary situation

There is a big difference between the peri-urban areas of Maputo and Beira as far as the sanitary situation is concerned. Apparently, this difference is caused by the fact that the city of Beira is situated below sea level. Building sanitary installations, i.e. latrines, is very difficult and dangerous because the underground water level is very near the surface and latrines would pollute the drinking water. Therefore, two thirds of the families in the peri-urban areas of Beira only use the bush for their sanitary needs (the IAF found 70 per cent in this condition), 7 per cent use a latrine together with one or more families, 22 per cent have their own latrine, 2 per cent have a flushing toilet and 2 per cent a septic tank.

Table 6.5 Sanitary facilities

	urban M	urban B	peri-urban M	peri-urban B	IAF 671 villages
bushes	—	—	2	66	71
shared latrine	—	—	7	7	—
own latrine	—	3	61	22	28
improved latrine	—	—	25	1	—
flushing toilet	100	94	4	1	1
septic tank	—	3	2	3	—
n	(26)	(32)	(243)	(85)	(5,758)

Contrary to Beira, in the peri-urban areas of Maputo only 2 per cent use the bush for their sanitary needs but like in Beira 7 per cent use a latrine together with one or more families and also 2 per cent have a septic tank, but 61 per cent have their own latrine, and in addition, 25 per cent already have an improved latrine[6] (see figure 6.9).

In the villages of the Sofala province, 88 per cent of the families use the bush for their sanitary needs, however, only in Nhangau the level of underground water is near the surface and not in Mutua. Here, the reasons for not having latrines are apparently different ones. In newly built up Massaca1 nearly all families have their own latrine which is again quite atypical for rural areas. The reliable results of the third stage of the IAF show that 71 per cent of the rural households do not have any sanitary facilities.

Having one's own latrine is not sufficient enough because it might not be hygenic. The aim must be to improve latrines for all, also in rural areas. In this regard Mozambique does not seem to be an exception because world-wide there are some three billion people without proper sanitary facilities (Wirasinha 1998). Concerted effort is needed to end those squalid, health-threatening conditions.

The water supply

The mode of the water supply in the peri-urban areas are fountains, followed by wells. In Beira the mode are fountains that are far away (39 per cent), followed by the far away wells (19 per cent) while in Maputo the mode are fountains (37 per cent) and wells (25 per cent) that are near. In Massaca 1 83 per cent have to fetch water from a nearby river.

124 *Globalization, urban progress, urban problems, rural disadvantages*

Figure 6.9 Improved traditional latrine with small hygienic slab

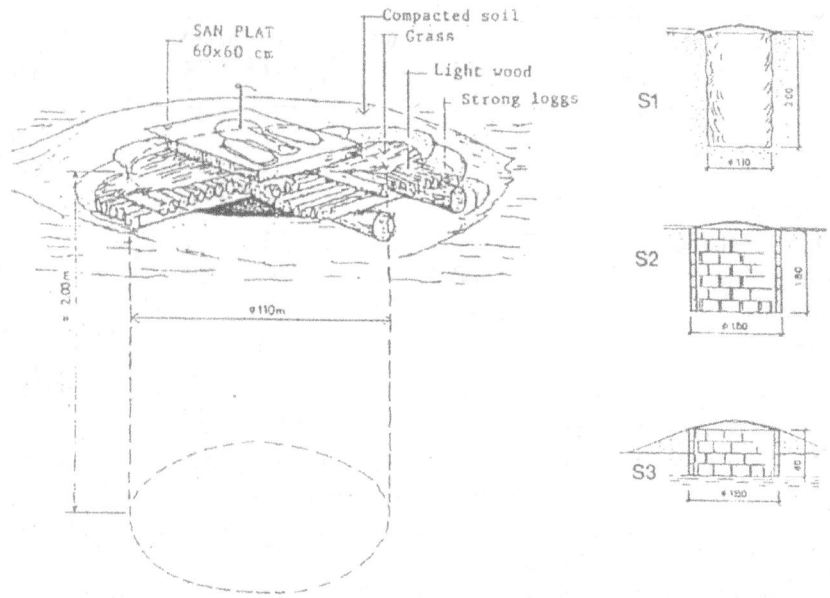

S1: Simple latrine for stable soil; water table 3.0 metres or more; volume 1.9 m^3; useful life 6 -16 years for 5 persons.
S2: Lined latrine for unstable soil (with cement/sand blocks); water table 2.4 metres or more; volume 2.1 – 3.2 m^3; useful life: 12 – 30 years for 5 persons.
S3: Elevated latrine, where it is difficult to dig; water table 0 to 2.4 metres; volume 0.9 – 1.6 m^3; useful life 6 – 10 years for 5 persons.   *Source:* UNDP Maputo 1991, Annex V.

Table 6.6 The water supply

	urban		peri-urban		rural	IAF 671 villages
	M	B	M	B		
rivers or lakes	—	—	—	—	31	38
distant well	—	—	5	19		
nearby well	—	3	25	13	66	58
distant public water outlet	—	—	13	39		
public water outlet close by	—	—	37	19		
water tap in our yard	4	31	13	8	—	0.6
piped water in our house	92	66	3	1	—	0.2
others	4	—	4	1	3	3
n	(26)	(32)	(243)	(85)	(63)	(5,758)

Figure 6.10 The water problem in the peri-urban areas of Beira
The water has to be carried long distances and is, in addition, often not clean. In the foreground the Beira-Corridor railway line.

In general, the supply of drinking water is better in Maputo than in Beira, but in both cities the water is not of good quality. More than half of the households in the peri-urban areas of Beira and almost a fifth in Maputo do not have access to public water near their homes and therefore have to buy water from the people who have a well, a fountain or a tap.

Water seems to be more expensive in Beira, where the water supply is a bigger problem: the majority of the households that buy water pay between 30 and 60 Mt. for a tin of water (about 25 litres). In Maputo the price mode is between 15 and 30 Mt.

Because the families in the peri-urban areas in Beira have to wait in a queue in front of a well or a tap to get water for a long time and then carry it a long distance and, in addition, because the water is more expensive in Beira than in Maputo, the families use less water. More than half use between 1 and 5 tins per day and two fifths use 6 to 10 tins per day, only 5 per cent use more than this. But in Maputo 60 per cent use between 6 and 10 tins and only a quarter uses 1 to 5 tins a day.

In the villages of the Sofala province, where the majority have a fountain or a well near their homes and where the household heads do not have to pay for water, the majority of the families still only use between 1 and 5 tins per day. The same relatively small quantity is used by the majority of the households in Massaca 1, here apparently because they have to fetch the water from far away, from the Limpopo River.

Transportation

Most people naturally walk to work in the villages but almost half have to walk also in the peri-urban areas and almost a third in the cement cities. Once again, we note the medium position of the peri-urban areas: 31 < 43 < 78 per cent go to work on foot. The second place of the means of transport used by the household heads to go to work in the peri-urban areas is taken by a 'chapa cem'.[7]

Table 6.7 Means of transportation to work

	urban		peri-urban		villages	
	M	B	M	B	M	S
on foot	40	31	45	54	71	87
'chapa cem'	10	4	27	17	—	13
bus/train	—	—	6	7	8	—
bicycle	—	—	1	8	13	—
motorcycle	5	8	1	1	—	—
car	20	15	3	—	—	—
transport of workplace	25	42	17	13	8	—
n	(20)	(26)	(183)	(71)	(25)	(40)

The privileged position of the urban household heads compared to the peri-urban and rural ones becomes once more apparent in the transport facilities. A considerable proportion of them is provided transport by the working place although they are the ones who could most easily afford to pay for public transport. In addition almost a fifth drives to work with their own car.

Forty per cent of the household heads in the peri-urban areas of Maputo and 36 per cent of those of Beira apparently work in the cement city because they say they go to 'town' 20 to 30 times per month. A quarter of the village household heads go to Maputo or Beira once a month and another quarter twice a month. For other errands and visits, the majority of the families of all areas use a 'chapa cem' most frequently as means of transportion, with the exception of Massaca 1 – people there use a bus most frequently.

Additional infrastructure

In the peri-urban areas of both cities, the majority of the roads are dirt roads; only for about a quarter the nearest road to their homes is a tarred road. Through squatter upgrading, which was never really carried out in Beira, the houses in the peri-urban areas of Maputo have a much better access to roads:

Access to roads in the peri-urban areas:	Maputo %	Beira %
direct access	38	11
next road in a distance of one hundred metres	25	44
next road in a distance of 100 to 500 metres	30	37

the rest of the houses are even further away from the next road which brings a lot of problems particularly in emergency cases.

Three quarters of the families in the peri-urban areas of Maputo, bury their waste and 60 per cent of the peri-urban areas in Beira do so; but unfortunately, still 35 per cent of the families of the peri-urban areas in Beira burn their waste, 33 per cent do the same in the villages of Sofala and 66 per cent in Massaca 1. As is well known, this does a lot of harm to the environment. Much of educational work will still be necessary to prevent this method of air pollution. Even in the cement city of Beira 6 per cent burn their waste and 28 per cent throw their waste on to a public place, 13 per cent bury it and only for 53 per cent of the families the waste is removed by the city council. In the cement city of Maputo the waste of all families is collected by the city council, however, not frequently enough – the containers are often overflowing. The importance of collecting organic waste and getting it composted for reasons of hygiene and plant nutrition is discussed in the section on urban agriculture in chapter 12.

Nearly half of the household heads of the peri-urban areas of Maputo, two fifths of Beira and the majority of the three villages, never use a telephone. But 5 per cent of the household heads of Massaca 1 already use a telephone at work and for 13 per cent of the household heads in the villages of Sofala telephones exist 'in other places' of the village. All household heads of the cement cities phone: one third in Maputo and nearly half in Beira already have a telephone at home. In Maputo 44 per cent phone at work and for one quarter other possibilities exist, there are telephones in the neighbourhood or in other places of the bairro. In the cement city of Beira only 13 per cent of the household heads phone at work, 36 per cent have telephones in the neighbourhood, and 3 per cent in the centre of the bairro.

In the peri-urban areas of Maputo only 1 per cent of the families already have a telephone at home but in Beira 3 per cent have. In the peri-urban areas of Maputo 23 per cent of the household heads and 26 per cent of those in Beira phone at work, 19 and 30 per cent respectively have a telephone in the neighbourhood, in the centre of the bairro or at another place in the bairro. In general the situation concerning telephones seems to be better in Beira as well as in the villages of Sofala than in Maputo and Massaca 1.

Supply of radios

> Radios are the best indication of our capacity to inform and communicate because, given our high rate of illiteracy and the very limited circulation of newspapers, only the spoken word can reach the people rapidly and effectively (Forjaz 1984).

Forjaz quotes the 1980 Census in his paper and states that then only 48 per cent of the urban households (61 per cent in Maputo) had a radio, but only 12 per cent in the rural areas. The situation in this regard has apparently improved considerably since.

The proportion of the families that do have a radio now is much higher but still decreases from area 1 to area 6:

urbM	urbB	periM	periB	villM	villS
100 %	94 %	82 %	57 %	50 %	38 %

The percentage of the families that do have a radio is smaller in Beira. If we consider both provinces together, then 97 > 75 > 42 per cent have a radio. This proportion is much too high for the entire rural areas as the IAF (1998) only found 22 per cent with radios but also 2 per cent with a TV set.

Supply of television sets

The proportion of the families that do have a television set decreases from area 1 to area 4. There is of course no television in the villages.

urbM	urbB	periM	periB
46 %	19 %	9 %	1 %

In Beira there are less families who have a television set than in Maputo. Those who do have one in Beira could only watch video-films at the time of the interviews in 1991. Only in the following year television broadcasting was installed in Beira.

Summary

Also concerning the infrastructure, which is an essential part of housing, the inner urban as well as the peri-urban – rural gap can be shown clearly in most aspects. Latrines, even though they have improved in the peri-urban areas, can in no way reach the comfort of a flushing toilet in the fully urbanized areas and using the bush for ones sanitary needs, as it is common in the rural areas, lacks any hygienic standards. Unfortunately, improving the sanitary facilities is hardly seen as a priority in development programmes and so it might take decades until the project of improved latrines will reach the countryside.

The urban – peri-urban gap is wide as far as water supply is concerned. Water from a well or a public water outlet, which has to be carried home and kept in a bucket or tin and which is, in addition, in most peri-urban areas of low quality, belongs to a different 'world' in comparison to clean piped water, which the inhabitants enjoy in the fully urbanized areas. However, even the village samples were too small, judging from other observations, there seems to be no peri-urban – rural gap as far as water supply is concerned. Just the opposite, this time the rural population could have an advantage insofar, as they do not have to pay for the water while in both peri-urban areas half the families have to buy water. As water supply is a much bigger problem in the peri-urban areas of Beira, the water there is also about twice as expensive as in Maputo. In addition, people have to queue up for it and carry it for long distances. For all those reasons it is more than understandable that the families in the peri-urban areas of Beira use less water than those of the peri-urban areas of Maputo. However, different reasons for the low quantity of water used in the villages of Sofala must exist, as the water supply there is sufficient and good.

The household heads of the cement cities are also privileged as far as transport to work is concerned. For almost a third of them this transport is provided by their employers and one seventh use their own car. One third has to walk. Transport to work is provided by employers for only one seventh of the household heads in the peri-urban areas and only three per cent drive to work with a private car. More than half go to work on foot. In the villages more than three quarters have to go to work on foot.

Waste is burried by the majority of households in both peri-urban areas, but about one third in Beira as well as in the villages of Sofala and two thirds in Massaca 1 burn it. Waste removal is still a serious problem even in the cement city of Beira.

More than 90 per cent of the rural household heads and about half of those in the peri-urban areas never use a telephone, while all household heads of the cement cities do phone once in a while. The more frequent telephones in Beira are – apart from the more durable, larger houses with more rooms – one of the few aspects where Beira has an advantage over Maputo.

Almost all families in the cement cities have a radio, compared to three quarters in the peri-urban areas and less than half in the villages. Almost half of the families in the cement city of Maputo and about one fifth in the cement city of Beira have a TV-set but only 9 per cent in the peri-urban areas of Maputo and 1 per cent in the peri-urban areas of Beira have.

Social facilities

Not so directly a part of the housing quality as the above discussed infrastructure, but just as essential, are the social facilities concerning the quality of a housing area. Nearby schools, health posts, shopping facilities, etc. are important for the quality and the security of life. The analysis of the insufficiency of social facilities particularly in the rural but also in the peri-urban areas will bring to light other facets of poverty as well as the privileged situation of the fully urbanized areas, i.e. other effects of Europeanization and globalization.

Schools

The two urban worlds manifest themselves not only, but also in the quality of schools, as far as building standards and equipments are concerned. Although this was not directly subject of this investigation, simply visiting schools in the two urban areas shows the great difference. Many schools in the peri-urban areas have no windows and are virtually empty. Pupils sit on the floor, while schools in the cement cities have at least a minimum standard of equipment.

In addition, a higher proportion of children attend school in the fully urbanized areas compared to the peri-urban areas. However, it should be noted that three quarters of school attendance for a poor country like Mozambique shows that the government and the people are trying hard to give all children at least a basic education. Primary education for all is the goal for the year 2001 (World Bank 1995, 13).

Unfortunately, for the time being the gap is still wide between peri-urban and rural areas. However, the low school attendance in the villages of Sofala which we found in our survey can, apart from the unreliability of the small sample, be attributed to the war situation and in addition to the fact that Sofala belongs to the central region. Also in this regard:

Figure 6.11 School children in a classroom in the peri-urban areas of Maputo

the government is focusing efforts to increase the overall participation of girls in primary education by targeting programmes in the northern and central region of the country where girls enrolment is relatively low. The objective is to bring the national share of girls in the students population in line of that with southern Mozambique by the year 2001 (World Bank 1995, 13).

The low school attendance in the rural areas is also due to the war. Almost half of the primary schools were destroyed by Renamo or had to be closed because teachers were tortured and killed. Massaca 1 is once more too atypical and too privileged to give a picture of the educational situation in the rural areas in general. Here just as many children attend school as in the peri-urban areas and also almost as many girls as boys.

Table 6.8 School attendance of children between 6 and 14

	urban		peri-urban		villages		IAF
	M	B	M	B	M	S	671 villages
proportion of girls attending school	86	83	76	76	80	17	42
n	(29)	(30)	(248)	(66)	(30)	(23)	(3,534)
proportion of boys attending school	90	100	76	83	82	48	53
n	(21)	(32)	(286)	(66)	(22)	(27)	(3,613)

According to the IAF, the percentage of children of this age who attend a school in entire Maputo (including the fully urbanized areas) is 3.5 per cent higher compared to the results of this research but the difference between the sexes is also only 2 per cent.[8] The equality of school attendance between the sexes in the peri-urban areas of Maputo and the almost equality in the fully urbanized areas becomes conspicuous and could be interpreted as one of the positive aspects of globalization.

The real picture of the school attendance in the rural areas in 1996/97 is shown by the results of the third stage of the IAF. According to these results, 42 per cent of the girls and 53 per cent of the boys attended school in those years. However, these figures are changing fast and, fortunately, this time in a positive direction. In his 'state of nation address' President Chissano of Mozambique said on 29 March 1999 that by the end of 1998 all schools destroyed during the war had been rebuilt (Mozambique News Agency, AIM, No.155, 1999).

Secondary schools and delayed primary school   Due to lack of places in school or because of the difficulties to pay school fees or other expenses, children start to go to school at a later age and therefore primary school is often finished at a later age than 14 or 15 in many African countries. Here Mozambique does not seem to be an exception, where a considerable proportion of juveniles still attend school.

Table 6.9   School attendance of juveniles between 14 and 20[9]

	urban		peri-urban		villages		IAF
	M	B	M	B	M	S	671 villages
prop. of females attending school	64	90	49	56	60	30	13
n	(11)	(11)	(121)	(36)	(10)	(13)	(1,855)
prop. of males attending school	67	92	53	69	50	25	32
n	(8)	(11)	(127)	(26)	(6)	(16)	(1,839)

In our sample, as so often, also here, the school attendance of the juveniles in Massaca 1 corresponds quite well with the peri-urban areas, but the proportion of the females of this age group was much too high in the villages of Sofala as the IAF sample census shows.

The results of all areas and both age groups show a better situation in Beira than in Maputo. This would be the third advantage particularly in the peri-urban areas of Beira: better houses, more telephones, and now higher school attendance.

The churches

The proportion of people who stated that they were not religious increases from the cement cities to the villages: 16 < 32 < 51. This time the increase of percentages has most probably not much to do with the rural – urban continuum as the 51 per cent could mean something completely different than the 16 per cent. The percentages are certainly not referring to religion in the proper sense namely, attachment to God or Gods, belief in supernatural forces. In Mozambique one understands under being religious belonging to a church or a sect. Nobody chose the code 'animist' – although this option was the first of the codes in the questionnaire and the meaning was explained to the interviewees. This is certainly a consequence of the specific Portuguese colonization, which was very different from the English one. In Zambia, for example, people did not have any problems in saying, 'I am an animist'. But apparently in Mozambique being an animist is the same as not being religious, being a 'pagan', which was considered very negative by missionaries and colonizers. It is very possible that those 51 per cent of the household heads in the villages who chose the answer 'no' to the question 'are you religious' actually are animists.

The interpretation of one third in the peri-urban areas who stated that they were not religious is more difficult. Here it is possible that part of those 32 per cent are not religious in the proper sense, meaning that they are agnostics or secularized. This possibility is even growing in the cement cities. Secularization is a modern phenomenon and is increasing – one of the causes being urbanization.

In spite of a trend to secularization, religion still seems to play an important role also in other African cities. In Lagos, for instance, Peil states:

> Religion is firmly based in local culture, as important to the successful as to the marginal. Adherence to religion, in their mainstream or separatist manifestation, provide a measure of security and also a source of support in times of trouble. Traditional religion is less visible because it is based on homes rather than special buildings, but it remains important in the lives of residents. Religion affects attitudes towards medical care and education; it structures social relationships, use of leisure time and even business ties. Small sects provide face-to-face relations in a situation of equality, which deflects attention from the problems of every day life and the leaders who may be responsible for them (Peil 1991).

Of those who are religious in the Maputo province the vast majority and in the province of Sofala also more than half have a church of their own denomination in the same bairro or village respectively. The reader should be reminded that the churches in the peri-urban areas and particularly in the villages are not concrete buildings but can be made out of caniço or other materials just like the houses in the respective area.

Table 6.10 The religion of the household heads

	urban		peri-urban		villages	
	M	B	M	B	M	S
Catholic	50	50	22	34	—	29
Moslem	4	19	3	1	—	2
Protestant	—	6	7	6	—	—
Mazione[10]	8	—	15	9	10	2
Assembly of God	4	6	4	8	17	10
Twelve Apostles	—	—	5	—	14	3
other	12	6	11	8	10	3
no religion	23	13	34	33	48	51
n	(26)	(32)	(242)	(85)	(29)	(41)

The most frequent religious denomination of the household heads in all areas, except Massaca 1, is Catholic. In Massaca 1 the mode is the Assembly of God. It is interesting that the large mainstream churches appear to be underrepresented in Massaca 1. The second most frequent religious denomination is the Moslems in the cement city of Beira and in the peri-urban areas of Maputo the Mazione. There is no statistical difference between men and women as far as belonging to a particular church is concerned.

If the frequency of going to church can be considered as a measurement of the degree of religiousness, then a large proportion of those household heads who said that they were religious are at the same time very religious.

136 *Globalization, urban progress, urban problems, rural disadvantages*

Table 6.11 The frequency of going to church

	urban		peri-urban		villages	
	M	B	M	B	M	S
almost every day	5	19	20	9	31	5
more than once a week	5	7	21	44	56	30
each weekend	35	56	28	39	—	45
sometimes	40	11	25	7	13	20
never	10	7	2	2	—	—
we go to the beach for ceremonies (Mazione)	5	—	4	—	—	—
n	(20)	(27)	(160)	(57)	(16)	(20)

In both provinces together 19 < 45 < 57 per cent go to church almost every day or more than once a week. But there is a big difference between these two provinces as one can see from the table above: 10 < 41 < 87 per cent of the religious household heads go to church almost every day or more often than once per week in the province of Maputo, but 26 < 52 > 35 per cent go to church this frequently in the province of Sofala. While we can conclude a diminishing religiosity through a higher degree of urbanization, taking into consideration peri-urban and fully urbanized areas only, the 35 per cent of the religious household heads who go to church very frequently in the villages of the province of Sofala can probably be considered as more typical for the villages than the 87 per cent of Massaca 1.

In the rural areas people often walk long distances to reach the church of their choice, but most go at least weekly. Massaca 1, situated relatively close to the district capital Boane, seems to be an exception once again. So the rural urban continuum of 19 < 45 < 57 per cent of very frequent church goers must be questioned this time. It is unlikely that people in the rural areas go to church more frequently than people in the peri-urban areas, but it is likely that people in the rural areas are more religious in the sense of belief in supranatural powers than people in the peri-urban areas and particularly than people in the cement cities. People in rural areas naturally value their traditions more than those in urban areas and traditionally it was not possible, also not in Europe, to be irreligious or an agnostic. This process of secularization started only with the era of enlightenment and industrialization. 'Hardly any non-religious individual can be found in a truly traditional culture. There is no conceptual cleavage between the natural and the supranatural' (Busia 1962, 50; see also Bolaji 1973).

In this context the research of Macamo (1999) among the Tsonga in southern Mozambique mentioned in chapter 2 (footnote 2) should serve as an example to show the vitality of local knowledge versus the claim of universal knowledge. The latter was represented by the Swiss Presbyterian missionaries who had internalized the Protestant ethic with its rejection of witchcraft, on the one hand, and the postulation of hard work and other ethical principles, on the other hand, which dominated their social action. Here a dialectical process started between the global and the local and continues up until today as the process of 'glocalization'.

No matter how hard the missionaries tried to discredit witchcraft and the belief in spirits and no matter whether the people converted to Christianity or not, Africans continued to believe in three categories of spirits: the powerful spirits of nature, the spirits of the ancestors and the spirits 'by chance' (accidental spirits). The latter can be used by people to achieve wealth, success or other advantages by dubious means on the cost of others. Traditional healers and other authorities of the Tsonga consider these as very bad practices. For them the world is not bad because those bad spirits exist, but rather because bad people use them too often. The missionaries were not able to reduce these practices considerably nor were they able to reverse the conception of reality of the Tsongas (which might not be much different from most other African peoples): reality in a western, scientific world view, including the view of the Swiss missionaries, is an optic illusion for the magic ontology of the Tsonga. Only the reality of the spirits and ancestors is the true reality, while the reality of the living is an illusion. Human beings are holograms housing spirits. Life derives its meaning from the spirits and is determined by them. Real life only starts after death.

All these beliefs, Macamo found, are still undiminished strong today and are not only an example for the vitality of the local versus the global but also an example for 'hybridization': people often converted to Christianity in order to be protected against bad spirits in which they continued to believe. However, it should also be mentioned that Macamo did his research in the rural areas. With urbanization religious beliefs weaken, be they traditional, Christian or of any other denomination.

For a country which had to endure so much hardship as Mozambique had to, religion is often the last resort. In addition, people belonging to a church or a sect apparently do have additional social bonds and support nets.

138 *Globalization, urban progress, urban problems, rural disadvantages*

Figure 6.12 Mutual help and contact with members of the same religion

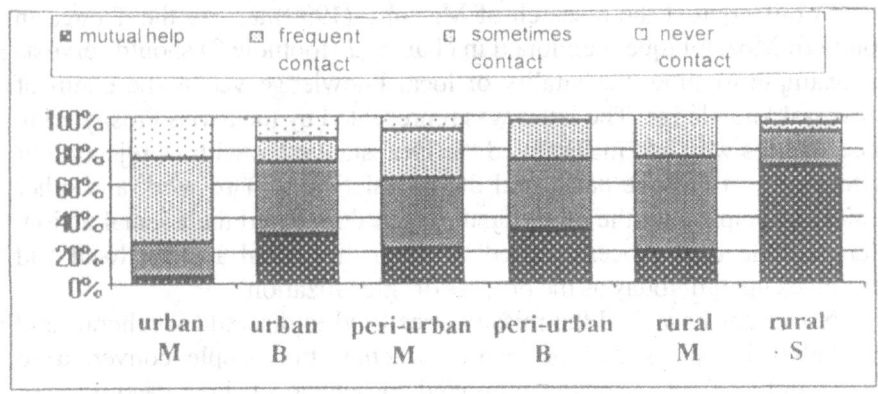

With the exception of the cement city of Maputo and the villages in Sofala, in all other areas the most frequent answer was, 'we have many contacts'. In Mutua and Nhangau, the villages of the Sofala province, almost three quarters of believers in the same religion help each other. In the cement city of Maputo half of the members of the same church contact each other only sometimes and one quarter never. This could be another indication of the secularization process through urbanization.

There is no difference between men and women as far as this kind of mutual help and contact is concerned, however, a higher percentage of women (73 per cent) stated that they were religious as compared to men (64 per cent) and a higher percentage of religious women go to church every day or more often than once per week (23 and 30 per cent respectively) as compared to religious men (17 and 23 per cent respectively).

Political and social centres

Political, administrative and party centre   All bairros and villages in Mozambique have a political and administrative centre which is called 'circulo' (circle). Since only one political party existed until recently in Mozambique, namely FRELIMO, this political centre was at the same time the centre for the party officials and their activists, the grupos dynamazadores. The majority of the household heads go to this circle sometimes. Only in the cement city of Beira less than half go to the circle sometimes and more than half never go. The percentages of people in the other two areas of Sofala who

Housing in the two urban worlds and the neglected countryside 139

never go to the circle are also much bigger than the percentage in the province of Maputo, which could be an indication that FRELIMO was less popular in the province of Sofala than in Maputo (compare also the variable 'aspects of life liked most' in chapter 11).

In both provinces 0 < 8 < 22 per cent visit the circle more often than once a week or once a week. 62 < 76 > 69 per cent go to the circle sometimes and 38 > 16 < 9 per cent never go there. The co-operation with these centres also seems to diminish with urbanization.

Opinion about the multi-party system As in most other African countries a multi-party system was introduced in Mozambique recently. There were elections in October 1994. Consciousness raising was part of the electoral process. However, what was the percentage of the population that really liked and wanted a multi-party system at the time of the survey? We simply asked the respondents 'do you like the multi-party system?' and the answer codes of the following table were presented to them.

Table 6.12 Opinion about the multi-party system

	urban		peri-urban		villages	
	M	B	M	B	M	S
yes	48	50	33	41	7	26
no	20	25	19	5	38	16
I am not interested in it	28	16	19	20	14	5
I don't know what it is	4	9	29	34	41	53
n	(25)	(32)	(241)	(81)	(29)	(38)

While the difference in the cement cities is not impressive, a higher percentage wanted a multi-party system in the peri-urban areas of Beira and particularly in the villages of the province of Sofala. But if the villages of Sofala could be seen as somehow typical, the proportion of the rural population which was in favour of more parties would, nevertheless, have been only a quarter. It was already mentioned that in Mozambique about 77 per cent of the population still live in rural areas and that from the urbanized population about 80 per cent live in the peri-urban areas; if we consider this, then maybe only one third of Mozambique's population really wanted more political parties in 1991. On the other hand the percentage can be considered as high, because it is a completely new system and also because it is difficult to explain to the rural population, where the majority has no formal education and less than half of the families have a radio.

So it is self-evident that half of the rural population did not know what a multi-party system was (although the interviewers had to explain that it means more parties instead of only FRELIMO). People had no opportunity to experience a multi-party system and particularly could not imagine, whether it would change their lives or not. Nevertheless, after an intensive campaign the elections were held and 88 per cent of those entitled to vote did so (44 per cent for FRELIMO, 38 per cent for Renamo, the rest for smaller parties, Fandrych 1994).

The ones who answered 'yes' or 'no' were asked to give their reasons. These reasons were given by the people, i.e. by the interviewees, during the pilot study and only thereafter included into the questionnaire. As they show a high degree of political awareness, they should be presented here, even though the number of the respondents, who then actually chose the codes, is very small.

Reasons for a positive reply

	f	%
More parties would improve the situation of the country	61	40
If we have more parties, we can see who will have capabilities and who will not	41	27
If we have more parties and one fails, the others can take over	39	26
Other reasons	11	7
	152	100

Reasons for a negative reply

	f	%
I only know FRELIMO	47	55
I only want FRELIMO	19	22
Because all the party officials have the same tendencies: they only want to improve their own situation	11	13
Other reasons	9	10
	86	100

The barracks Barracks (barracas) is the name for places of entertainment in Mozambique. They are small structures, normally of precarious material, in the peri-urban areas and in the villages. They are, of course, bigger and partly of permanent material in the cement cities. People go there in the evenings to drink locally brewed or imported beer as well as other drinks. They can listen to music – normally from cassettes – and they can dance.

Table 6.13 The frequency of visits by the household heads to the barracks

Chi^2 sign.=.2787	urban		peri-urban		villages	
	M	B	M	B	M	S
more often than once a week	—	3	1	4	3	—
once a week	3	3	3	5	8	3
sometimes	31	10	23	12	29	11
never	65	87	72	82	58	8
n	(26)	(31)	(240)	(85)	(24)	(38)

The frequency of visits to the barracks by the household heads is one of the few variables, which show no difference between the areas. The proportion of those who go to the barracks regularly is very small. In the cement city of Maputo and in Massaca 1 less than a third visit these places of entertainment 'sometimes', but in all other areas this proportion is even smaller. The vast majority never goes to the barracks.

The sports centres Other places of entertainment are the sports centres, which in the peri-urban areas and in the villages only consist in an open space (field) – for playing football. Also here, the percentages of the household heads who go to the sports centre regularly to watch a match is small, but almost two fifths in the fully urbanized areas of Maputo go there sometimes and about a quarter in both peri-urban areas.

Table 6.14 The frequency of watching football of male household heads

$Chi^2=.0897$	urban		peri-urban		villages	
	M	B	M	B	M	S
more often than once a week	4	3	—	3	—	—
once a week	8	6	5	7	8	10
sometimes	38	19	27	19	12	11
never	50	72	68	71	80	79
n	(26)	(32)	(238)	(84)	(25)	(38)

Also here there is no statistically significant difference between the areas as this entertainment is not related to costs. The big difference though lies in the facility as such, as a big football stadium exists in the cement city of Maputo.

Shops and markets

There is a relatively large central market in each cement city, but there are not too many food stores for the Mozambican people, but a big so-called 'loja franca', which until recently served foreigners only or a local elite having US Dollars at their disposal. Shops for other commodities vary a great deal. From reaching European standard, particularly in the fully urbanized area of Maputo, to being often very poorly equipped. There are few shops in both peri-urban areas and only one in each village centre of the investigated villages in the Sofala province, but there was none in Massaca 1. People who want to buy in shops there go to the near district capital, Boane. There are a number of markets in both peri-urban areas, which vary in size and quality. In some cases their legal status is difficult to determine, because also the so-called black illegal markets are often quite well established, they can be seen on the same place every day, the authorities know about their existence. Nevertheless, they are now and again harassed by the police. Black markets are called 'dumba nengues' in Maputo and 'chunga moios' in Beira. Both mean 'trust your legs' (when the police is approaching).

Figure 6.13 Kind of shopping facilities used

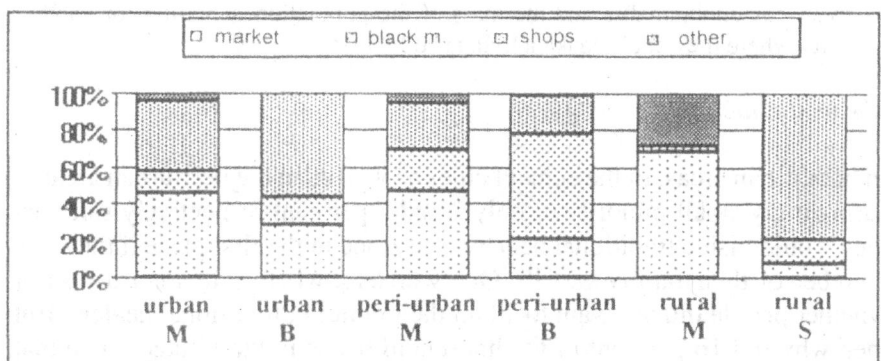

The mode of shopping facilities used in the cement city of Maputo is the central market, but in Beira the shops. The quality of the central market in Beira is probably considered insufficient by the inhabitants of the fully urbanized areas and in addition shops are all over the place and much nearer and therefore most frequently used. Also the villagers of the Sofala province mainly buy in shops there, whereas in Massaca 1 the majority goes shopping in the market and a considerable proportion apparently goes to Boane to shop (see 'other' in table). Black markets are particularly popular in the peri-urban areas of Beira. The popularity of buying at 'dumba nengues' and 'chunga moios' increased when people were asked about their second choice of shopping facilities; then in both provinces together, following the usual order of areas, 38 > 31 < 43 per cent buy at black markets. This shows, on one hand, that a considerable percentage of households use the opportunity to buy cheaper as those who sell on the black market – or one could also say, as those who sell in an informal way – avoid to pay taxes to the city or local authorities. In this way part of the revenue is lost, on the other hand, we saw that 24 per cent of the family income in Maputo city and 19 per cent in the other provincial capitals comes from trading, which means to a large extent illegal trading. In this light the steady attempt of the authorities not only in Mozambique but also in other African countries to abolish this part of the informal sector becomes questionable as it would mean more poverty for the households – for those who sell as well as for those who buy.

Also Peil sees the necessity of allowing to trade on markets and streets for Lagos when she states:

144 *Globalization, urban progress, urban problems, rural disadvantages*

If all trading were removed from the streets, Lagos might temporarily resemble a European city, but it would soon close down – its people unfed, services unobtainable and the mass of the population departing for another city where they could make a living (Peil 1991).

The health facilities

In both urban areas, in the cement cities as well as in the peri-urban areas, a surprisingly small minority of only 2 and 5 per cent respectively said that they would visit a traditional healer or mazione in the first place if they or a member of their family was ill. One wonders, whether this is truly so or whether people did not want to admit their belief in traditional healers. But then why did 16 per cent of the household heads in the villages state that they would go to a traditional healer or mazione in the first place? In the second place, apparently after modern medicine has failed, a somewhat higher percentage tries to take advantage of traditional medical knowledge in all three areas. In this regard the social change is more pronounced in the first stage of urbanization, namely, from the villages to the peri-urban areas than in the second stage of urbanization from the peri-urban to the fully

Figure 6.14 People awaiting treatment in front of the hospital in Beira

urbanized areas. The people in the rural areas are not necessarily inert when consulting traditional healers, but it can often become a necessity, because modern medical facilities are so insufficient. They could well be longing for this kind of social change, but cannot make it happen. As we will see below, the majority, also in the villages, does consider it as necessary to have more health centres and hospitals; only 5 per cent of the village household heads in Sofala want more traditional healers.

Church persons are normally not consulted in order to get medical aid but psychological and particularly spiritual and supranatural one. For 6 per cent of the families in the peri-urban areas this has apparently priority, even for 2 per cent in the cement cities and 5 per cent in the villages. These proportions do not increase drastically in a second attempt.

Table 6.15 The use of health facilities in the first place

	urban	peri-urban	villages
traditional healer/mazione	2	5	16
religious healer	2	6	5
health post/health centre	54	65	72
hospital	16	23	7
central hospital	26	1	—
n	(57)	(326)	(65)

Table 6.16 The use of health facilities in the second place

	urban	peri-urban	villages
traditional healer/mazione	9	13	24
religious healer	5	8	9
health post/centre	2	11	38
hospital	9	27	10
central hospital	75	41	19
n	(44)	(270)	(58)

The vast majority visits health posts or health centres, either in their own or in another bairro, in the first place in all three areas. In Mozambique there exists an official distinction between health posts and health centres. The later normally being equipped with a medical doctor and some hospital beds, while in health posts only the assistance of nurses is available. However people often mix up these two entities: a post can be called a centre and vice versa. For this reason – although the questionnaire distinguishes between posts and centres – in the presentation of results the respective percentages are summarized.

In the second place, this obviously means in more serious cases, that the majority of the people in the urban areas go either to a hospital in another bairro or to the central hospital, which has in both cities, but particularly in Maputo, by far the highest standard of medical care. There is hardly any specialist in the other hospitals. As hospitals and particularly a central hospital is often too far away from the rural areas and transport is in most cases too expensive, only about a quarter of the villagers can go there even in the second place. In addition, since the structural adjustment programme was introduced, medical care is no longer free in Mozambique.

In response to the question, which categories of medical facilities should be increased, the mode is health posts followed by health centres in all the different areas of the province of Maputo, while in the province of Sofala, in all the areas, more than two fifths think it is necessary to have a hospital. Only 0.4 per cent in the peri-urban areas of Maputo wish there would be more traditional healers, but 5 per cent of the investigated village household heads of Sofala think there should be more traditional healers. Only 7 per cent of the household heads of the peri-urban areas of both cities and 10 per cent in the cement city of Beira think there are already sufficient health facilities, however, two fifths of the interviewed household heads in the cement city of Maputo share this opinion. While about a third of the household heads in all three areas consider the supply of medicine in clinics and hospitals as sufficient, the majority in all three areas think that it is insufficient.

Summary

School attendance of children from 6 – 14 increases particularly with the first stage of urbanization. It increases from less than half (or one fifth of girls respectively) in the villages to three quarters in the peri-urban areas.

From there, school attendance increases up to about 90 per cent in this age group in the cement cities. While we found considerable inequality in the proportion of school attendance between the sexes in the rural areas, there almost seems to be equality between the sexes in both urban areas, another positive aspect of social change, of the process of urbanization and globalization. In this regard the rural – peri-urban gap is undoubtedly wider than the inner urban gap.

About three quarters of juveniles from 14 to 20 in the cement cities, half in the peri-urban areas and more than one third in the villages still attend delayed primary school or secondary school. Beira has an advantage over Maputo as far as school attendance is concerned.

In regard to the quality and accessibility of health facilities the rural – peri-urban gap also seems to be wider than the inner urban gap. In the rural areas only one fifth of the household heads have the opportunity to reach a central hospital if they or a member of their family is seriously ill (second place, second attempt), two fifths can do so in the peri-urban areas and three quarters in the cement cities. In addition, more than a quarter can at least go to another hospital in the peri-urban areas, but only 10 per cent can do so in the villages, the rest there has to remain in health centres or health posts or go to a traditional healer. Although the value of traditional medicine is more and more discovered, for the time being people long for modern medicine, even though it also has so many shortcomings.

Churches are a valuable social facility, too, as the majority of the urban Mozambican people are religious: Catholic or Moslem or members of a sect. Judging from the frequency that people attend church services, a large proportion is very religious. Almost half of the peri-urban household heads go to church more often than once per week while 'only' one fifth does so in the fully urbanized areas where also a higher proportion never goes to church. Both of these results can be considered as a hint towards secularization through urbanization. A slightly higher percentage of women is religious and they go to church slightly more frequently.

The co-operation with political and administrative centres seems to diminish with urbanization and probably only about a third of Mozambique's population wanted a multi-party system in 1991. The vast majority of the investigated household heads in all three areas never go to drinking places but two fifths of the fully urbanized area of Maputo and about a quarter of both peri-urban areas watch a football match sometimes.

Central market and shops are the most frequently used shopping facilities in the fully urbanized areas. Households in the peri-urban areas of

Maputo shop at markets most frequently, while households in the peri-urban areas of Beira do so on black markets. About a third in both urban areas of both provinces use black markets as their second choice and two fifths in the villages. This illegal, informal trading alleviates poverty for the families who sell as well as for those who have the opportunity to buy cheaper.

Notes

1. With respect to the housing situation, wherever a comparison with the cement cities does not make much sense, the results of the peri-urban areas, the main focus of the study, will be presented and compared with the villages only.
2. Administração do Parque Imobiliário do Estado, the agency responsible for the administration of state-owned housing and other buildings.
3. These differing results can be due to the fact that in the 2nd district – close to the cement city – 37 per cent of the houses have corrugated iron walls (IAF 1919, 12). However, in this district, we chose only a small area, Minkadjuine. (By using table 18.2 (IAF 1991, 52), it was possible to calculate the absolute numbers without district 1.)
4. Wooden sticks are fixed vertically and horizontally in about 10 to 15 cm distance and the process is repeated parallelly also in about 15 cm distance. The space in-between is filled with clay and small stones (see the figures 6.4 and 6.5). These walls are very resistant.
5. On the basis of the IAF of the CSO results only 11 per cent of the houses in peri-urban Maputo have one room, but 44 per cent have two rooms. The other percentages correspond more or less: 3 rooms: 19 per cent, 4 rooms: 17 per cent, 5 and more rooms: 10 per cent (IAF p. 55; author's calculations without district 1). The higher percentage of one roomed houses in this study could be due to the fact that the Portuguese question: 'quantas divisoes tem a casa' has a twofold meaning: firstly, it does mean the number of rooms but secondly, it could also mean the number of walls which divide one room from the other. Although it was explained to the interviewers that only the first meaning counts, it could have been forgotten by some of them. If there are more such walls (divisions) the danger of counting them is smaller, one more or less automatically starts to count the rooms.

    The IAF results of Beira include the cement city there. However, as only 20 per cent of the population live there, the results correspond, nevertheless, quite well with the much larger peri-urban areas as can be seen in table 6.5.

    In Zambia 16 per cent of all the urban dwellings consist of one room only, but in the rural areas this proportion is 31. In urban areas only 4 per cent of households with 7 or more persons live in one room only, but 15 per cent of these large households do so in the rural areas. 'The problem of an adequate number of rooms for a household appears to be more accute in rural than in urban areas' (CSO 1980).

    Conditions seem to be quite different from country to country. Peil found in a study of three towns in Sierra Leone that 45 per cent of the households have one room only. The mean density was 2.4 people per room (Peil 1984, 376).
6. Improved latrines exist of a concrete shaft, about one and a half meters deep, with a very thick concrete cover with a diameter of also about one and a half meters which makes the latrine completely hygienic. In the centre of the big cover there is a small

Housing in the two urban worlds and the neglected countryside 149

cover, which can be opened and closed easily for daily use. The entire cover was constructed by a Swedish architect in 1979. Soon after the government of Mozambique launched a nationwide programme for the improved latrines or 'Low cost sanitation programme'. Today this is already a huge project financed by the United Nations and big NGOs of different states, using an annual budget of about one million US$ (MOZ/91/014 Low cost sanitation). There already exist 23 workshops with about 200 workers who produce the huge concrete covers (Project terminal report November 1991). The household heads may buy the cover for a third of the price; the rest is subsidized by the government and the above mentioned organisations, considering the already discussed very low wages in Mozambique.

7 'Chapa cem' are private mini-buses which used to charge each passenger one hundred (cem) Meticais. Because of high inflation, the fare was already three hundred (trezentos) Meticais in 1991, but the name remained. 'Chapa' means number plate.
8 The IAF found that 82.7 per cent of the children between 6 and 14 attend a school in entire Maputo: 81.8 per cent girls and 83.6 per cent boys (IAF 1993, 13).
9 The IAF found 42.3 per cent females and 52.3 per cent males in this age group attending school; in Maputo 47.4 of both sexes (IAF 1993, 13).
10 The mazione are a sect whose members often also function as traditional healers and who carry out their ceremonies on the beach, where they also admit new members after they have passed tests with special hardships.

7 Housing and services as problems

An analysis of the subjective judgement of the household heads of the different areas concerning their habitation is just as relevant as the objective analysis of the housing situation, the infrastructure, and the social facilities. People were asked whether they considered their house, their water supply, or the schools, for instance, as a serious problem, as a problem but not a serious one, or as no problem.

The results are shown in the following table. The variation of a few per cent is treated as being equal. The village Massaca 1 has been excluded in this analysis because of its privileged position.

Table 7.1   Proportion of evaluation of housing and services as problems

	house[1]	sanitation	water
a serious problem	15 < 43 < 68	23 < 42 < 63	16 < 48 > 18
a problem	30 = 34 > 20	25 = 27 > 22	14 < 24 > 10
no problem	55 > 23 > 12	52 > 31 > 15	70 > 28 < 72
n	(53) (315) (41)	(57) (328) (40)	(56) (324) (40)
	waste removal	transport	primary schools
a serious problem	25 < 30 > 5	23 < 52 = 55	11 < 36 < 52
a problem	23 < 29 > 22	26 = 30 = 32	28 < 39 > 24
no problem	53 > 41 < 73	51 > 18 < 13	61 > 25 = 24
n	(57) (321) (40)	(57) (325) (38)	(47) (192) (25)
	health facilities		
a serious problem	41 = 43 < 52		
a problem	29 < 38 > 31		
no problem	30 > 19 = 17		
n	(56) (318) (35)		

Highly significant, significant or no significant difference between:

	urban and peri-urban areas	peri-urban and rural areas
house as problem	.000	.007
sanitation as problem	.001	.012
water supply	.000	.000 (negative t-value: -5.29)
waste removal	.169	.000 (negative t-value: -4.12)
transport	.000	.514
primary schools	.010	.395
health facilities	.247	.427

This subjective evaluation of the people shows us, firstly, the big difference of negative or positive judgement, respectively, between the urban and peri-urban areas (with the exception of the judgement of waste removal and health facilities), secondly, it shows us a significant difference between peri-urban and rural areas but only as far as housing and sanitation are concerned; the judgement of housing being the only highly significant difference. Water supply and waste removal are judged much more positively in the villages. The evaluation of transport, primary schools, and medical facilities is more or less equal between peri-urban areas and villages, at least there is no statistically significant difference.

Adding the first two negative categories only and showing the differences of these two categories between the areas is another possibility of a more simple illustration of the differences, equalities or 'negative' differences of the judgement by the people concerning their houses and services.

Table 7.2 Proportions of evaluation of housing and services as a serious problem or a problem, with the differences between the areas

	difference between urban and peri-urban		peri-urban and rural areas
house	45 < 77 < 88	32	11
sanitation	48 < 69 < 85	21	16
water	30 < 72 > 28	42	- 44
waste	48 < 59 > 29	11	- 32
transport	49 < 82 < 87	33	5
schools	39 < 75 = 76	36	1
health facilities	70 < 81 = 83	11	2

Concerning the house, there is a highly significant difference of evaluation between urban and peri-urban as well as between peri-urban and rural areas and this corresponds with the empirical findings, namely that the conditions of the house are, on the one hand, much worse in the rural than in the peri-urban areas but on the other hand much worse in the latter than in the fully urbanized areas. We have also seen that the sanitary situation is much less satisfactory in the peri-urban than in the urban areas and worst in the villages. Also here the subjective evaluation of the household heads corresponds with empirical facts, the more so, as the difference between peri-urban and rural areas is, this time, not highly significant but still significant. The somewhat smaller difference compared to the housing evaluation is obviously due to the fact that the sanitary situation in the peri-urban areas of Beira is also very problematic, similar to the situation in the villages. We have seen that in the peri-urban areas of Beira a large proportion of families do not have any toilet at all at their disposal.

Water supply in the villages of Sofala (and these are the only rural areas considered here) is much better than in both peri-urban areas and therefore it could be expected that three quarters of the families have no problem with it and that the percentage of those who, nevertheless, do have some problems is much smaller than in the peri-urban areas.

As far as waste removal is concerned, the situation is similar. It does not come as a surprise that only about a quarter of the household heads in the villages have problems with the waste because, on the one hand, few consumer goods exist and the problem of packing material does not arise, on the other hand, the awareness that burning waste is harmful to the environment also does not yet exist.

A very different interpretation is required for the equal or almost equal evaluation of transport, primary schools, and medical facilities between peri- urban and rural areas. The transport system is much worse in the rural areas but has been judged almost equally; this could be due to the fact that the lack of transport is not felt so desperately in the rural areas, at least not in every day life, as people go to the fields on foot. However, there are many other occasions where transport is needed, for instance, for visiting far away relatives, going to buy something for the little money available in the district-, the provincial- or the national capital, going to a clinic, etc. For all these reasons the interpretation that the need is not felt so urgently, is not satisfactory.

The schools have also been evaluated with no difference between the peri-urban areas and the villages but in reality the difference is considerable: in the villages of Sofala less than half of the children go to school. It is probably dangerous to interpret this result as if the household heads in the villages would be more or less indifferent to the question whether a child goes to school or not. Three quarters of the household heads with children at school age actually do consider the primary schools as a serious problem or at least as a problem, also in the villages. As half of the children go to school, it is difficult to expect that in order to correspond with the much worse situation of the primary schools in the villages, also 88 per cent should have seen them as problems (as it was the case with housing).

Eighty-three per cent did consider the health facilities as problems or even as serious problems in the rural areas but an almost equal percentage also did so in the peri-urban areas. As this proportion is not far away from hundred per cent anyway, it is difficult to find out, why not a higher proportion considerd the health services as a problem in the villages as they are much worse there than in the peri-urban areas. One answer could be that less than a fifth of the household heads and their family members do or did not have health problems in recent times. Fortunately, even in a poor country like Mozambique not everybody needs medical treatment at all times, but there are always also people who are quite healthy. On the other hand, the health facilities which do exist in the villages might have been useful in some cases. Some could also be quite satisfied with traditional healers.

The other possible explanation (beyond all the already mentioned interpretations) of little or no difference in the evaluation of transport, primary schools and medical facilities between peri-urban and rural areas would be the concept of relative deprivation. According to Harvey (1973, Ch. 3) groups or individuals feel relatively deprived, 'who do not receive goods or services which they see other people receiving, which they want and regard as feasible that they should receive them'. People in the villages are not always confronted with the relatively better transport system which exists in the peri-urban areas, they are not constantly confronted with (although they know about their existence) the relatively better schools there, and the high percentage of children attending schools and they are also not always confronted with the relatively better medical facilities than they themselves have at their disposal. Together with being far away, the rural population obviously does not yet regard it as feasible to have this better transport, these better schools and these better health services which, in addition, are still full of shortcomings and one might also, therefore, not long for them so much. Yet, apparently they do regard it as feasible to have the relatively better houses of the peri-urban areas and the much better sanitary situation at least as the peri-urban areas of Maputo are concerned. It is likely that visits to relatives in the provincial and national capital end up in the peri-urban areas so that direct confrontation with the relatively highly developed fully urbanized areas hardly takes place.

The situation is completely different in the peri-urban areas. A large proportion of the household heads work in the fully urbanized areas or go there frequently for other reasons. They know the beautiful houses there even if run down buildings also exist (which were selected for this research) they know about the large flats with two or three bedrooms, flushing toilets and piped water and they know the better transport system there, the buses and numerous cars. All these are wanted badly by the peri-urban population, they find it feasible to participate in this wealth and feel relatively deprived as they cannot have these needs fulfilled. In all these aspects the difference of evaluation between peri-urban and fully urbanized areas is highly significant. It is interesting that the difference is not highly but only significant concerning the evaluation of primary schools. More than three quarters of the children at school age in the peri-urban areas attend a school and not yet one hundred per cent do so in the fully urbanized areas. Although the schools are much better equipped in the cement cities, the difference is not so extreme as in the other four aspects. People can also see that waste removal is still a big problem even in the fully urbanized areas, particularly in Beira, and therefore the difference in evaluation between urban and peri-urban areas is not significant.

It is surprising that almost three quarters of the household heads in the cement cities have problems with the health centres and the central hospital (while in the judgement of all other services the proportion of discontented is only about half or much less than half in the cement cities). The reason could be that even in this big but understaffed hospital people normally have to wait very long to be treated and if they want to visit a specialist they have to wait for months. These facts obviously lead to discontentment and this in turn could be the cause for the small difference between urban and peri-urban areas concerning the evaluation of the health facilities.

In general it can be said that both, the objectively big difference in the quality of the houses and services between urban and peri-urban areas as well as the awareness of the people in the latter, the feeling of relative deprivation – in this research of the household heads only – lead to the big difference in the subjective evaluation. The equality of evaluation of transport, schools and health services between peri-urban and rural areas is more difficult to explain, but not yet feeling relatively deprived might to some extent be the cause.

The phenomenon of relative deprivation is also relevant in Peil's survey of three towns in Sierra Leone. She found that ordinary people in the capital felt less satisfied than residents of provincial towns, because the former were aware of the elite standard of living and saw the limitations of their own position (Peil 1984, 367).

Note

1   Here the codes: from v 80 (see questionnaire in appendix 1) 'I suffer a lot because I do not have a good house', 'I suffer but not too much', and 'I do not suffer' have been used because they mean exactly the same.

8 Female household heads

Definition of terms

We speak of a female household head only if an unmarried woman, single, separated, divorced, or widowed is leading the household. A married woman has little chance of being considered a household head, particularly if the husband is present. And yet, there is actually no reason for assigning the headship of a married couple automatically to the man, except a tradition as old as mankind with probably only one period of mother right, about which the discussion has intensified again recently (see Bachofen 1975, Orig. 1861, Maged-Scherney 1995), and a few exceptions even in modern times (Mead 1937, Malinowsky 1962, Brauen 1994, Luczak and Ernsting 1995). There is no evidence that women are not just as capable of leading the household as men. To designate one person in the household, woman or man, as 'reference person' with no implication of headship as it is done in some industrialized countries, such as France, the United States and others (UN 1986a), would be more adequate. However, as 'reference person' is not yet commonly used, in this chapter 'head' means the person recognized by other members of the household as head, in other words, the 'reported head'. This reported head means in the case of female headship mainly moral authority and regular presence in the household but not primary economic contribution, while in the case of male headship primary economic contribution is the norm as well as moral authority. However, a male head can be absent for long periods of time, as is the case of labour migration from Mozambique mainly to South Africa; by sending regular remittances and visiting (returning home) regularly he is still considered as head.

As the household has been defined earlier as either one person living alone or two or more persons sharing a residence and essentials for living, by sending remittances, the sharing of essentials for living is still given in spite of long lasting absence.

Problems of comparison

Usually the female household heads, the widows, the separated, and divorced are compared with male household heads who live with a partner (UN 1995), although it would be much more appropriate to compare them with male household heads who also live without a partner, who are also widowers, separated or divorced. Unfortunately, in the sample of this research only 5 per cent of male household heads without a partner were found and these 5 per cent comprise only 25 persons. Apparently no other study exists so far, which investigates specifically widowers, separated and divorced male household heads in Africa or the Third World in general.

In the overall sample 13 per cent were female household heads, which means 57 persons.[1] From this small proportion as well as from the 25 male household heads we have deducted another 10 persons each, namely those who stated that they were single. As these were, in most cases, younger persons who planned to get married and often had already a partner staying more or less permanently with them but who, nevertheless, did not want to choose the code 'informally married', it is justified to deal only with the widows, the separated, and divorced. Of the remaining 47 female household heads 72 per cent are widows, 9 per cent are divorcees and 19 per cent are separated. Those whose husbands work in South Africa – 6 per cent of the overall sample – were not considered as female household heads. Regular returns show that there is still a relationship with wife and children. On the other hand, the wife left behind, is really managing the household and making the decisions although with the economic support of the absent husband, if he sends remittances. Nevertheless, it was a difficult decision and is still open to debate. Green (1992) does also not consider wives whose husbands work in South Africa as female household heads but the IAF does and at the same time makes the most appropriate distinction, namely, between those who receive remittances and those who do not. The results of this distinction will be shown below.

Although the low percentage of female household heads found in this investigation is supported by 'the study of the five provinces', and if the 6 per cent whose husbands work in South Africa would have been included, the proportion would have increased to 19 per cent, generally, the proportion of female headed households is estimated higher in Sub-Saharan Africa. Davidson and Dankelman (1990, 19) found 22 per cent female headed households and Green (1992, 13f) estimates 20 to 25 per cent for Mozambique. If these later two estimates are more correct than the results of the 'study of the five provinces', then one could argue that the low percentage of female headed households could be due to the heavy urban bias. In the villages of the Sofala province 25 per cent of female household heads were found. As the majority of Mozambiques population is still rural, it could well be that one fifth or even one quarter of the households are headed by a female.

If we – contrary to all statistical principles – nevertheless, dare to compare the tiny sample of 15 male household heads without a partner, the widowers, the separated, and divorced, to the 47 widows, the separated, and divorced female household heads, we find that, firstly, these few persons are well distributed over the different codes of most of the relevant variables (40 per cent are widowers, 33 per cent are divorcees and 27 per cent are separated) and, secondly, we find that, although the male household heads without a partner are much higher educated than the female heads, their personal income as well as the income of their entire households is very much the same as that of the female heads. There is, in addition, no difference between these two kinds of households as far as their housing situation is concerned. We could probably conclude with much caution, because of the smallness of the sample, that families with male household heads without a partner are just as poor as those with female household heads. However, a lot more research would be necessary to substantiate this finding. In the following comparison all male headed households are included, regardless whether the head lives with or without a partner.[2] Wherever new insights can be gained, the female household heads will be compared with the wives of the male household heads. The distribution of the female household heads over the three investigated areas somehow corresponds to that of the male household heads, although they are over-represented in the villages and under-represented in the fully urbanized areas.

Table 8.1 The distribution of the two kinds of household heads by area

Chi^2=.2557	female household heads	male household heads
fully urbanized areas	4	14
peri-urban areas	75	71
rural areas	21	15
n	(47)	(304)

Socio-economic characteristics of the female household heads and their families in comparison to the male household heads and their families

The income situation

If only the personal income of female household heads without a partner is considered, then this is much lower than that of the male household heads with a partner and even lower than the monthly income of the wives of the male heads. Almost three quarters earn nothing or next to nothing as against one in eight of the male household heads, who are so extremely poor.

Table 8.2   The monthly income of the female household heads, the male household heads and their wives

| | heads | | wives |
	female	male	
no income	37	6	35
less than 50 contos	34	6	29
50 – 100	21	41	22
100 – 200	5	32	8
200 – 400	3	10	3
400 +	—	4	2
n	(38)	(277)	(170)

A very different picture emerges if not the personal income of the heads but the income of the two kinds of households are compared. Although the degree of poverty still remains to be very serious, the difference between the two kinds of households diminishes considerably. Almost half of the female household heads indicated a monthly family income of less than 100 contos – which was considered as being below the poverty line in chapter 3, – but also more than one third of the male headed households have to live in this extreme poverty.

Table 8.3 The monthly income of the female and male headed households

		female headed hh	male headed hh
no income		4	1
less than 50 contos[3]	extreme	16 } 48	4 } 37
50 – 100	poverty	28	32
100 – 200		32	35
200 – 400		16	22
400 +		4	6
n		(25)	(257)

As the number of respondents concerning the female household income is even smaller than when the personal income of the female heads was inquired, the table can only be considered as a hint on the situation, it must be supported by other sources, and further research is necessary.

Presently (mid 1998) the only other source available[4] which deals with income in the urban areas of Mozambique comprehensively is the here frequently quoted IAF. Although in this inquiry of families, Beira was not dealt with separately but only within all provincial capitals and no rural area was included, the comparison with the results of Maputo only could be seen as some support for the results shown above, as also in the sample of this research Maputo is heavily over-represented.[5] The tables in footnote 5 show an average income of male household heads of 200 contos and an average monthly income of female household heads who do not receive remittances (and only those are dealt with in this chapter) of 151 contos. As in this research only income groups were processed, the average can not be calculated but from table 8.3 it can at least be estimated. The results of the two investigations seem to be very close again. Female headed households that do not receive remittances are poorer than male household heads, they receive three quarters on average of the latter.

However, the IAF also gives us the eye opening information – at least for Maputo – that female headed households which receive remittances are much better off than those which do not and that they are even better off than the male headed households, receiving well over one third more than the latter. So if wives whose husbands are absent for long time periods for economic reasons would be included into the group of female household heads and a considerable proportion of them receives remittances then we could no longer speak of the disadvantages of the female headed households in general.

However, the difference of income even between those female headed households which do not receive remittances and the male headed households is by far not as extreme as the gap between the personal income of female and male heads. The question arises, what the factors responsible for this relatively small difference between the two kinds of households are?

The first factor accounting for the relatively small difference could be the family field (which will be discussed in more detail in chapter 13). Sixty-eight per cent of the families with a female household head do have a field, but only 45 per cent of the male headed families and for 35 per cent of the female headed families this field produces the major part of the food (a percentage almost identical with those female household heads who said that they had no income) while this is the case only for 12 per cent of the male headed families. Food for one's own consumption must be considered here as a separate important factor contributing to the well being of the female headed households, not only because it guarantees a better nourishment, but also because self produced food can be used to acquire other things in the barter system as we will see in chapter 9. And apparently, when one produces most foodstuff on the family field it is also possible to sell some of these agricultural products. Urban and/or rural agriculture seems to be the last resort to survive. As Streiffeler (1993) pointed out, the worse the economic situation of a city the more the inhabitants have to resort to agriculture. In this case we could add: the worse the economic situation of a certain category of households the more they have to cultivate.

This is again supported by the second table of footnote 5: for families with a female household head who do not receive remittances, wages and salaries constitute less than half of their income but income from trading, family production, and other income are more important than wage earning. Only 11 per cent of the female heads are formally employed but 71 per cent of the male household heads are. How can then wage earning make up for more than two fifths of the female headed households? One of the answers could be that in a higher proportion of female headed households, namely in 38 per cent, other family members apart from the household heads work as compared to 29 per cent of the male headed households. The vast majority of female household heads seems to be integrated into families with other adults, but unfortunately not all. As will be shown below, 13 per cent live alone and those are the ones living in real misery.

Liquor, however, is not more often produced by the female heads than by the wives of the male headed households. We asked all the women who said that they were mainly housewives: 'You are a housewife, but are you doing other things as well?'

Table 8.4 Other activities of housewives (multiple response)

	female heads	wives Maputo	wives Sofala
working on the field	60	35	71
producing liquor	5	9	—
trading	30	45	12
other	–	6	2
no other activities	5	5	15
n	(40)	(121)	(48)

In sum, the families with female heads who do not receive remittances are poorer than the male headed households but more than one third produce the major part of their food themselves. Part of their own agricultural production is obviously sold, as the IAF found out, since 12 per cent of the family income in Maputo is constituted by selling one's own produce, and even 27 per cent by trading, which must not necessarily always exclude self produced products. All these factors can be seen as contributing to the relatively small income gap between the two kinds of households.

Statistically there is also no difference between male and female household heads as far as satisfaction with one's income is concerned ($Chi^2 = 0.3542$). However, only 3 per cent of the female household heads as against 18 per cent of the male household heads are very satisfied or at least satisfied with their income.

Lundin makes another, maybe crucial, distinction within female headed households. In a survey of the Green Zones of Maputo (Benfica and Machava) of 1988 she observes female heads with no adult male in the family. Unfortunately, no figures are given apart from the estimate that, according to her, about 10 per cent of the households in the Green Zones would be without any adult male.

Within a research we carried out in the Green Zones of Maputo City we met a group with a very weak social network – woman headed households with no adult male. These households have no extended kinship bounds and great difficulties to survive in a situation of crisis.

These households are mainly engaged in agricultural work, though they are not able to obtain a production neither big enough to feed themselves, nor a surplus to fulfil their social obligations ... (namely) to exchange agricultural products in order to strengthen their social bonds. They plant on very poor, sandy soils and live in a situation of continuous vulnerability.

These kinds of households comprise roughly 10 per cent of the total of the households of the Green Zones of Maputo. They are in a difficult situation because of two different factors. First, the poor quality of the soil they cultivate (sandy soils). Second, the lack of potential income earners (adult males) within the households in order to get a salary outside the agricultural sector (Lundin 1989).

Also in this respect further research is essential in order to find out the proportion of female headed households with no adult male in the different kinds of areas, not only in the Green Zones of Maputo. It would also be important to gather more information about whether female headed households with no adult male are generally poorer than those with adult males or whether those with several adult females, a sister and a grown up daughter, for instance, who are formally employed or help on the family field, can be economically just as well off as those with adult males.

Lundin found female heads working mainly on sandy soils. This is obviously a consequence of patrilineal inheritance customs of central and southern Mozambique, where the separated, divorced or widowed have no right to own land. Land is inherited by the sons only. A widow is supposed to marry the brother of the late husband. If she refuses or there is no brother, it depends on the good will of the chief whether he allocates some land to her or not – and which kind of land (Lamadé 1997, Centro de Estudos Africanos 1994). On the other hand, in some districts and particular situations households without a male are not worse off than those with a male as men are often not working on the land. If there is no wage employment available, the survival of the family depends entirely on the hard work of the women (Lamadé 1997).

Surprising are the findings of Nelson (1988), in her interesting study of the informal sector of Mathare Valley in Nairobi. Although the research was carried out twenty years ago, it is still surprising that she did not mention agricultural activities of women at all. Even more surprising is her estimate that 60 – 80 per cent of all the adult women in Mathare are heads of households. Anyway, judging from her description, particularly from that of the entertainment industry and the self built housing for rental, the squatters of Nairobi on one side and the peri-urban areas of Maputo and Beira on the other side seem to be different worlds altogether, reflecting amongst others two opposing political systems: capitalism in Kenya and socialism in Mozambique, which she had attempted to build, but which she had to abandon. However, some sectors of society seem still to be shaped by it. Hardly any self built houses for rental exist in the peri-urban areas of Maputo and only about a fifth of the houses are rented in Beira. An entertainment industry in the peri-urban areas of Maputo one cannot imagine, at least not to that extent as Nelson describes it for Mathare. In addition to all the other difficulties of comparison, we are not provided with the income distribution of the female headed households (Nelson in Gugler 1988).

Additional socio-economic characteristics

The female household heads are older than the male household heads and the difference is still greater compared to the age of the wives. However, between 10 and 20 per cent of these relatively young, mainly urban wives will most likely become female household heads in the next decades.

Figure 8.1 Proportion of age groups of the female household heads compared with the male heads and their wives

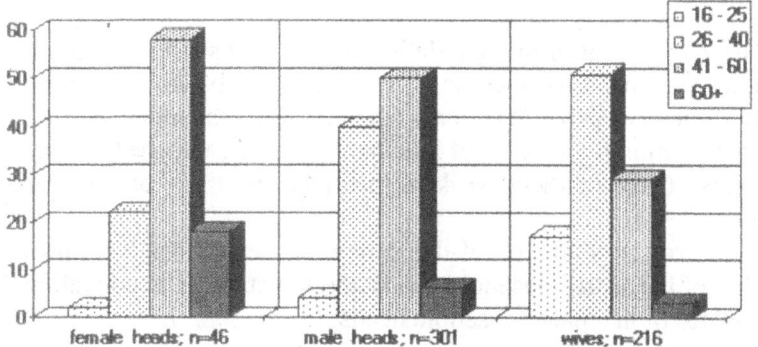

The higher age compared to the male heads – three times as many are over 60 is, on the one hand, due to the higher life expectation of women apparently all over the world, on the other hand, particularly in the countryside of Mozambique, many husbands had not been able to reach a high age because they died in the war.

The two main differences concerning the household size between the two kinds of households consist, firstly, in the already mentioned fact that 13 per cent of the female household heads live alone while this is the case only with 1 per cent of the male household heads. Secondly, female heads less often have very large families. While the percentage of those households with 2 to 7 members is almost equal, only 23 per cent of the female headed households have 8 and more members as against 39 per cent of the male headed households.

Figure 8.2 The size of the female and male headed households

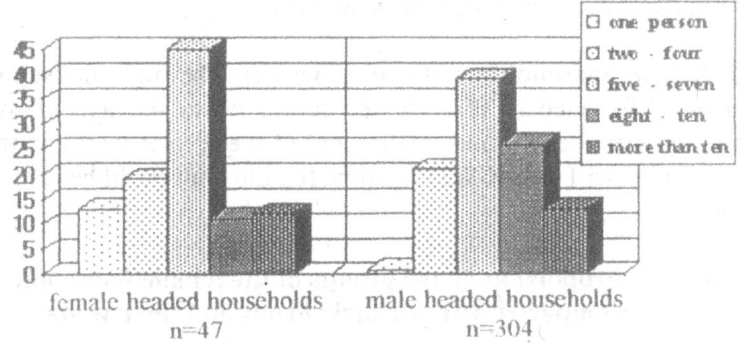

The 13 per cent of the female household heads who live alone are the destitute, their personal income is, of course, equivalent to the household income. These 13 per cent are only six persons in our small sample. Five of them have a monthly income of less than 25 contos and one between 25 and 50 contos. Three of them work in the field and three of them are small traders.

The level of education of the female household heads is much lower than that of the male household heads and lower than the educational level of the wives of the male household heads.

Figure 8.3 Educational level of female household heads, male household heads and their wives

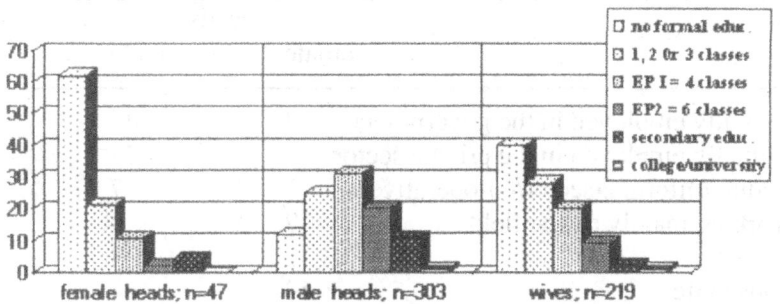

More than three fifths of the female heads have no formal education,[6] while this is the case only for one eighth of the male heads and two fifths of their wives.[7] The reasons are obvious: access to formal education is made difficult for women in most developing countries, due to a complex traditional value system in which discrimination of women is manifold.

The household heads in general are very dissatisfied with their education, so are their wives with no difference between these two groups. (Chi^2=0.8319) Although the difference in the degree of satisfaction between female and male heads is by statistical measures also not relevant, (Chi^2=0.4301) we can, nevertheless, find some differences: two thirds of the male household heads are dissatisfied or very dissatisfied with their education, but almost three quarters of the female heads are. In addition, in the categories of contented or very contented we find only 11 per cent of female but almost a quarter of male heads.

As one can expect, the kind of participation in the labour force of the female household heads is very different from that of the male household heads, but they are not very different from those of the wives. More than half are house wives, more than a quarter work mainly on the field, 5 per cent in the informal sector, and 2 per cent in a co-operative. Only 11 per cent are formally employed and 2 per cent are retired.

168 *Globalization, urban progress, urban problems, rural disadvantages*

Table 8.5 Position in the labour force of the female household heads, the male household heads and their wives

	heads female	heads male	wives
formally employed in the government	4	45	4
formally employed in the private sector	7	23	4
trading/informal sector/co-operative	7	7	8
working mainly on the field	27	9	19
retired	2	3	—
housewife	53	—	64
others	—	12	1
n	(45)	(297)	(218)

Statistically there is again no significant difference between the female and male household heads as far as satisfaction with their occupation is concerned ($Chi^2=0.2417$) but twice as many male household heads are very satisfied with their job (32 per cent) as of the female household heads (15 per cent).

The housing situation of the female headed households

It is also difficult to determine whether the gap in the housing situation between male and female headed households who do not receive remittances is bigger than the income gap. Considering some crucial elements of housing one would be inclined to affirm the question as in these specific housing aspects, showing great poverty, the proportion of female headed households is about two times higher than that of male headed households and in the last positive aspect the proportion of the female headed households is only almost half.

About one third of the houses of the female headed households have soilfloors and grassroofs, while this is the case only with one fifth and one seventh, respectively, of the houses of the male headed households. In about a tenth of the houses with female heads the rain enters through the roof and one quarter is already 'very old', while this is the case only in 6 per cent and one tenth, respectively, of the houses with a male head. Two fifths of the female headed households use a candle as illumination, but less than a quarter of the male headed households do so. More than one third of the female headed households have no toilet but have to use the bush for their sanitary needs while less than one fifth of the male headed households lack this essential facility.

	female hh per cent	male hh per cent
soilfloor	28	12
grassroof	14	3
rain enters through the roof	17	7
the house is already very old	33	14
using a candle as illumination	33	16
no toilet	36	18
cement blocks as house walls	25	40

· While only one fifth of the female headed households have cement blocks as material for their house walls, more than one third of the male household heads enjoy this relatively good quality of walls. No essential difference exists in the water supply between the two kinds of households.

One could be inclined to interpret some of the differences as coming about because of the over-representation of female heads of the rural areas. However, this is not the case as the same comparison with the urban households only gives us almost identical relations between the respective percentages, except the roofs consisting of grass.[8]

And yet, women are obviously used to disadvantages. There is hardly any difference between the two kinds of household heads in seeing their house, the infrastructure, and the social facilities as problems. Only a higher proportion of female heads sees sanitation as a serious problem.

Summary

In order to assess the specific situation of female household heads and their families, it would be more adequate to compare female household heads without a partner, the separated, divorced or widowed with male household heads and their families, who also live without a partner, who are also separated, divorced or widowed. Some indication was found in this research that the latter could be just as poor as the families with a female head.

Following the usual comparison of female headed families without a partner with all male headed families with a partner, it was found that female household heads are much older and have a considerably lower level of formal education than male heads; it is also lower than the educational level of the wives of the male household heads; a higher proportion of female household heads lives alone and the size of their households is generally smaller than the size of male headed households. Their participation in the labour force is very different from that of the male household heads, but very similar to that of the wives of the latter.

Female household heads themselves are much poorer than male household heads, however, the relation of the entire monthly income of the two kinds of households seems to be about 3/4 to 1 in Mozambique. The reasons for the much smaller gap between the two kinds of household incomes compared to the personal income are the integration of the vast majority of female heads into families with other adults, except about one seventh who live alone in severe poverty. In a higher percentage of female headed households than male headed households other family members apart from the household head are employed. In addition, the vast majority of female headed households have a family field and for about one third this field produces – with the help of family members – the major part of their food as well as a surplus, which is sold to increase the household income. Female household heads themselves as well as family members trade legally and on the so-called black markets.

The difference in the housing situation between the two kinds of households seems to be greater than in the income situation. Building material, the state of the house, as well as the infrastructure show severe poverty on the side of the female headed families and yet there is little difference between the level of satisfaction of the two kinds of household heads.

Notes

1. The 'study of the five provinces' found also only 14 per cent female household heads and this in the rural areas (DNE, 1990, 10). Unfortunately, the percentage of female household heads has not been presented in the IAF.
2. Subtracting the 25 persons does not influence the results as the number of male headed households is 304.
3. The categories have been doubled in this as well as in the previous table as has been done in chapter 3: People who responded 'less than 25 contos' were put at less than 50 contos, those who said that their income was 25 – 50 contos are shown in the category 50 – 100 contos a.s.o. because the IAF found that households in general receive only 52 per cent of their income for employment in Maputo. In an ad hoc answer – as it was required in this survey – it was more likely that people included

mainly the monthly wages of the family members and not all the other forms of income which are shown in the tables in footnote 5.

4   Although another household survey, another IAF inquiry of families which included again all urban and – for the first time – even large parts of the rural areas was completed in 1996, the official results were not out mid 1998.

5   MONTHLY HOUSEHOLD INCOME OF THE DIFFERENT KINDS OF HOUSEHOLDS ACCORDING TO TYPE OF INCOME (IN CONTOS)

TYPE OF INCOME	male hhh	female hhh without remittances	female hhh with remittances	ALL HH
income from formal employment	118	64	36	103
income from family production	15	18	7	15
income from trading	49	41	53	48
income from property	2	1	1	1
remittances	3	—	118	9
other income	9	26	108	18
interests and loans	4	1	8	4
TOTAL	200	151	332	199

MONTHLY HOUSEHOLD INCOME OF THE DIFFERENT KINDS OF HOUSEHOLDS ACCORDING TO TYPE OF INCOME IN PERCENTAGES

TYPE OF INCOME	male hhh	female hhh without remittances	female hhh with remittances	ALL HH
income from formal employment	58	42	11	52
income from family production	8	12	2	8
income from trading	25	27	16	24
income from property	1	—	—	1
remittances	1	—	36	5
other income	5	17	33	9
interests and loans	4	1	8	4
TOTAL	200	151	332	199

Source: IAF of the CSO: Direcção Nacional de Estatistica, Relatorio sobre os resultados finais do inquérito às famílias na cidade de Maputo, Volume I, Maputo 1993.

6   It is important to stress *formal* education as normally too little attention is given to traditional education, where an enormous amount of knowledge, skills, wisdom and ethical principles are transmitted by the older to the young (Mbikusita-Lewanika 1979).

7   According to the Statistical Yearbook of UNESCO also in neighbouring Zimbabwe as well as in Kenya 40 per cent of adult women have no formal education. In many African countries this proportion is 70 or even 80 per cent (UNESCO 1993).

	urban female hh per cent	urban male hh per cent
soil as floor	28	12
grass as roof	14	3
rain enters through the roof	17	7
the house is already very old	33	14
using a candle as illumination	33	16
no toilet	36	18
cement blocks as house walls	25	40

9 Urbanization and the decline of specific social interactions

Group solidarity constitutes an essential value of traditional African and many other traditional cultures. With a high group solidarity social interaction is frequent and intensive. Where urbanization, modernization, and globalization have not yet led to a substantial social change this frequency and intensity can be observed up until today. In chapter 2 competition was discussed as one of the essential characteristics of globalization. With the increase of competition also individualism increases and replaces group solidarity more and more and with it the frequent and intensive private personal social interactions. These developments are also a concomitant of the process of urbanization as such. Not only the increase of competition and individualism leads to a decline of frequency and intensity of private social interactions and at the same time to an increase of impersonal contacts but also the social character of city life. According to Simmel, rapid crowding of changing images and the unexpectedness of new impressions uses up, so to speak, more consciousness than do the regular habitual impressions of rural life which, in addition, rests upon more deeply felt emotional relations. All the numerous contacts with different people in a city cannot result in so many inner reactions. People reserve for themselves even the right to distrust; neighbours can remain unknown for years in fully urbanized areas (Simmel 1964). However, emotional ties within the nuclear families must therefore not become weaker in the city than they are in the rural areas. Although the family life is not dealt with in this research, it should at least be mentioned that the family in urban areas loses functions it had in completely traditional rural areas such as being a production -, educational -, religious -, recreational and even a political unit but that it gains instead importance as being an emotional resort against stress, competition and the impersonal city life (Morris 1968, 95 – 100). According to Pfeil, social life in cities has three levels. Firstly, the level of confidentiality, friendship, and familiarity, secondly, the level of impersonal, partial acquaintance, thirdly, the level of anonymity. The behaviour of urbanites is characterized by a high degree of reservation (on the one hand) but also by a considerable degree of close contact on the other hand. Through urbanization the respect and the esteem of the privacy of each individual has been developed. Reservation makes urbanites appear cold and not interested in the fate of their fellowmen and yet, it is often merely a form of protection against over taxation of stimuli. The apparent indifference can change into readiness to help at any time (Pfeil, 1972, 238 – 241) and apart from family life, emotional ties with other people can – in spite of the decline in frequency – be lifted to a different level. City life can, but must not necessarily, lead to more isolation of the individual.

In this chapter mainly the social interaction between kin, friends and neighbours will be investigated. These interactions are basically social networks but can also be called informal exchange groups or self-help groups. Stacher sees these groupings based on kin, friends, and neighbours but also imbedded in religious or ethnic affiliations. (Religious networks have been dealt with briefly in chapter 6, but ethnic networks have not been considered separately in this research, however, they might fall partly under either of the three categories: relatives, friends, and neighbours). In the poor urban areas at least some access to resources and to some infrastructure is made possible through networks based on mutual help and solidarity, shared cultural values and behaviour patterns. They also foster personal orientation against marginalization, frustration and loss of identity (Stacher 1997b, 165). However, in this context the validity of a comparison between rural, peri-urban and fully urbanized areas becomes apparent again, because it puts the description above and the often cited social network groupings mainly observed in poor urban areas into a different perspective. All these social networks are there now and have existed also in the countryside for centuries or millennia. Religion and group solidarity rank not only high in the hierarchy of the traditional African value system (Knauder 1975, 23 – 30) but in most traditional cultures. It is likely that networks in poor urban areas are of a different character than the traditional ties in the countryside but it must also be seen that all the group solidarity in the rural areas as well as in the poor city areas cannot essentially raise either the standard of living or the degree of happiness. The other aspect which puts the often cited social networks of poor city areas into a different perspective is the existence of very similar networks in the fully urbanized areas where people in general are not at all or by far less marginalized and frustrated and normally do not suffer from any loss of identity. What is crucial, however, is the decrease of such networks, for reasons discussed above.

One difference between social networks in the rural, peri-urban and urban areas is the increase of free choice. While these networks are much more ascribed in the more or less traditional areas than freely chosen, they are to a higher degree 'chosen' even often out of necessity in the peri-urban areas and this freedom increases in the urban areas. This view is based on the theoretical positions trying to explain the concept of social networks which considers them as social preferences based on cognitive consistent, balanced patterns of relationships.

Social networks can also be explained as stable relationships where costs outweigh the benefits and where non-material and material goods are exchanged. This consideration of costs and benefits in social interactions might be there unconsciously and collectively in rural areas with many traditional aspects but is likely to start in peri-urban areas only and increase approaching social interaction with such rationality in the urban areas.

However, the symbolic interactionistic approach to the concept of social networks can be fully applied to the rural as well as to the other two areas. This theory considers them as relationships without which life would not make sense, relationships which are collectively created and cultivated as social reality. They have to be seen in their cultural context and in their meaningful symbolic substance (Roehrle 1994, 12 – 15).

Apart from being relationships without which life would not make sense, social networks are also substitutes for the social security which the state refuses to or cannot give (Komlosy et al. 1997, 18). This applies mainly to the rural and peri-urban areas, yet to a lesser extent to the fully urbanized areas where some state social security is already available.

Social networks gain importance insofar, particularly in the peri-urban areas of the Third World cities, as planned economies and full scale state interventions have disappeared and, on the other hand, the negative effects of the so-called free market system are in general more visible in these areas, although the effects are the same or worse in the rural areas. Social relations and social networks could – like urban agriculture – also be seen as survival strategies in times of crises. In the last decade they did not only attract ethnologists and sociologists, for whom this area of studies is not a new one, but also economists, political scientists, urban geographers and development researchers (Schneider and Vorlaufer 1997, 233). However, as we have seen in the previous chapters and as we will see in the next chapter even the most closely knit social network in the rural areas cannot alleviate the hardship there.

It might be questioned why social interaction is measured within one respective bairro only. However, apart from restricting the questionnaire to the manageable, localities can be considered as a specific social base.

> They are the places where people find their sense of belonging. The majority of people, even in the largest of cities, have some sense of identification with a locality. It's their part of the city, their place, their (bairro). The basis of this identification arises from the sets of activities which take place within the local areas and are affected by the boundaries which exist (Thorns 1992, 250).

However, before looking into the respective social networks, the feeling of isolation should be dealt with briefly. City life can – but must not necessarily – lead to a higher degree of isolation of the individual.

The feeling of isolation and loneliness

It was hypothesized that unlike the material situation, which is worst in the villages and best in the cement cities, social interaction would be the opposite: highest in the villages and lowest in the cement cities, with the peri-urban areas taking on a middle position. While this is the case with most of the variables in this chapter, it does not apply to feelings of isolation and loneliness. Feelings of isolation appear to occur most frequently in the peri-urban areas and least frequently in the fully urbanized areas.

Figure 9.1 The feelings of isolation and loneliness

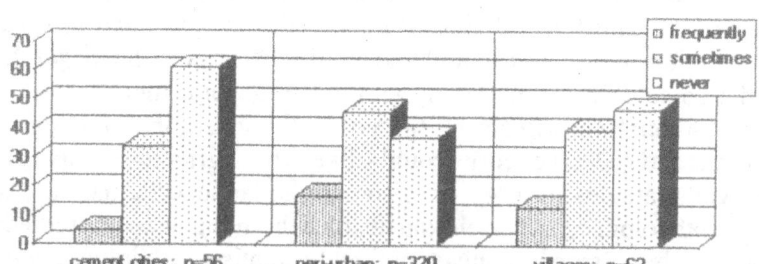

This time the villages take on a middle position: 39 < 63 < 53 per cent of the household heads frequently or sometimes feel lonely and isolated.

One explanation for the finding that the household heads in the peri-urban areas feel most frequently lonely could be that those who have migrated recently and/or have no relatives in the same bairro miss the closer affiliation in the villages. The fact that in both areas, in the villages as well as in the peri-urban areas, the household heads feel lonely more often than in the cement cities could on the one hand be surprising because, as we shall see in this chapter, there are more frequent contacts in those two areas than in the fully urbanized one. On the other hand though, it is no special characteristic of Mozambique's peri-urban areas (and even villages) that people feel more often lonely even though they are not really alone more often than, for example, those in the more modernized cement cities. In the villages as well as in the peri-urban areas household heads still belong to traditional societies where people are oriented towards and dependent on community.

> It is important to remember that the body of theory that has grown up around the concept of the study of African society is not a purely abstract formulation by the social scientist but that Africans themselves conceive of social relations in terms of group membership with its duties and privileges and symbols of identity (Ottenberg 1965, 20).

We have not measured whether the household heads of the cement cities are really more often alone than those in the other two areas. The considerably higher percentage of those who never feel lonely there can still be considered as an indicator of the process of urbanization and with it as westernization, where being alone and having time just for oneself, enjoying privacy, can even be appreciated as a value. In a small sample of mainly married male workers in Vienna also 67 per cent never, 28 per cent sometimes, and 5 per cent frequently feel lonely (Knauder 1994, 115), which is a similar distribution to the one of the fully urbanized areas of Mozambique shown in the previous graph.

In case they are in fact less frequently alone, this could also be due to a social and psychological change, namely the change of the concept of partnership. In the cement cities any kind of living together between a woman and a man is more frequently based on a free choice of partners and is, therefore, also more frequently understood as companionship. The sexes are no longer so strictly separated in most of the activities as in the villages. In addition, city life entails more professional and private contacts, not just contacts with relatives, friends and neighbours. On the other hand as most of the household heads are males, one could also take into consideration that in the cement cities more entertainment for men is available outside home.

In order not to expand the questionnaire to the unmanageable, the following social interactions between relatives and friends were investigated only within the same bairro or village. Although this might not always have been adhered to in a very strict sense by interviewees and even interviewers, particularly if a family lived at the border of two bairros and some relatives a few meters across the border in the other bairro. But at least it gave some limitation, meaning relatives and friends nearby or in the area in order to exclude interaction between rural, peri-urban and fully urbanized areas. To measure this kind of interaction was not the objective of this study, but to compare social interaction within the three types of areas. We touched upon rural urban interaction in the chapter on migration.

Interaction with relatives

All people have sets of kin. The extent to which these are utilized varies. Kinship links are usually reciprocal particularly in traditional communities where they were and often still are a key feature of stability (Thorns 1992, 254). All these aspects will be analyzed in this paragraph including the considerable variation or decline respectively of frequency of interaction and kind of mutual help among kin from rural via peri-urban to urban areas. The reciprocity was investigated (see questionnaire, v183 to v195 in appendix 1) and the results show almost identical tables of giving and receiving. However, to spare the reader from even more tables and figures, only the active side is presented here.

Half of the household heads in the cement cities have no kin living in the same bairro, compared to more than a third in the peri-urban areas and only about a quarter in the villages.

The more than one third of peri-urban household heads who have no relatives living in the same bairro corresponds with the proportion of household heads who have arrived in this bairro during the last 10 years. This does not mean that also those who have arrived earlier can have no relatives in the same bairro. It simply means that a considerable proportion of the peri-urban household heads (and more than one quarter of those in the investigated villages) has moved recently (maybe even only from one bairro to another) and has apparently left all relatives behind. Relatives living in the same household are of course not considered here, because they belong to the (extended) family.

It is not surprising that half of the household heads of the cement cities have no kin living in the same bairro, because these are truly urbanized areas, with one word modern cities where mobility is high.

The percentage of spouses (in the vast majority wives) who have no relatives in the same bairro is higher in the peri-urban areas and in the villages than the corresponding percentage of household heads. However, it is not higher in the cement cities: 47 > 41 > 37 per cent of spouses have no kin living in the same bairro (as compared to 50 > 35 > 27 per cent of the household heads). This could be due to the fact that women move more often when getting married as the southern half of Mozambique is patrilinear. Also in the rural areas of Austria wives often move to their husbands' places and leave relatives behind but in the urban areas changing one's residence when getting married is not sex specific. The correspondence of percentages between heads (50 per cent) and wives (47 per cent) who have no relatives living in the same bairro in the fully urbanized areas can, therefore, be considered as another indication of modernization.

Social interaction is closely related to social integration. People who have nobody to interact with outside the narrow circle of their family or household, cannot be called socially integrated. Mutual visits are one way of interaction. The frequency of visits must not – but can – be an indication of a cordial relationship, of affiliation.

Figure 9.2 The frequency of visits by household heads to relatives in the same bairro

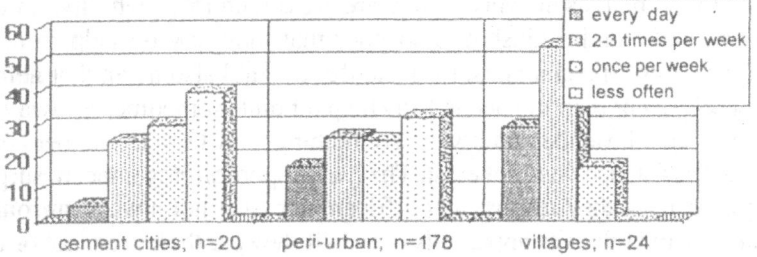

The frequency with which household heads visit their relatives in the villages is impressively high. It declines drastically from the villages to the peri-urban areas, but the changes are moderate from the peri-urban areas to the fully urbanized areas: 60 < 68 < 100 per cent visit their relatives once or twice or three times per week or even every day. Only daily visits decline also from the peri-urban to the fully urbanized areas. Although the control groups are even smaller here than normally, as those who do not have relatives in the area were not asked and there were, in addition, a number of missing observations, we can still cautiously conclude that the frequency of visiting relatives declines with urbanization and somehow also with the stage of urbanization. There is also not much difference between visiting and receiving relatives as visitors: 63 < 66 < 96 per cent are visited frequently by relatives. This is not surprising as these kinds of social interaction are normally based on reciprocity.

Apart from the frequency of visits we also tried to find out what kind of assistance relatives give each other or if there is mutual help. As with many other variables the different kinds of assistance were named by the people themselves in the pilot study, when most of these kinds of questions were still open questions.

The interviewees in the survey proper were allowed to indicate up to three different kinds of assistance they give to their relatives. Although it is possible that those who named only one kind of assistance give this kind three times as often as those who mentioned three kinds, it is quite unlikely. Therefore, the result that 48 < 62 < 80 per cent mentioned a third kind of assistance they give to relatives, allows us to conclude cautiously that the multiplicity of help amongst relatives decreases with urbanization and the level of urbanization. More research would be necessary to substantiate this finding particularly as the average number of answers does not differ between fully urbanized and peri-urban areas. The mean is 2.4 in both of these areas but 2.7 in the villages.

In the pilot study people also mentioned: 'we have nothing to help our relatives with' or simply stated that mutual assistance between relatives did not exist for some reason. Maybe they are cross with those who live in the same bairro or the entire kinship is so poor that they rely on help from friends, neighbours or the churches, for instance. It could also mean that neither they themselves nor their kin needed any help for quite sometime. Anyway 3 < 10 = 10 per cent chose the code: 'we have nothing' and 13 = 13 > 5 per cent chose mutual assistance does not exist. The two proportions together are surprisingly high. At least they tell us, that Africans are also not always surrounded by relatives and relatives apparently – even if they are there – cannot or must not necessarily always help each other. This could also be seen as a trend towards the nuclear family with some negative effects. In several peri-urban areas of investigation particularly in Maputo we met children alone, without any adults. In many cases, they told us that mother and father were working. There were apparently no relatives living nearby or they were not able to take care of the children during the day.

The following table shows the different kinds of assistance the household heads give to their relatives and the frequency with which each kind of help was mentioned.

Table 9.1 Kinds of assistance the household heads give to their relatives who live in the same bairro

	urban	peri-urban	rural
food	15	24	28
money	17	17	19
exchanging goods	16	13	14
helping in the case of illness	27	23	22
helping in ceremonies	20	21	16
others	6	2	1
positive responses/n	64/27	444/185	132/49

Food is the most common form of assistance in the peri-urban areas and in the villages followed by helping out in the case of illness, which takes on first place in the fully urbanized areas. In the next chapter we will see that food is also named as the number one problem in the peri-urban areas and in the villages, which is not surprising if we remember the extremely low average wages and salaries and the fact that one third of Maputo's children is undernourished and half the population of Maputo gets less than half of the necessary food (Ministerio do Comercio 1988). The situation in Beira is not better and it is much worse in the rural areas.

Assisting at ceremonies (such as weddings and funerals) takes on second place in the cement cities and third place in the peri-urban areas. The other two forms of assistance: helping out with money and exchanging goods, have been named with almost the same frequency and there is little difference between the areas.

After five years of field work in Maputo city Lundin stresses the importance of a kinship network in the strategies for survival.

> If your needs can be fulfilled by someone who belongs to the category of a relative then you have met your maxaka (a Ronga term) – your own kin – and that places you in a position ... that guarantees you to obtain all the help available at present, be this food, clothe, shoes, home appliance or jobs (Lundin 1989).

Since she includes food in the barter system, which she has observed in kinship networks and which she calls 'craft-economy', existing alongside the official economy, the first category 'helping out with food' would belong to this system. In her enumeration of the goods that are exchanged she again mentions 'foodstuff'.

> The exchange is basically a non-monetary exchange where the value of the merchandise depends on the relationship between the supply and the demand together with the social relationship between the partners. The range of these exchanges comprises products from foodstuff (vegetables, roots, flours, fruit, etc.), craft production (home-made alcoholic beverages, shoes, simple mechanics, furniture, clothes, some household goods, sculptures and similar things), manufactured goods (materials, tires, batteries, household goods, fuels, etc.), it may include also service areas (registers, certificates, requisitions, and so on) (Lundin 1989).

It is surprising that Lundin looked at the kinship network only to develop her concept of the craft-economy – which is basically a barter system – while exchanging goods is also practised between friends and neighbours. She reports that in the extremely difficult struggle for survival new categories of relatives have been invented, which have been given a classificatory place: one is 'swali' (Ronga, an African language spoken in Maputo apart from Changana):

> Swali is a variation of the African term of kinship for a brother-in-law. In Maputo this term is being used at present for a close friend (male or female) that is in a position to give some kind of help (Lundin 1989).

The other category is (va)maseve and basically means parents-in-law.

> This term of kinship is being used to day to someone of a very high status in the community that gives his/her name to a baby. The name giving used to be an internal affair among the kin themselves. Nowadays the parents are using this strategy to enhance their social network with view to increase chances of survival and increase absorptive capacity for stress in a situation of crisis (Lundin 1989).

This invention of new categories of kinship is interesting but it does not explain why – if kinship plays such an important role – exchanging of goods is also practised between neighbours. On the other hand, she does mention that associations are set up where colleagues, neighbours and friends join and participate on various levels. This is supported by the findings of this research. Much mutual help goes on outside the kinship network and interest associations spontaneously and out of necessity. It is interesting though that respondents in the pilot study did not mention 'helping out with food' as a form of mutual help, neither between friends nor between neighbours. This kind of assistance seems to take place only or mainly between relatives.

Interaction with friends

Friendships are another indication of social integration. The intensity of friendship depends on the frequency and quality of contacts of different kinds – of which visiting is only one. However, friendship must not necessarily include assistance when friends do not need it. On the other hand, friendship means assistance in the wider sense as it improves the quality of one's life. Friendship is developed voluntarily, in contrast we normally cannot choose our relatives.

This investigation only asked for the frequency of visits amongst friends living within the same bairro or village and some forms of interaction which again where named by the people in the pilot study. First we had to ask how many had friends within the bairro/village. Unfortunately, there is no empirical proof, but again from our impression during the long time period of interviewing, it could be, that people who had no friends within the same bairro had also no friends in another bairro. Contrary to the results of the question regarding the relatives there is no difference between the areas of investigation concerning the question whether household heads have many, some or no friends in the same bairro.

Table 9.2 Friends of household heads in the same bairro

$Chi^2=.7320$	urban	peri-urban	villages
many friends	16	14	19
some	60	57	57
none	24	29	24
n	(57)	(328)	(68)

There is hardly any difference between the areas concerning the household heads in having many, some or no friends, but there is a difference between women and men in all the areas. The proportion of women (mainly wives, but also singles, separated, divorced, and widowed) who have many friends is 8 per cent lower than that of the men and the proportion of women who have no friends is 10 per cent higher.

In the following graph only those household heads are taken into consideration who do have friends in the same bairro.

184 *Globalization, urban progress, urban problems, rural disadvantages*

Figure 9.3 The frequency of visiting friends in the same bairro

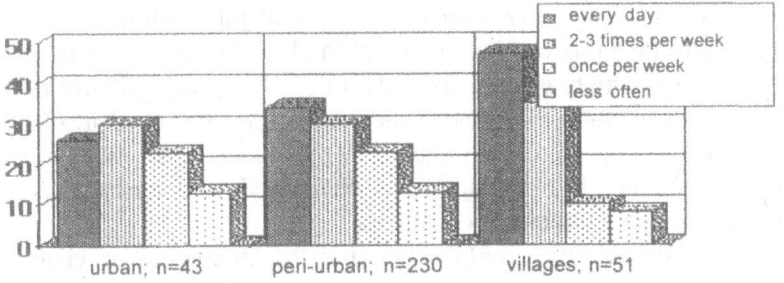

Similar to the frequency of visiting relatives, the frequency of visiting friends also declines from the villages via the peri-urban areas to the fully urbanized areas, in other words, it declines with urbanization and the level of urbanization. If we would include visiting once per week into a first category, as we did with discussing frequency of visiting relatives, then 74 < 87 < 92 per cent visit their friends frequently. These proportions are much higher in the peri-urban areas as well as in the cement cities than they were visiting relatives. Frequent visits to relatives indicated 60 < 68 < 100 per cent. This is interesting and can be interpreted in the way that kinship loses importance with urbanization while friendship gains importance. Apart from the fact that migrants leave relatives behind when they move to an urban area, we can also consider the trend towards the nuclear family as a reason for this phenomenon.

Although, as mentioned above, helping each other is not necessarily and always a characteristic of friendship. Nevertheless, we did ask the people whether and in what way they help their friends and get assistance from them. The different possibilities of mutual assistance were again mentioned by the people in their answer to an open question in the pilot study. Helping out with food was not mentioned as a form of mutual assistance, neither amongst friends nor amongst neighbours. It could be that for this kind of help kin takes priority. Not even having enough food is already a very serious crisis in which relatives apparently are the first ones who are asked for help.

> Kin living in town are the chief source of help for serious difficulties, even by people who do not otherwise have much to do with their kin. Friends take second place, but they provide considerable support for individuals who do not happen to have kin in town (Peil 1981, 265).

The proportions of those who neither give to nor receive help from friends, 19 > 14 > 6 per cent, are similar to those of relatives who do not practise mutual assistance (13 = 13 > 5), but the proportion is higher in the cement cities. The proportion of the household heads who named a third form of assistance is lowest in the cement cities: 33 < 55 < 65 per cent. Both show a characteristic of urbanization, where friendship without or without much mutual help gains importance, or where mutual help is a non-material, psychological one as, for instance, giving moral support. The latter increases from the villages via the peri-urban areas to the cement cities as the following table of the different kinds of assistance shows.

Table 9.3 Assistance household heads give to their friends in the same bairro

	urban	peri-urban	villages
lending goods	30	25	30
lending money	21	22	17
exchanging goods	9	21	22
helping out with labour	6	15	17
giving moral support	28	16	11
others	6	1	3
positive responses/n	67/43	503/230	98/50

Lending goods appears as the most frequent form of help amongst friends in all three areas, followed by giving moral support in the fully urbanized areas, lending money in the peri-urban areas and exchanging goods in the villages. Helping out with labour decreases somehow with urbanization but more so with the level of urbanization.

Interaction with neighbours

We have seen that the proportion of those who frequently feel isolated is highest in the peri-urban areas, that the percentage of those who do not have any friends in the same bairro is also highest there and now we see that the proportion of those who do not have contact with at least one of their neighbours is also highest in the peri-urban areas.

Household heads where asked: 'How many neighbours do you have' and then 'with how many of those neighbours do you have contact?' As neighbours were considered only the houses directly next to the house where the interview was carried out. In the peri-urban areas and the villages this was usually the inner circle around the interviewed household. In the case of the flats only those next door as well as one floor above and one floor below were considered as neighbours.[1] The sum of the neighbours with whom the three samples have contact expressed in percentages is 87 > 80 < 90 or stated negatively with 13 < 20 > 10 per cent of all the neighbours the household heads of the three samples do not have contact.

In the cement cities 24 per cent of all household heads have only one neighbour and 46 per cent have 2 to 3 neighbours, only 30 per cent have more. One neighbour exists only for 2 per cent in the peri-urban areas and all households in the villages have more than one neighbour. In the last two areas more than 80 per cent have 3 to 6 neighbours.

As the control groups are small and the percentage of those who do not have contact with at least one of their neighbours is even smaller, only for the peri-urban areas with 66 cases the reasons for not having contact will be shown:

30 per cent stated 'we don't trust them', 21 per cent 'we are not yet accustomed to them', 15 per cent 'the house entrance is on the other side', 11 per cent 'they have inferiority complexes', 6 per cent stated 'the neighbours are proud' or 'they don't want contact with us', and 3 per cent said 'we do not understand each other's language'.

In the frequency of visiting the same pattern emerges as in the interaction with relatives and friends: The frequency of visiting neighbours declines with urbanization.

Figure 9.4 The frequency of visiting neighbours

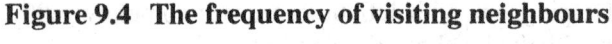
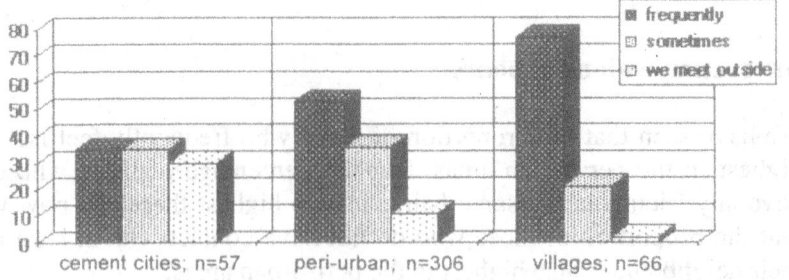

The 30 per cent of the household heads in the cement cities who always meet their neighbours outside, in the corridor, staircase, or near the house entrance can hardly be considered as a substitute for direct visiting as the latter is much more intimate.

As in the case of relatives and friends, people were also asked if and in what way their neighbours assist them and vice versa. Similar patterns emerge as with relatives and friends, mutual assistance among neighbours declines with urbanization: $26 > 11 > 4$ per cent do not give help to their neighbours as compared to $16 > 14 > 8$ per cent of household heads who do not give help to friends and $12 = 13 > 5$ per cent who do not give help to relatives. While the percentage of those who do not give help does not differ much in the villages and peri-urban areas concerning friends and relatives the percentages of household heads in the fully urbanized areas who do not give help increases from relatives via friends to neighbours: 12 per cent do not give help to relatives, 16 per cent do not give help to friends, and 26 per cent do not give help to neighbours.

Interestingly enough, this time the highest proportion of those who named a third kind of assistance they give to neighbours cannot be found in the villages but in the peri-urban areas: $33 < 77 > 66$ per cent mentioned a third kind of assistance. On average, in the cement cities 1.2 kinds of help were indicated, 2 in the peri-urban and 1.8 in the rural areas. A satisfactory interpretation is difficult: it could be that village household heads are already saturated with such high percentages of mutual help between relatives and friends or that neighbours are at the same time relatives or friends. On the other hand, a higher percentage of the peri-urban household heads has no relatives and friends in the same bairro than of the rural household heads and it could well be that, therefore, mutual assistance among neighbours is practised more frequently.

The different kinds of assistance named by the interviewees as response to an open question in the pilot study are identical with those of mutual assistance among friends with the exception that people exchange personal advice with neighbours while in the case of friends it was characterized as moral support. There is a difference between the two but for the purpose of this study the difference is not crucial.

Table 9.4 Kinds of assistance the household heads give to their neighbours

	urban	peri-urban	villages
lending goods	44	34	36
lending money	14	13	14
exchanging goods	13	25	28
helping out with labour	7	13	8
giving personal advice	14	13	12
others	10	2	2
total of positive replies/n	71/57	617/317	121/68

As was the case with friends, if we add all three positive answers, lending goods appears as the most frequent kind of help in all three areas. Exchanging goods takes second place in the peri-urban and rural areas, but not in the cement cities. Lending money and giving personal advice were mentioned with almost the same frequency, and there is hardly any difference from area to area. Only few help their neighbours with labour in the fully urbanized and rural areas. This proportion is higher in the peri-urban areas.

It is most probably possible to generalize the existence of a higher degree of mutual assistance in a situation of economic deprivation compared to a situation of relative prosperity. In a very different Southeast Asian cultural setting, namely in a poor city area of Jakarta, Jellinek (1991) also found that people created for economic reasons extended but fluid kinship and neighbourhood ties. On the other hand, 'economic necessity' might be too narrow an interpretation as we also have to take into account the existence of the traditional behaviour and cultural norm of solidarity as it can be found in most or all rural societies. These traditional behaviour patterns do not disappear abruptly just by moving to an urban area. Even for those born in a city, traditional values fade only slowly in a long process of social change.

Conflicts

The household heads were asked: 'All people have conflicts once in a while with relatives, friends or other persons. What – according to your opinion – are the main reasons for your conflicts?' Just not getting along with each other, for whatever reason, seems to be the cause of conflicts for almost half of the household heads in the villages, more than one third in the peri-urban areas and more than a quarter in the cement cities. Envy was mentioned as the second most frequent cause of conflict in the peri-urban and rural areas but people in the cement cities mentioned 'other' sources for conflict in the second place, perhaps because of the more complex social relationships there.

Table 9.5 Main reasons for conflicts

	urban	peri-urban	villages
we do not get along with each other	29	36	48
people envy us	22	30	27
people have inferiority complexes	11	8	2
they are proud	11	12	2
others	27	14	21
n	(52)	(267)	(56)

Apparently, the problems the people do have with each other are not the same in all these areas. Inferiority complexes, for instance, or – most of the time just the other side of the same coin – behaving proudly and looking down on other people hardly exists in the villages were social differentiation does exist but probably not to the same extent as in the two urban areas.

Summary

The hypothesis that the frequency of social interaction with relatives, friends, and neighbours and with it this specific kind of social integration decreases with urbanization and the level of urbanization was verified in a manifold way. It was measured by the frequency of visits, by the percentage of those who do not normally assist relatives, friends, and neighbours and by the number of kinds of mutual assistance. However, also other aspects, as the number of relatives, friends, and neighbours, the different kinds of assistance and conflicts as well as the question on loneliness shed some light onto the relationship between social integration and the process of urbanization.

In spite of less frequent social interaction with relatives, friends and neighbours household heads in the cement cities feel lonely less often than those in the other two areas. This could have various reasons. (1) With higher education, westernization and a higher level of urbanization people do not feel lonely, even if they are alone once in a while. (2) The living together between the sexes, married or not married, has become a different kind of partnership as it has been the case traditionally. (3) City life brings with it more professional and private contacts than just with relatives, friends, and neighbours. (4) A higher percentage has cars and public transport is much better than in the other two areas so one can travel across the city. (5) Time might already have become an interval for them that has to be filled with achievements and there are much more activities possible than in the other two areas.

About half of the household heads in the fully urbanized areas, a little more than one third in the peri-urban areas, but only about a quarter in the rural areas have no relatives in the same bairro or village. This could be one reason for the decline of mutual visits with urbanization. However, frequency of mutual visits does not only decline drastically among relatives, but also among friends and neighbours.
38 < 51 < 85 per cent of household heads visit their relatives frequently,
37 < 64 < 82 per cent pay frequent visits to friends and
35 < 53 < 77 per cent pay frequent visits to neighbours.

It was assumed that the mentioning of three different kinds of mutual assistance at the same time means more frequent assistance. Also this frequency declines almost as drastically with urbanization and the level of urbanization as the frequency of visiting:
48 < 62 < 80 per cent of household heads mentioned a third kind of help to relatives
35 < 55 < 65 per cent named a third form of assistance to friends
33 < 77 > 66 per cent mentioned a third kind of help to neighbours.

The frequency of assisting neighbours does not decline with the first level of urbanization; having less relatives and friends in the peri-urban areas could be one reason. For the drastic decline in the second level of urbanization the reasons could be, having less neighbours and not needing so much mutual help in the cement cities.

The percentage of those who do normally not give help to relatives, friends and neighbours increases with urbanization but with the level of urbanization only in the case of neighbours.

$12 \cong 13 > 5$ per cent of household heads do not help relatives
$16 > 14 > 8$ per cent do not help friends
$26 > 11 > 4$ per cent do not help their neighbours.

Interesting is the increase from relatives via friends to neighbours to whom this relatively small percentage of household heads in the fully urbanized areas does not help, apparently, because even in the cement cities relatives are still closer than friends and friends closer than neighbours.

As far as the different kinds of mutual assistance between relatives friends and neighbours are concerned, helping out with food and in the case of illness – two more intimate forms of assistance – are apparently practised mainly between relatives; at least they were not mentioned by the interviewees in the pilot study as kinds of mutual help between friends and neighbours. Lending goods, actually the easiest thing to do, takes first place as kind of help between friends and neighbours in all areas. Giving moral support or personal advice, more spiritual or better psychological forms of assistance, take second place only in the cement cities. The following table should give an overview over the manifold kinds of assistance between relatives, friends and neighbours as far as they occupy the first three ranks.

	relatives			friends			neighbours		
	urban	peri-urb.	rural	urban	peri-urb.	rural	urban	peri-urb.	rural
1.	health care	food	food	lending goods	lending goods	lending goods	lending goods	lending goods	lending goods
2.	ceremonies	health care	health care	moral support	lending money	exchanging goods	money, personal advice	exchanging goods	exchanging goods
3.	lending money	ceremonies	lending money	lending money	exchanging goods	lending money, labour	exchanging goods	money, labour, advice	lending money

Note

1 The number of all neighbours was considered as 100 per cent. Then all neighbours with whom the household heads did have contact were added. On this basis the percentage of neighbours with whom the entire sample or control group did have contact was calculated.

10 Satisfaction and depression in favourable and extreme adverse conditions

Few countries have gone through as much hardship in recent times as Mozambique. As several questions of the questionnaire, the results of which are discussed in this chapter, relate to the various difficult time periods, the reader should be reminded on them briefly:

- The colonial oppression and the successful fight against it from 1962 – 1975, which brought political independence for Mozambique in 1975.
- The construction of a new society from 1975 to around 1980. During this time there were constant attacks by the Smith Regime of Rhodesia with heavy losses for Mozambique.
- From 1981 to 1987 the war was initiated mainly by the then racist South Africa and the secret service of Rhodesia shortly after independence. It affected the lives of all Mozambicans with famine even in the capital Maputo around 1983.
- In 1987 PRE, an economic structural adjustment programme, was forced on Mozambique by the IMF and the World Bank while the war was still going on. It worsened the material situation of the majority as we will see in this chapter.
- In 1991/92 Mozambique also suffered under the most horrible drought of this century which affected most parts of Southern Africa. Hundreds of thousands of people lost their lives.

After all the unimaginable sufferings of the Mozambican people there were also three positive events while writing this report. On October the 4th, 1992 a cease-fire agreement was signed in Rome and shortly afterwards, the drought came to an end: it rained and it rained sufficiently. In October 1994 the first general elections were held and won by FRELIMO. So, the results of the survey which will be analysed in this chapter, must be understood in the light or better in the darkness of Mozambique's history before the end of the war. It would be very interesting to repeat some of the questions since peace has been restored. Would the answers be significantly different, would people be less depressed or would it not make so much difference, since the structural adjustment programme has not yet hieved substantial improvements particularly in the countryside? As this survey was carried out in 1991, we can only examine peoples' sufferings, their problems, and their depressions at the time when the war was still going on, but we will also look into their pleasure and their satisfaction which existed even then alongside all the sufferings.

In the discussion of the areas of inquiry Maslow's (1954) hierarchy of needs was mentioned and this hierarchy is one of the theoretical bases for the hypothesis of this chapter, namely, that the degree of happiness is lowest in the rural areas but increases via the peri-urban to the fully urbanized areas. In the rural areas neither the first stage of human needs, the basic human needs, such as food, housing, sanitation, medical care, etc. is fulfilled nor is the second stage, human security. Lack of human security is not only due to the war but also due to the economic situation and, therefore, relevant even now that the war has ended. Security does not only mean peace and absence of crime and banditry but also to have no doubt that one's basic needs will be fulfilled in the future. Where both these essential features of human needs are not fulfilled, one cannot expect much happiness. It has been established for industrialized countries, where extreme poverty is the exception although a certain amount of poverty and insecurity has been on the increase in recent years, that a higher amount of material goods, as well as satisfaction with work (see high proportion of satisfied with participation in the labour force also in the villages and the peri-urban areas in chapter 4) and leisure time are not unimportant but are not at the top of the list of components essential for the overall happiness of a person (Schulz et al. 1985, 28). A higher standard of living increases happiness only up to a certain level. Too much money and affluence can even have the opposite effect (Gehmacher 1994). There certainly does exist an absolutely tiny minority with too much affluence in Mozambique who might not be very happy, but those were not the objective of this study. What is important to bear in mind here is that an increase in the standard of living does increase happiness, even though only up to a certain level. However, this level has not been reached yet, neither in the villages nor in the peri-urban areas and, therefore, the highest degree of happiness can naturally be expected in the cement cities. Here, where extreme poverty has also become the exception and a decent standard of living has been reached, the components which are more important for a person's overall happiness than the increase on material goods can come to bear, namely, self-actualization, physical well being, and happiness derived from partnership and other social relations (Schulz et al. 1985, 28).

One of the characteristics of depression is absence of joy, cheerfulness, and happiness. Unhappiness and depression are more or less equivalents and are, therefore, used here interchangeably. This is the case also as far as the concepts of happiness and satisfaction are concerned. Both are used to indicate well-being although satisfaction in comparison to happiness means a more cognitive evaluation and depends on comparisons with relevant reference groups. Satisfaction also depends on a person's wishes, expectations, hopes, and aspirations while happiness is to a large extend an affective state derived from positive experiences and events (Bradburn 1969). Satisfaction is a precondition for happiness but not a sufficient condition (Michalos 1980). Although the term 'quality of life' as such has never been used so far, this entire research is implicitly also an analysis of the quality of life primarily of the household heads and their wives but to a lesser extend also of their families. People's judgement has been taken seriously all along. Life cannot have a high quality without happiness. Even if in the following scales people were not asked to judge their quality of life, but their happiness, cheerfulness, depression and suffering directly, the following sober definition of happiness can still be useful in understanding the following graphs and tables: 'happiness is defined as the degree to which an individual judges the overall quality of her/his life favourably' (Veenhoven 1993, 6).

Depression – happiness scales

A scale from very unhappy (1) to very happy (5) was presented to the interviewees. The results show the rural household heads as the most unhappy, the urban household heads as the happiest, and those of the peri-urban areas in a middle position: 23 < 48 < 69 per cent said that they feel very unhappy or unhappy, a little more than a third is neither happy nor unhappy over all three areas, and 41 > 14 > 5 per cent stated that they are happy or very happy.

Figure 10.1 Scale from 'very unhappy' to 'very happy'

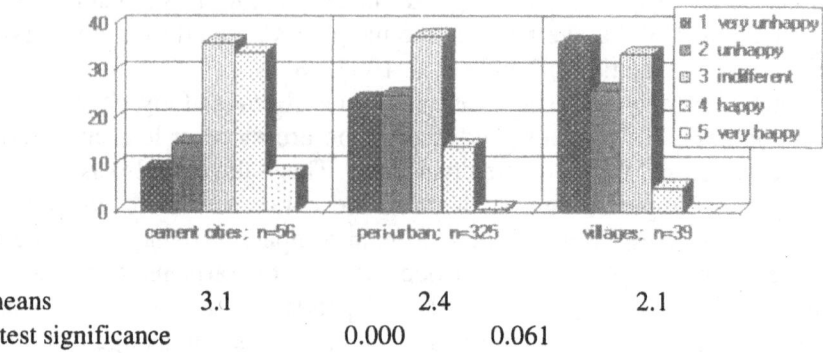

	means	t-test significance		
	3.1		2.4	2.1
		0.000		0.061

The difference between the cement cities and the peri-urban areas is greater than the one between the latter and the villages, which is statistically only almost significant. As a whole it is a very tragic result because only such a small percentage in the rural areas is happy and nobody very happy, particularly when we bear in mind that 77 per cent of the total population of Mozambique still live in rural areas.

The village in the Maputo province, Massaca 1, as mentioned several times before, was a very atypical one, even more privileged than the other two and for that reason it was excluded from the depression – happiness variables as far as the presentation of data of the two provinces combined is concerned as well as for the LISREL model at the end of this chapter. (The results of Massaca 1 for the depression – happiness variables are shown in appendix 3, tables 10.1a to 10.4a.)

The second statement was supposed to measure satisfaction and depression in terms of cheerfulness. Apparently, it is easier for people to state whether they are cheerful or not than whether they are happy or not. Cheerfulness is a more immediate emotional state and more directly perceived than happiness. In the cement cities one quarter indicated that they are cheerful almost every day as against 6 per cent and 3 per cent respectively in the peri-urban areas and the villages. Frequently cheerful are 28 > 19 > 8 per cent and the statement 'I have not been cheerful for a long time' was chosen by 4 < 15 < 39 per cent. There is no doubt that people in the villages are less cheerful than the people in the peri-urban areas and particularly less cheerful than those in the cement cities.

Figure 10.2 Scale of being cheerful from 'very rarely' to 'almost every day'

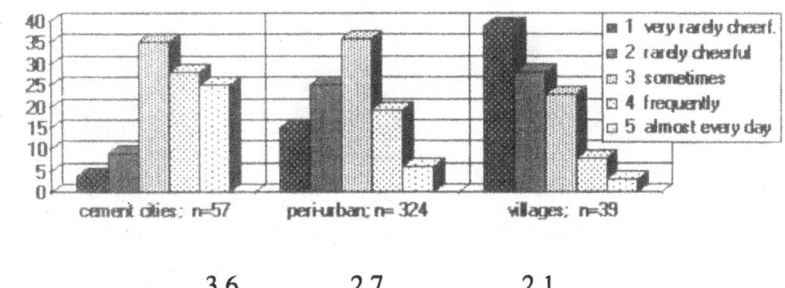

	cement cities: n=57	peri-urban: n=324	villages: n=39
mean	3.6	2.7	2.1
t-test significance		0.000	0.000

This time there exists a highly significant difference not only between the fully urbanized and the peri-urban areas but also between peri-urban areas and villages.

In the cement cities and in the peri-urban areas the statement 'I am cheerful sometimes' was most frequently chosen, namely, by more than one third and it corresponds with the answer 'indifferent' in the previous graph. However, the most frequent statement in the villages is sadly enough: 'I have not been cheerful for a long time'.

The responses to the question: 'at this time are you suffering very much, you suffer but not too much, you do not suffer at all?' show once again less difference between the peri-urban areas and the villages – the difference between the latter is not even significant statistically – than between cement cities and peri-urban areas where the difference is statistically highly significant again.

198 *Globalization, urban progress, urban problems, rural disadvantages*

Figure 10.3 Degree of suffering at this time

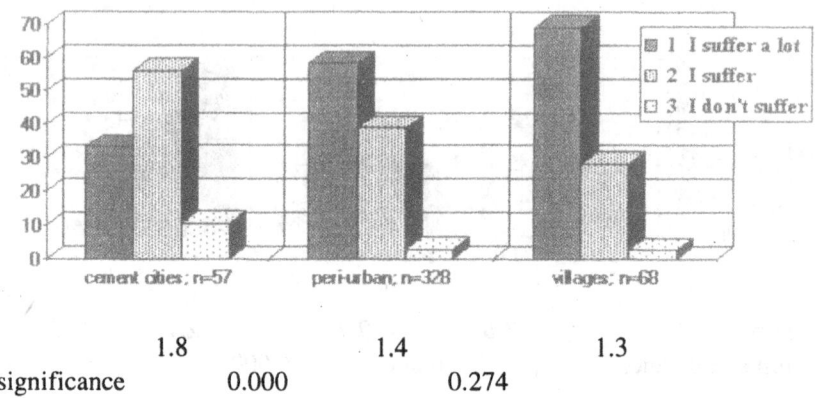

mean	1.8	1.4	1.3
t-test significance	0.000	0.274	

As in the two previous scales the two urban worlds vary greatly also in the degree of subjective suffering. Even though the difference between the other two areas is statistically not significant, it should not be overlooked that the proportion of those who suffer a lot is 11 per cent higher in the villages than in the peri-urban areas.

In the responses to the scale whether the interviewee was very depressed to not at all depressed on the day of the interview, the pattern remains the same as in the previous variables: the highest percentage of very depressed household heads was found in the villages while the peri-urban areas take on a middle position again. The difference between the peri-urban and the rural areas is also smaller than between the two urban areas but this time also the peri-urban rural gap is statistically close to being significant.

Figure 10.4 Degree of depression on the day of the interview

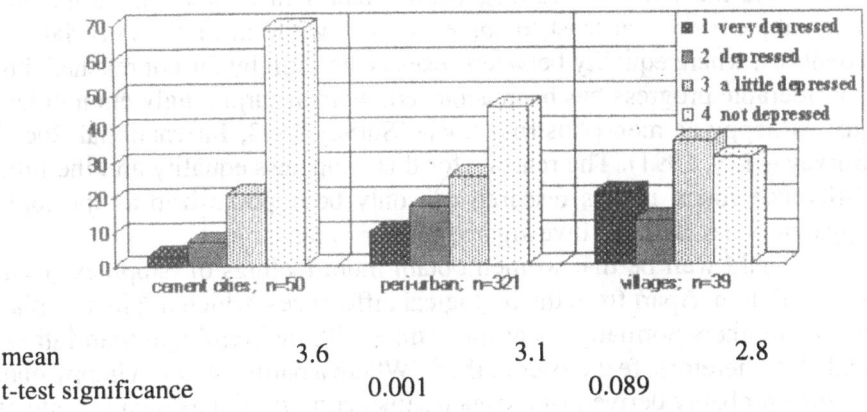

	cement cities; n=50	peri-urban; n=321	villages; n=39
mean	3.6	3.1	2.8
t-test significance		0.001	0.089

The middle position of the peri-urban areas becomes apparent in the codes 1, 3, and 4. However, a higher proportion is depressed in the peri-urban areas than in the villages.

There is no statistical difference between female and male household heads and no statistical difference between women and men in general when both provinces are combined and no difference was found in the province of Sofala between women and men in all these four depression–happiness scales. However, there is a statistically significant difference between women and men in the Maputo sample in the degree of suffering at this time with a Chi^2 sign. of 0.03757 and an almost significant difference in the cheerfulness-scale with a Chi^2 sign. of 0.05501, which could actually be treated also as being significant. The magnitude of importance of these two significant differences against the background of so much correspondence is very difficult to assess. On the one hand, it should probably be taken seriously as the sample in the province of Maputo was much larger than that in the Sofala province. It would also not be difficult to find causes for a higher degree of unhappiness of women. Considering the well documented manifold and serious discrimination of women in almost all countries and especially in Africa (UN Department of Public Information 1996, OECD 1994, Wichterich 1996, Hedman et al. 1997). One would expect a just as highly significant difference between women and men in the happiness variables as was the case between the urban and the peri-urban areas. However, we found only two significant differences out of four happiness variables and this only in one of two provinces. There was no difference between female and male household heads. A lot more research would be necessary to reach the conclusion that women in Mozambique – or all over Africa and the Third World in general – feel their serious discrimination also subjectively – at least to some extent – while in most industrialized countries, where equality between sexes is also still by far not reached, but considerable progress has been achieved, women surprisingly enough feel just as happy as men (Austrian Social Survey 1993, International Social Survey – ISS, 1991). The reasons for this happiness equality and the little difference found in this research can only be hypothesized as the topic apparently has not been investigated further so far.

It could well be that women obtain more feelings of happiness from their children. Apart from the biological differences, which might also play a role, mothers normally spent more time with their children than fathers and also, therefore, feel closer to them. Where a partnership is a happy one, women probably derive just as much satisfaction from it as men in spite of hierarchical structures and overall discrimination. Apart from a partnership and having children satisfactory relationships with other persons such as relatives, friends, and neighbours are normally a source of happiness where poverty is overcome. So, for parts of the peri-urban and the urban areas the assumption might well be relevant that the ability to set up and maintain such relationships is evenly distributed between the sexes and contributes to this happiness equality. In addition, it is a well established fact that childhood shapes the personality. It could well be that even in Africa, in spite of other forms of discrimination, girls are loved just as much as boys, or in the negative sense, that they are not beaten more often than boys. If the quality of childhood were the same, then this would be another essential cause for this happiness equality. Equal quality of childhood does not necessarily mean the same child rearing practices for both sexes. Girls are already influenced in childhood to be more modest than boys. This can lead to a lower aspiration level of the adult women and at the same time women can be satisfied easier and happy with conditions men would not be satisfied with. Differential child rearing practices could also lead to a more altruistic behaviour of women, which would constitute another compensating factor in spite of discrimination. Boys are raised to be braver than girls. One consequence of this is the incomparably higher criminality and the much higher suicide rate among men[1] which could be another reason for men not to be hppier in spite of not being discriminated. However, as mentioned before, these remain hypotheses for the surprising happiness equality (or almost equality) between women and men, as long as further research is lacking.

Satisfaction and depression in favourable and extreme adverse conditions 201

There is in essence little difference in the degree of happiness between the urban area of Maputo and the urban area of Beira. This becomes apparent if we add the first two and the last two statements of the four depression–happiness scales. Although there are, for instance, 8 per cent more unhappy household heads in the urban area of Maputo this is almost made up for by 5 per cent more happy ones. The rest of the variables could be a hint that the household heads of the urban area of Beira feel slightly better, but some of the small differences could also be due to the standard deviation (see tables 10.1a to 10.4a in appendix 3). The correspondence between the two peri-urban areas is impressive.

Table 10.1 Comparison of combined happiness variables between Maputo and Beira

	urban		peri-urban	
	M	B	M	B
very unhappy or unhappy	28	20	47	51
very happy or happy	44	39	14	16
not cheerful for long or rarely cheerful	12	12	50	49
frequently cheerful or almost every day	48	56	25	22
I suffer a lot or I suffer	92	88	97	98
I don't suffer	8	12	3	2
very depressed or depressed on interview day	12	9	27	28
a little or not depressed	88	91	73	72

As in the chapter about the consideration of housing as a problem, also here the urban – peri-urban gap is considerably larger than the peri-urban – rural gap. The difference is statistically highly significant in all four scales between the urban and the peri-urban areas while this is the case only once between the other two areas. This means the first level of urbanization does increase happiness compared to the rural areas but by far not to the same extent as the second level of urbanization.

The factor analysis of the depression and happiness variables
(v220, v221, v226, v227; see questionnaire, appendix 1)

The factor analysis shows that the four variables are determined by one factor only, in other words, they all do measure happiness and depression and that the variables 221 (very unhappy to very happy) and 226 (very rarely cheerful to cheerful almost every day) which show a higher loading, measure depression better than the other two variables, 220 (I suffer a lot, I suffer or I don't suffer) and 227 (very depressed to not depressed on the day of the interview). But even the last two variables show a considerably high loading.

	factor loading
V221 degree of happiness	0.81
V226 degree of cheerfulness	0.77
V220 degree of suffering at this time	0.65
V227 degree of depression on the day of the interview	0.61

The four variables result in one factor only. This factor explains 51 per cent of the variance of the different responses.

Time period in which life was or is most difficult

Life became successively more difficult for the Mozambican people in the last two decades. This is reflected in the answers to the question: When was life most difficult for you? The mode in all three areas is 'now'. 39 < 40 > 34 per cent said that life is most difficult for them at this time.

Table 10.2 Time period in which life was or is most difficult

	urban	peri-urban	villages
before independence	2	4	2
after independence	16	9	5
from about 81 to 87	27	14	31
after 87	16	33	28
now	39	40	34
n	(56)	(326)	(67)

The answer 'after 1987' could also mean that life became most difficult after 1987 and has not improved since then. Insofar it is justified to add the last two categories and then life was and is most difficult from 1987 until now (1991) for 55 < 73 > 62 per cent. While the proportion is the same in the peri-urban areas of both cities, it is lower in the fully urbanized area of Beira (52 per cent) and the villages of Sofala (58 per cent) than in the fully urbanized area of Maputo city (60 per cent) and the village of the province Maputo (70 per cent; see table 10.5a in appendix 3). However, for the cement city of Beira and the villages of the province of Sofala the lower proportion is made up for by a higher proportion for which life was already most difficult in the early 1980s. This can be explained by the fact that in 1983 and 1984 there was a terrible drought in Mozambique with famine even in the cities and that from 1980/81 onwards the war started to escalate.

It might astonish particularly those non-Mozambican readers who have sympathised and supported the liberation struggle of FRELIMO against Portuguese oppression that few people stated that life was most difficult for them before independence. One could argue that to remember things clearly for more than 16 years is too long a time period. People may have forgotten their hardships before independence. On the other hand, we must bear in mind that the successful liberation struggle was mainly carried out in the North of the country, (though psychologically, morally and through sporadic action also supported, of course, by the majority of the population in the South; Newitt 1995), that it was a very noble cause people were fighting for and particularly that there was hope, which not even half of the household heads had at the time of the survey (see Figure 10.5).

After achieving political independence, life improved for the majority only in the first five years. Then the undeclared war of the, at that time racist, South Africa against Mozambique supported by other rightist politicians, organisations and business communities (Austin, 1994) started to escalate. These brutal forces destroyed the country and with it the economy. Drought did the rest and now the IMF and the World Bank have brought more hardship for the majority. So, the high percentages of people who stated that life has been most difficult after 1987 up until now are not surprising.

As many other developing countries in the last two decades, in 1987 Mozambique had to agree to the introduction of the structural adjustment programme (programa da rehabilitação economico = PRE), which will be dealt with in more detail in chapter 12. In the survey we wanted to find out whether PRE has affected the lives of the people in general to the better or worse and what the difference between the areas was. Although the abbreviation PRE is commonly used in the cities among the educated people, we did not, of course, use it in the question referring to the changes of life in the last three years as people with little or no formal education who, in addition, do not have access to newspapers or a radio do not know about it: 28 < 56 < 76 per cent of the household heads did not know what PRE is all about.

Life became more difficult or much more difficult for 45 < 63 < 69 per cent in the last three years, which means after the introduction of PRE. The effects of PRE were apparently felt most negatively in the villages but also in large parts of the peri-urban areas. However, in the cement cities benefits and negative effects seem to be more or less equal.

Figure 10.5 Overall changes of life since the introduction of PRE

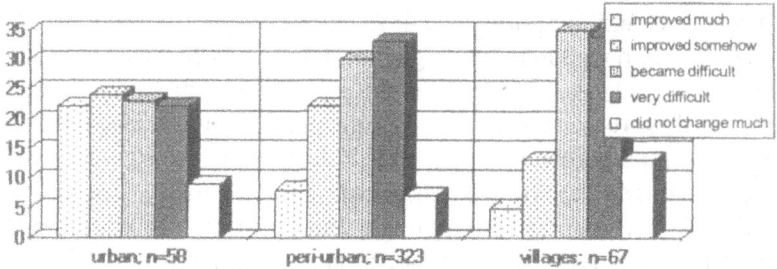

In the peri-urban areas life has improved for 30 per cent and in the villages even only for 18 per cent. As 77 per cent of Mozambique's population still live in rural areas, the proportion for whom life has improved through PRE is really small. We cannot generalize the result from this small village control group for the entire rural population but according to the already quoted investigation in the five provinces (Direcção Nacional de Estatistica, 1990, x) 31 per cent of the rural population near the district centres live in constant risk because of insufficient food, and 38 per cent live at high risk of starvation matching the 69 per cent of the rural group who said that life became difficult or very difficult in the last three years. Even though, it could well be that some of those who indicated no change could be also undernourished while part of those who said that life became very difficult may still get adequate food, the matching of the percentages remains nevertheless not completely irrelevant. The situation is worse in Beira and the Sofala province. Life improved for a considerably lower percentage in the peri-urban areas of Beira compared to that in Maputo and in the fully urbanized areas of Beira as well as in the villages of Sofala the proportion for whom life became very difficult is almost twice as high compared to Maputo and Maputo province, respectively (see table 10.6a in appendix 3).

Satisfaction and depression in favourable and extreme adverse conditions 205

In this economically extremely difficult time the conditions of the house also worsened in the last three years for 21 < 29 < 44 per cent, and only improved for 36 > 18 < 19 per cent. For the rest the house remained the same.

The differences between Maputo and Sofala are great. While the percentage for whom the house became worse is only half in the cement city of Beira in comparison with Maputo, the conditions of the house worsened for about twice as many in the peri-urban areas of Beira in comparison to those areas of Maputo and the houses deteriorated three times more often in the villages of the province of Sofala than in Massaca 1 (see table 10.7a in appendix 3).

The main problems

Although Mozambique is one of the poorest countries in the world and has gone through extreme hardships in recent times, it is necessary to bear in mind that the problems mentioned by the interviewees in this survey do most probably and unfortunately not only apply to Mozambique. At the beginning of this decade there were wars going on in a number of developing countries and where there is no war, poverty is still the lot, particularly for the majority of the rural population. We can speak of 'two lost decades' for the developing world in general – with only a few exceptions – since the debt crisis started in the early 1980s and the structural adjustment programme is forced upon the majority of governments in the Third World with all its negative consequences particularly for the lower strata. It is not unlikely that the same question put forward in many other developing countries would have brought similar results.

People were allowed to mention three problems. On average 2.5 < 2.8 > 2.7 problems were named by the interviewees, an indication that the problems in the peri-urban and rural areas are not only much more serious but also quantitatively greater than in the cement cities.

Table 10.3 The main problems of the household heads

	urban	peri-urban	villages
food	15	25	23
war	29	20	26
low wage	21	18	5
house	8	13	12
crime	13	7	1
banditry	—	6	11
unemployment	3	2	4
health	2	2	5
others	9	7	13
designations/n	144/57	937/329	184/67

In the last chapter we saw that helping out with food was the most frequent kind of assistance among relatives in the peri-urban areas and the villages; in the answers to this question food was named most frequently as main problem in the peri-urban areas but war takes the first place of main problems in the other two areas.

There is a big difference in the first ranking problem 'food' between the peri-urban areas of Maputo and Beira. The proportion (20 per cent) who named food as the main problem in their first reply in the peri-urban areas of Beira was only half of that in Maputo (40 per cent). The cause for this difference can obviously be found in the much higher percentage of households who have family fields in Beira (66 per cent) as compared to Maputo (38 per cent). Finding enough food for the family where there is no family field is related to the low wages in the cities because there would be sufficient food in the markets and shops but people do not have enough money to buy it. The fact should again be stressed that food was mentioned in the second place of the main problems, even in the villages. This can, but must not, be due to the war situation. Two ILO-studies have proved, for instance, for Zambia, where there has never been war in recent history, that poverty and with it even the percentage of undernourished children was much higher in the rural areas (ILO/JASPA 1977, 58 and ILO/JASPA 1981, 25).

Banditry was related to the war. People not only suffered from organized brutal Renamo attacks but also from the attacks of single bandits, who broke into the houses during the night and took the few things which were left. It is not surprising that crime became a problem for people in the cement cities with so much poverty in the near by peri-urban areas. On the other hand, it is not only poverty as such that leads to frequent crime against property but it is rather the change in the value system and norms of a society as well as the change in the social structure,[2] in the case of Mozambique, the advent of capitalism as most modern and even some older theories concerning the causes of crime confirm (Taylor, Walton and Young 1979, Pfeiffer and Scherer 1979, Knauder 1994, 35 – 49).

The housing situation is number four amongst the main problems in the peri-urban areas and number three in the villages, but ranges much lower in the cement cities. It actually surprises that unemployment and health problems range so much lower than the other four problems. On the other hand few household heads are unemployed themselves and not everybody is frequently ill, while everybody suffers from the food shortage, the war, the low wages and the housing situation.

The list of problems presented to the interviewees was longer than is shown in the previous table (see v222 in the questionnaire, appendix 1). But the rest of the problems: having no family field, water supply, transport, not enough vacancies in schools and the original 'others' were all summarized under a new 'others' as these last four problems received only from less than one to almost three per cent of the designations.

Most appreciated aspects of life

Although the situation was grim in Mozambique during 1991, there were also positive factors. During the interview phase we encountered much kindness, openness and warm welcome. It was justified to ask people not only about their sufferings and problems but also about their likings. Most of the codes were named by the household heads themselves, again during the pilot study.

Table 10.4 The most appreciated aspects of life

	urban	peri-urban	villages
life in the city	22	16	5
life in the rural areas	9	23	29
occupation	21	22	22
church	19	18	16
music	14	6	7
sports	7	7	7
one of the new parties	1	1	7
Frelimo	7	6	7
others	—	1	1
designations/n	159/58	776/321	163/68

Here we have just the opposite situation in comparison to the variable of the main problems: on average 2.7 > 2.4 > 2.4 most appreciated aspects of life were named. This can be seen again as a weak but, nevertheless, as an indication that the household heads in the urban areas can appreciate more aspects of life because their basic needs are better fulfilled than those of the household heads in the other two areas.

The results also give an additional indication that people in the cement cities are more urbanized than those in the peri-urban areas because only 9 per cent appreciate life in the rural areas most, as against 23 per cent in the peri-urban areas. These 23 per cent are the mode of the most appreciated aspects in the peri-urban areas which shows, on the one hand, that a considerable percentage would probably like to go back to the countryside, if they had the opportunity to do so. On the other hand, the result that in addition to the 16 per cent who appreciate life in the city most, 22 per cent appreciate their occupation which they could not have exercised in the rural areas, allows the interpretation, that almost two fifths of the peri-urban household heads appreciate life in the city most.

There exists a striking similarity between all three areas as far as the appreciation of occupation, church, sports and Frelimo is concerned. However, a considerable higher percentage in the fully urbanized areas likes music and a higher percentage in the rural areas likes one of the new parties. The appreciation of one's church takes on third position in all three areas which again shows the high importance of religion in Mozambique.

Prospects for the future

Finally people were asked: 'Do you think life in general will improve in the next five years, not change much, or deteriorate?' A considerable proportion has not lost hope, in spite of all the difficulties.

Figure 10.6 Prospects for the future

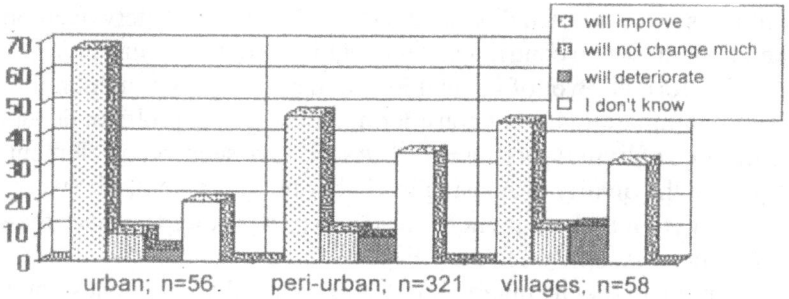

Almost half in the peri-urban areas and in the villages but more than two thirds in the fully urbanized areas remain optimistic. Few are completely pessimistic. This proportion is highest in the villages. However, there is no statistically significant difference between the areas.

The linear structural relations

The manifold differences between the three areas of living have been dealt with all along in this research. With the LISREL-model it is now possible to show the intensity of the influence that the area of living as an independent variable has on the dependent ones: income, formal education, the housing situation or quality of housing, social interaction (here measured only as frequency of visiting relatives, friends and neighbours), considering housing as a problem, and, finally, satisfaction. On the one hand, it is surprising that the influence of the area of living on the housing situation is so dominant over all the other influences with a gamma value of 0.76, on the other hand, if we remember all the big differences in the chapter on the housing situation, it does not come as a surprise.

The other surprise at first glance is the relatively low influence of the area of living on imcome: gamma = 0.40, which is, of course, only low when compared to the influence of the area of living on the quality of housing. As mentioned earlier, the data on income in the villages are not very reliable in this research; other more comprehensive sources had to be consulted. However, those could not be included in the LISREL-model as they were not comparable with the chosen income groups. On the other hand, as low wages and food take on second and third place even in the cement cities as main problems of the household heads (as the run down buildings were selected there), poverty is not yet completely overcome even there. All these can contribute to the relatively low gamma value.

The formal level of education also depends very much on the area of living, gamma = 0.47, but considering housing as a problem depends least on the area of living: gamma = 0.21. As we have seen, many elements which consitute the quality of housing are either not a problem, like water supply and waste removal, or are not considered as a problem because the specific need is not felt so much in the villages.

Personal social interaction (here only the frequency of visiting relatives, friends and neighbours) as it decreases with the process of urbanization is influenced negatively by the area of living, gamma = -0.30 and the gamma value concerning the influence of the area of living on satisfaction is also not extraordinarily high with only 0.31.

What was not dealt with throughout the research, was the influence of the dependent variables on the other dependent variables. And we can see now: the frequency of the measured social interaction is not only influenced negatively by the area of living but also by the level of formal education, beta = -0.13 and the housing situation, beta = -0.25.

We have seen that the area of living has only a slight effect on considering housing as a problem, however, the quality of housing does affect this consideration strongly: beta = 0.48. In addition income with a beta value of 0.14 influences the consideration of housing as a problem slightly.

Apart from the area of living the degree of satisfaction is also influenced by income, beta = 0.30, considering housing as a problem, beta = 0.30, and the frequency of personal social interaction, beta = 0.20, but surprisingly enough, it is neither influenced by the quality of housing as such nor by the level of education.

Table 10.5 Correlation matrix for selected single or combined variables

	income	formal educ.	quality of housing	Interaction	housing problem	satisfaction	area
income	1.00						
formal education	.38	1.00					
quality of house	.39	.51	1.00				
interaction	.06	.22	.34	1.00			
housing as problem	.20	-.11	.35	.05	1.00		
satisfaction	.37	.20	.27	.10	.36	1.00	
area	.40	.47	.76	-.30	.21	.31	1.00

The selected and combined variables

household income = v036
formal education = v012
quality of housing = v063 + v064 + v065 + v067 + v069 + v076 + v088 + v090
interaction = v188 + v197 + v210
housing as problem = v080 + v089 + v094 + v099 + v103
satisfaction = v013 + v037 + v220 + v221 + v226 + v227
area = v003

212 *Globalization, urban progress, urban problems, rural disadvantages*

Figure 10.7 The linear structural relations with one independent variable – model 1

All household heads (only the total effects equal or greater than .10 are shown)

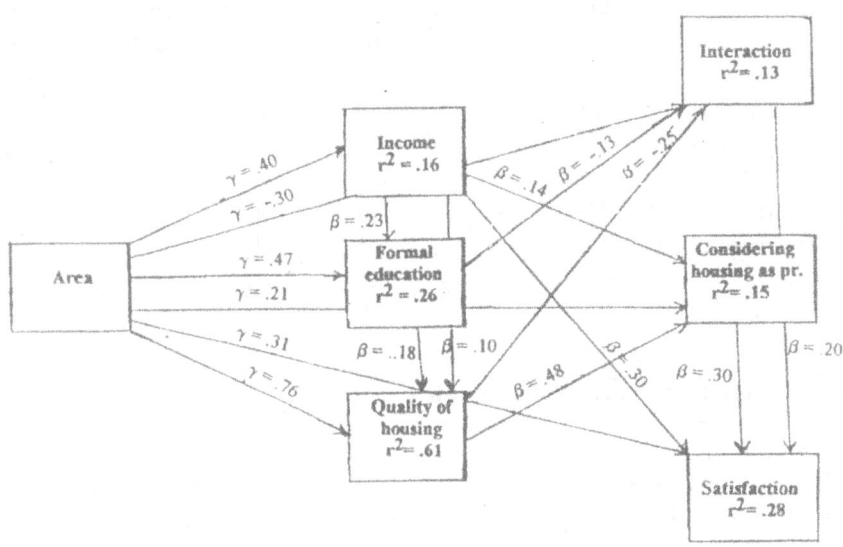

Figure 10.8 The linear structural relations with two independent variables – model 2

All household heads (only the total effects equal or greater than .10 are shown)

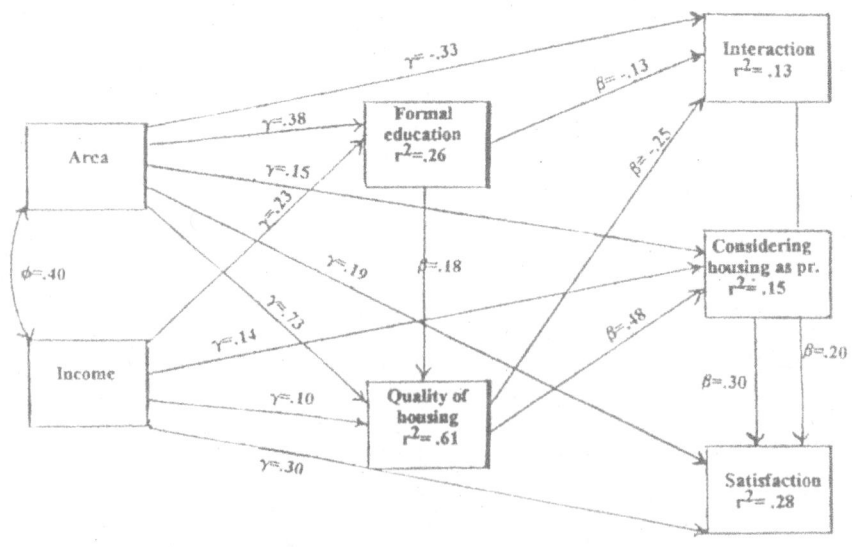

The beta values remain the same if income is also considered as independent variable apart from the area of living. According to the gamma values, the influence of the area of living becomes weaker on formal education, considering housing as a problem, as well as on satisfaction.

In both models the explained variances are not very impressive except the one of the housing situation of which 61 per cent of the variance are explained. For the level of satisfaction, as we measured it in this research, only 28 per cent of the variance can be explained by the independent and all the dependent variables together. This means that a lot of other variables which are not included in these models must be responsible for peoples' satisfaction and depression.[3] Some might not even have been dealt with in this research, others have at least been brought to light in the questions about the main problems and likings but could not be included into LISREL as they were named only and not measured as interval variables.

Summary

The results of the depression – satisfaction measurements show that – similar to the judgement of housing – also here in these subjective feelings the inner urban gap is considerably larger than the peri-urban – rural gap. Also in this respect the most probably lower level of the feelings of relative deprivation in the rural areas due to the remoteness and fewer contacts with the fully urbanized areas as compared to the frequent contacts with the latter of the peri-urban population could be made responsible for the smaller gap. On the other hand, the level of depression and sadness is so high in the villages that one could say, it has almost reached the maximum of a still 'normally' functioning society where, life goes on in spite of all the difficulties, (in contrast to even more extreme situations, say concentration camps, where life does not go on anymore) so that also for that reason a bigger difference to the peri-urban areas is hardly possible. In any case, the hypothesis that the degree of happiness increases with the process of urbanization was not falsified. Considering the fact that the majority of Mozambique's population lives in the countryside and only a tiny proportion in the cement cities, the results are sad indeed as they show that the majority is unhappy and suffering.

Life was surprisingly enough not most difficult before independence. In spite of racial discrimination, forced labour and other oppressive measures by the colonial power. People apparently had hope. They fought a liberation war for a noble cause. Only for a few years after achieving independence life improved but after that it soon deteriorated for the majority. For a considerable proportion life became most difficult in the time period of 1981 to 1987 but for the vast majority particular in the peri-urban areas, life became most difficult after 1987 or it was most difficult at the time of the survey as they felt the burden of the structural adjustment programmes, although, for almost half of the households in the cement cities life improved after the introduction of these programmes. But this was the case only for about a third in the peri-urban areas and not even for one fifth in the rural areas.

The conditions of housing worsened for one fifth in the cement cities in the last three years before the survey, they worsened for more than a quarter in the peri-urban areas and for almost half in the villages. The house improved for more than one third in the cement cities but only for one fifth each in the other two areas.

Almost all household heads mentioned three main problems in the peri-urban and rural areas, the avarage of replies was two and a half in the cement cities. Most of the main problems people have (and also named) are caused by their low wages and salaries and these in turn are caused by the ailing economy which again has many causes, as deglobalization, the war, the drought. But low wages are in addition forced upon by PRE. The wages are so low that getting enough food belongs to the major problems in all three areas, even in the cement cities as only families living in run down buildings were investigated there. The conditions of the house named amongst the four major problems are also a concomitant of poverty and even crime and banditry are related to it, although crime – a new phenomenon in Mozambique, almost absent after independence – is also closely related to the advent of capitalism, its change of values, and its change of the social structure in the sense of the widening of the gap between rich and poor.

However, in spite of all these sufferings life goes on also in Mozambique and side by side with depression and desperation there also exists much kindness, cheerfulness and liking of certain aspects of life. Concerning the answers to the latter we found the opposite to the answers of the main problems: the household heads of the cement cities mentioned almost three aspects of life which they like most while the respondents in the other two areas named less than two and a half.

To the most appreciated aspects of life belongs 'life in the city' in the fully urbanized areas and 'life in the country side' in the other two areas.

Occupation takes on second and one's own church the third place. Music, sports, new political parties and Frelimo were mentioned but remained below 10 per cent in almost all areas. As far as the prospects for the future are concerned more than two thirds of the household heads are optimists in the cement city but less than half in the other two areas.

Notes

1. Only 5 per cent of the entire prison population of Austria were women in 1994 (BMfJ, Statistische Uebersicht ueber den Strafvollzug 1994, 19). Even in a culturally very different society, such as Zambia, also only 5.4 per cent of the entire prison population were women in 1980 (Prison Department, Annual Report 1980, 4 and 7; quoted in Knauder 1994, 60). In 1994 72 per cent of those who committed suicide in Austria were men (STAT, Bericht ueber das Gesundheitswesen in Oesterreich 1994, 190).
2. In 1980 one could walk freely through the streets of the cement city of Maputo after midnight, while this was already extremely dangerous in Lusaka, the capital of Zambia. Mozambique had one of the lowest crime rates (and for sure the lowest corruption rate) in Africa in the years after reaching independence as socialism was put into practice, while Zambia had already a capitalist class society, even though the official state philosophy was Humanism with a few socialist elements. With the advent of capitalism high criminality is also one of the negative by-products in Mozambique.
3. Margaret Peil explained 34 per cent on the average of the variance of satisfaction in three towns in Sierra Leone although with very different variables such as standard of living, job, income, neighbourhood, town as a whole, getting ahead, and not comparing rural, peri-urban and urban areas (Peil 1984, 369).

PART III
GLOBALIZATION
AND POVERTY

11 The root causes of Third World poverty in a globalizing world

The reader might ask why after the rounding up of the empirical evidence through the path analysis a further chapter on the root causes of poverty and an attempt to show a way out of it are added. This is necessary because the many facets of poverty brought to light by the survey – low income, lack of sufficient food, insufficient housing conditions, lack of infrastructure and social facilities, and above all unhappiness and depression – are not isolated or ahistorical reality, but depend on numerous external factors and forces, have been shaped and will be shaped by global historical processes. The next two chapters are an attempt to provide a sketch of these forces and processes. The concentration on the root causes of poverty and an alternative development should, on the other hand, not blur the view on the rest of the findings, be they the manifold aspects of social change from the rural via the peri-urban to the urban areas in general, the decline of specific social interactions in particular, the influence of relative deprivation in considering housing and services as problems or the situation of the female household heads, just to mention a few.

Since the view that rapid urbanization in the Third World is a negative phenomenon and the poorest would be the inhabitants of the peri-urban areas is still extraordinarily widespread, it is necessary to include into the chapter of the root causes a paragraph about what is for sure not a cause for poverty and give evidence for it in the presence and past.

Rapid urbanization does not cause poverty

Rapid urbanization as such is often considered erroneously as a cause for urban and rural poverty. This view normally stems from a negative attitude towards urbanization, sees the urban poor as the worst off and is accompanied by rural romanticism. This research shows that urbanization neither causes urban nor rural poverty, as it analyzed urban progress and documented the relative advantage of the urban poor over the rural poor in numerous aspects. In all these aspects the inhabitants of the fully urbanized areas appear as winners on the national level. The problem of injustice inherent in this development can only be solved by massive positive interventions in the rural areas and not by curbing urban development. In the majority of Third World countries a higher degree of urbanization also shows a higher economic development even when measured by the GDP only. The latter correlates with $r = 0.6$, with the level of urban development. (r calculated by the author on the basis of table 1, Gugler 1988, appendix 2). Even though the GDP as measurement of development is by far inferior to the newly established Human Development Index (Nohlen and Nuscheler, Volume 1, 1993, 92), it has, nevertheless, some value, as it shows, that in very poor countries the level of urbanization is also low. People have to remain in the rural areas, because there are not enough urban areas to go to, but at the same time rural development does also not take place. (Prestom in Gugler 1988). The above mentioned table also shows that between more than 50 per cent and 85 per cent of the population of almost all major developing countries with a per capita GDP of more than US$ 2,000 live in urban areas. It would not be justified to conclude: because of those countries' high level of urbanization their economies are somewhat better off but rather because of some economic growth the pull factors joined the push factors and people flocked to the cities. As Hardoy and Satterthwaite put it:

> (The) process of urbanization is not itself 'the problem' indeed, in many instances, it has arisen from the development of stronger and more diversified economies. In many nations, it also reflects their increasing incorporation into a global economy (Hardoy and Satterthwaite 1989, 7).

In the following table the correlation of the level of urbanization with the GDP per capita for 1995, calculated by the author on the basis of table 3 in appendix 2 will be shown as well as the correlation of the level of urbanization with the Human Development Index (HDI) and the Human Poverty Index (HPI).

Table 11.1 Correlation of the level of urbanization with GDP per capita, HDI and HPI of 1995

	level of urbanization with GDP	level of urban. with HDI	level of urban. with HPI
Developing countries with 10 million + inh.	0.80	0.75	- 0.64
Asia	0.72	0.65	- 0.39
Africa	0.81	0.65	- 0.56
Latin America	0.67	0.64	- 0.84

Sources: Table 2 and Table 3 in appendix 2 (calculations by the author)

While the correlation coefficient of the level of urbanization with the GDP per capita for all major developing countries was 0.60 in 1985 it increased to 0.75 in 1993 (calculation on the basis of table 2 in appendix 2) and to 0.80 in 1995. It is highest in Africa the least urbanized continent. The similar correlation of the level of urbanization with the GDP per capita as well as of the former with the HDI shows that urbanization does not only mean economic advancement but also human development, even though the second column of correlation is in all cases slightly lower, but in Africa considerably lower. This could be interpreted in the way that even countries without a high HDI have a relatively high degree of urbanization: urbanization without growth, and widespread urban poverty.

The correlation of the level of urbanization with the HPI must, of course, be a negative one. The lower the HPI the higher the GDP and, normally the higher the level of urbanization. The correlation is relatively low in Asia. This could firstly be due to the low HPI of China, in spite of a low level of urbanization, (which could mean alleviation of poverty without rapid urban growth or, in other words, relatively high rural development) but secondly, it could also be due to the many missing cases, as the HPI is a new measure and for a number of countries it has not yet been calculated (see table 3 in appendix 2).

Mass poverty was – and is – nowhere a consequence of urbanization and industrialization. In this regard, Engels was wrong when he showed the misery of the urban poor of Manchester in his *Conditions of the working class in England* of 1844, in that he considered all these as inevitable consequences of urbanization and industrialization and did not compare the urban with the rural conditions. Abel, citing Bruno Hildebrand, remarks that 'poverty was greatest (in Germany) where there was no industry' (Abel 1972, 7 quoted in Wallerstein 1992, 28). Also Henderson mentions in his editor's introduction to the 1958 edition that Engels had overlooked the bad conditions of the working class and their children in the pre-factory period (i.e. in the rural areas): spinners and weavers were extremely exploited, sewing girls were overworked and shirt makers treated cruelly. However, factories brought the workers under one roof, so it became possible to detect bad conditions which were formerly hidden in isolated cottages and workshops (Henderson in Engels 1958, xiv).

One often gets the impression that for some contemporary Third World urban sociologists or even economists, rural poverty is also hidden too far away, they only stare at urban poverty and do not compare it with rural conditions. On the other hand, the advantages of the peri-urban population over the rural population are exaggerated as Jamal and Weeks have found (see chapter 3). The IMF and World Bank massively intervened in these allegedly 'unhealthy' urban privileges. Unfortunately, their policies increased urban poverty dramatically in too many countries and did not at all alleviate the rural plight.

Some comparative historical aspects: poverty in Europe

In an historical perspective the poverty in the Third World today is not unique. Unique is the affluence of a considerable proportion of mankind which never existed before. Poverty was the lot of the masses for centuries and even millennia in Europe. From the mid seventeenth to the mid nineteenth century, after the Thirty Years' War (1618 – 1648) the marginal classes grew inexorably. In Germany those who lived on or below the poverty line, who where particularly endangered in times of crisis, were estimated at 50 to 60 per cent of the population. Conditions in Austria were similar (Stekl 1978, 41). In Paris under the reign of Louis the XIV one fifth of the inhabitants were estimated to be beggars (Stekl 1978, 27). The situation was much worse in the countryside than in the cities. An Austrian historical document from 1682 describes the misery of people coming to Vienna (which had at that time about 80,000 inhabitants) from the rural areas.

It is a widespread daily experience that various sick persons come to this city from the hinterland and sit down or even lay down near the hospital ... in a way that one feels urged to take them in and feed them if they otherwise should not die or perish in the streets. However, in doing so this city would have unnecessary costs, which in the long run would become unmanageable (Codex Austriacus, 2, April 8th, 1682, 74; cited by Stekl 1978; 41; translated by the author).

Later on such conditions led to the prohibition of begging for rural-urban migrants, firstly, because city dwellers did not want to be harassed, secondly, for economic reasons, and thirdly, also for health security reasons (plague years 1679 – 1692). Those found begging without a city pass were either immediately brought back to their rural district, had to undergo corporal punishment or were confined in work camps for forced labour. Poverty was considered as one's own fault.

The conditions in Europe, at least until the middle of the nineteenth century, can thus be considered in many aspects worse than they are in most developing countries today. At least one cannot imagine 20 per cent of the population being beggars in the city of Maputo or any other capital in Southern Africa. The 22 per cent unemployed in the peri-urban areas of Maputo are at least in a certain way integrated into their extended families.

However, the rural poverty of Mozambique today is comparable to the rural poverty in Europe after the industrial revolution up until even shortly after the Second World War. Small peasant farmers were very poor and, in addition, there existed a considerable proportion of landless agricultural workers who were even much worse off than the poor peasant farmers. They could not work for huge commercial farmers as the landless in Latin America today, who have even started their oganized struggle, but they had to work for the poor peasants who could not or did not pay them any wages. They had to work extremely hard, often sixteen hours a day, for food and the most necessary clothes only. They had to sleep in cellars or stables not far from the animals. Being absolutely powerless, they could have been beaten and fired anytime. It is interesting to note that the turning point of European rural poverty to affluence occurred only recently while urban poverty, which Engels describes for Manchester, was the situation one and a half centuries ago, and which improved rapidly thereafter. Emigration to North America was one of the reasons why European poverty could be aleviated relatively rapid at least in the city, while it is not possible for the poor masses of the Third World to emigrate in large scale. Rural poverty seems to be much more difficult to overcome than urban poverty. Unfortunately,

Engels' analysis of the situation of the working class in Manchester is still tragic actuality for Maputo and Beira and other Third World cities concerning the majority of aspects. Engels describes, for instance, the poor housing conditions: the poor have to sleep in cellars where water seeps through the floor or in attics were rain comes through the roof; sometimes up to a dozen workers are packed into one room, they are deprived of all proper refuse disposal. Workers are deprived of the necessities of life, they do not receive medical care, they do not have proper sanitation and hygiene and they do not have enough food. Education is withheld from them and there is a high child mortality rate and low life expectation (Engels 1958, chapter 3).

Even though poverty is on the increase again for the lower strata of the affluent societies of Europe and the USA, this new poverty is first of all not comparable with the one just described. It can not be justified in any way, but one, nevertheless, has to admit that it is less inhuman. Secondly, there is a crucial structural difference between the old and the new poverty in Europe, on the one hand, and the Third World poverty of the pre-colonial, colonial, and neo-colonial times, on the other hand. While the poor European masses have been repressed and exploited by the powerful of their own societies – and this is also the case for the proportion of losers in the North today – the poor masses of the developing world have been and are today repressed and exploited in many cases, not only by the powerful of their own countries but in addition and more effectively by the affluent part of mankind, the North, which benefits from this inhumane economic system and remains the winner on the international level, while the majority of the developing countries remain losers.

Historical perspectives in particular

The slave trade

Although poverty, wars, natural disasters and even slavery existed in the developing countries before the arrival of the Europeans, the situation often worsened drastically thereafter. The most tragic example of the negative influence of the Europeans in Africa is the slave trade, which has been mentioned briefly in chapter 2, but should be dealt with here more comprehensively as one of the root causes of Africa's and Mozambique's poverty today.

Although slavery evolved independently in different societies, it often remained a marginal phenomenon over long periods, without disastrous effects on the political and economic structure of a country. After war captives were no longer killed and a certain structure of property relations had developed, slavery came into existence in China, India, and the Old Orient already between the 4th and 2nd millennium B.C. It reached its peak in Europe in the Greek and Roman Empires (Brockhaus 1998, 294).

> Only slavery made the division of agricultural and industrial labour on a large scale possible and with it the height of Helenism. Without slavery the Greek state would never have developed, no Greek art and science; without slaves the Roman Empire would never have existed either. However, without the basis of the Greek and Roman Empires also no modern Europe would have developed. We should never forget that our entire economic, political and intellectual development has an era as its basis where slavery was just as necessary as it was generally accepted (Engels 1894; quoted in Brossboetzl 1995,1; translated from German by the author).

When reading this quotation one would expect a most reactionary or neo-liberal writer undersigned. But it was Engels. Nevertheless, at the end of the 20th century it is truly repulsive to consider slavery as necessary at any one time in history. Most unfortunately, it has by far not been overcome in all its forms, even at present.[1]

Like most social phenomena, slavery is not easy to define. Here only the most striking criteria should be mentioned: it is the exclusion of the slave from the category 'human being'. The existence of such 'creatures' was seen as based on the laws of nature. According to Aristotle some are born to be free, others to be completely dependent. Politics was the realm of liberty and economics the realm of necessity. For the latter slaves were simply necessary. Although thereafter slavery was marginal for many centuries in most societies, the basic attitude apparently did not change until the 19th century and has in too many countries and groups of people not changed until today. Such deep rooted beliefs are comparable to the modern, neo-liberal 'credo' in the 'free' market laws, which are also considered as unquestionable, God-given, inherent in human nature and based on natural laws. From the 15th to the end of the 19th century, during the Atlantic slave trade, it was normal for Europeans to treat slaves as commodities. They were considered as savages without any intellect, without any culture, and any knowledge of Christianity. Slaves could be bought, sold, inherited, or even killed. They were the property of a person, who could use them to his or her own ends (Grossboetzl 1995, 2-6).

The Christian churches as well as the Moslems (Moslems traded with slaves particularly in East Africa long before the arrival of the Europeans) did not basically question slavery but tolerated it all along or were even actively involved in it. It was the Catholic monk De las Casas, who persuaded the emperor Karl V – out of pity for the enslaved Indians, who died in large numbers because of diseases and the extremely hard work for the white settlers – to allow stronger slaves to be imported from West Africa. Only the Second Vatican Council banned slavery officially in *1965*.

Why were slaves sold? The Europeans appealed mainly to the political and economic needs of those Africans who held at that time a certain position of power and had a strong interest to hold on to it. Fire-arms, liquor, textiles, metal goods, etc. were offered in exchange for slaves and armed support in conflicts with neighbouring empires, kingdoms and chieftaincies was promised. Slaves were captured by ambush attacks and assaults on settlements, by wars against weak neighbours, and raids. An already quite well developed trade net in Africa served the Europeans in their most inhuman endeavour (Grossboetzl 1995, 13-4). The Arab slave trade will not be dealt with here; it should only be mentioned that it was less cruel than the Atlantic trade. Slaves did not lose their human dignity completely, were treated in a similar way to domestic servants today and during the Arab slave trade the existing social structure of Mozambique, for example, was not destroyed (Madeiros 1988, 6). All these facts should, of course, not be misunderstood as justification, but rather show the difference between two tragedies.

Until the middle of the 17th century slave trade was the right of privileged trade companies and Portugal held the monopoly but permitted also private merchants to get involved for a share in their profits. Later Great Britain, France and Holland took part in the most profitable trade of that time. According to Wirz, Great Britain had a quantitative share in the trade of 41 per cent, Portugal 30 per cent, France 19 per cent, Holland 6 per cent, British North America/USA of 3 per cent, Denmark 1 per cent, and Sweden and Brandenburg 0.1 per cent only (Wirz 1984, 51; figures rounded off by the author).

The following graph shows the countries of origin and those of destination of slaves in the respective countries and centuries.

The root causes of Third World poverty in a globalizing world 227

Figure 11.1 Source areas of slaves[2] and countries of destination
(two graphs combined to one)

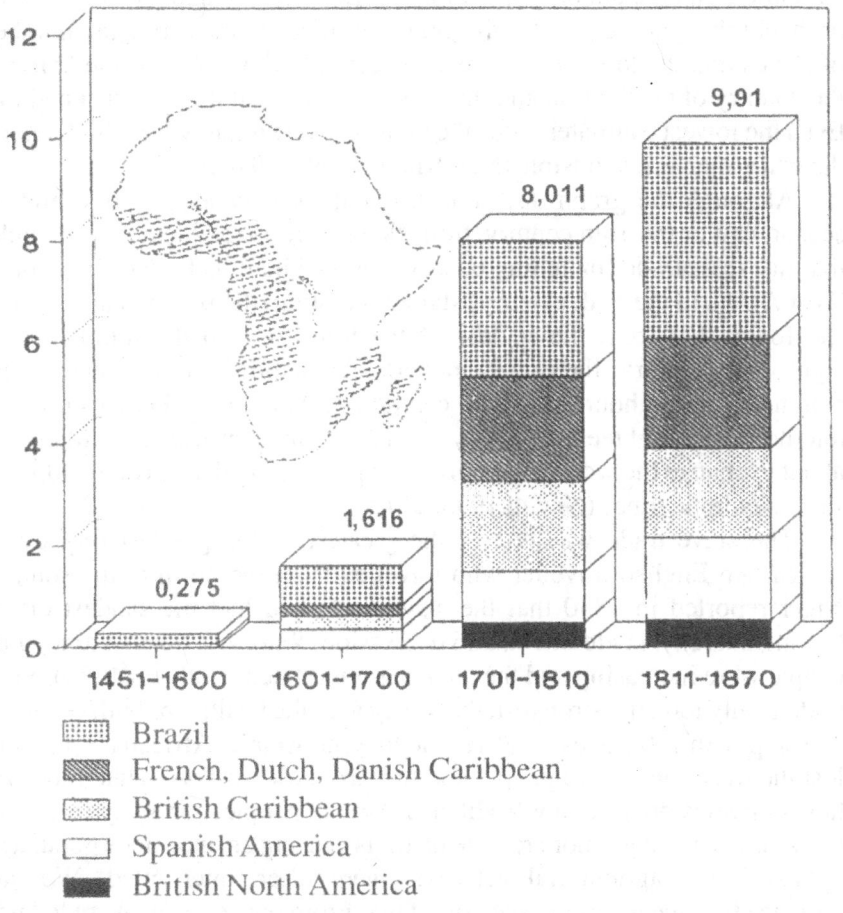

Sources: Source areas: Loth, H., 1981, 30; Graph: Grossboetzl, G. 1995, 14; Countries of destination: Kriedte, P., 1980, 104; Graph: Nussbaumer, J., 1999, 390.

The graph shows by far the lowest estimated number of exported slaves, who reached the respective countries of destination alive. The estimates of the majority of authors are between 50 and 100 million slaves, which Africa lost during the 400 years of trade. Those authors rightfully assume that for each slave who reached the country of destination alive four or five others died during their cruel capture and transportation, while awaiting shipment in the most inhuman conditions or because they commited, suicide out of desperation (Ki-Zerbo 1979, 228-9).[3] This is most probably the main reason for the great difference in the estimated numbers of slaves that the lower estimates consider only those who arrived alive in the country of destination and the higher consider all those Africa had lost. Even the lowest estimates show the unimaginable tragedy for which mainly the white man is responsible (Nussbaumer 1999, 391-2).

Although the graph does not differentiate between the first and the second half of the 18th century, from Newitt's research it can be concluded that full scale trade (including East Africa – while it had affected seriously West Africa in the 17th century) started mainly in the second half, because she found that from the middle of the fourteenth to the middle of the eighteenth century there was remarkable stability in production and commerce throughout the whole central African region. However, by the middle of the eighteenth century the European industrial revolution was about to change the world economy more profoundly than any development since Neolithic times (Newitt 1995, 244).

The slave trade was one of the greatest or the greatest tragedy for Africa. An English traveller who travelled from the north to the south of Niger reported in 1830 that the slave trade had had the saddest effects leaving anarchy, lawlessness, and depression. Wars and distrust among the people were increasing and the area was devastated (Loth 1981, 30). Slave traders only took the strongest, the young and, the healthy of both sexes. On one ship with 130 slaves 25 were able to write Arabic. African civilizations lost the most innovative people and the strongest workers. This trade with human beings drove many frightened African peoples far away from their home areas into ever more remote districts causing an enormous population upheaval and agricultural activities were often interrupted. War and violence became a chronic state of affairs. From now on wars were led with devastating means. More sold slaves meant more money to buy more guns, and more guns made it possible to capture more slaves (Ki-Zerbo 1997, 230-1). Although less than half of the area of sSA was affected by the slave trade, such a large proportion of the population in the affected countries died in all the upheavals and cruelties that population estimates show a zero growth rate considering the entire continent over 200 years.[4]

The French were the first who purchased slaves from Mozambique for their sugar plantations on the islands of the Indian Ocean. They had to pay a considerable amount of money to the governor of a district, who passed on a certain amount to the local traders. In the 1770s the French exported about 1,500 slaves from Mozambique (Newitt 1995, 246-7).

The slave trade developed separately from the ivory trade. In the 1780s ivory caravans were frequently impeded by the slave wars among the Mukua in northern Mozambique. Long lasting droughts and civil wars as they occurred also in the mid 1790s and particularly the great Mozambican drought around 1820 were fuelling the expansion of the slave trade, which was not simply an export trade, as slaves were sold also internally and kept in large numbers by chiefs and war lords.

The French introduced firearms and those who obtained guns in exchange for slaves became more powerful than those who controlled the resources of the land. Slavers from Cuba, the United States or Brazil were eager to load the slaves, where they were most plentiful and where they could obtain food supplies, so the fertile Zambezi region became the best source for slaves and Quelimane the port of departure (Newitt 1995, 248-9; compare also Madeiros 1988, 9).

Finally, under pressure from Britain, but also because of increasing slave uprisings,[5] the campaign against the slave trade started in 1817. But, Portugal with the greatest colonial tradition, had not been able to produce a metropolitan class capable of trading with industrial products. So, this campaign was the biggest threat to Mozambican trade. With the prices of sugar rising in the 1840s also the price for slaves soared and it is estimated that between 1840 and 1847 450,000 slaves were shipped from Mozambique to Brazil. Brazil closed its markets for slaves in 1851, but the trade continued unhampered to Cuba and the United States, as they closed their ports for slaves only in the early 1860s. Although the slave trade had officially ceased to exist after 1842, all indications suggest that in the 1840s and 1850s the number of slaves exported equalled or exceeded that of the 1820s or 1830s.

Conditions for the captured slaves deteriorated during the times of clandestine trade. A British intelligence officer received reports from hundreds burning alive in a baracoon, hundreds drowning or dying from disease before being loaded and half the consignment dying on board (Newitt 1995, 268-71).

As mentioned in chapter 2, Mozambique, where clandestine slave trade lasted well into the 20th century, has not fully recovered from the tragedy. It lost between 600,000 and 1 million people (Medeiros 1988, 59) mainly in the 19th century. Niassa, where clandestine slave trade intensified even in the beginning of the 20th century is still the most thinly populated and least developed province. All the human, cultural and economic losses mentioned in the slave trade affected areas in general might be particularly relevant for Mozambique because of the intensity of trade and the more recent occurrence and can, therefore, be considered as one of the root causes of poverty.

The transatlantic slave trade was the biggest forced transfer of people the world has ever known, with considerable consequences on the course of history, the interactions of civilizations and the construction of the Atlantic world. The degree of suffering it caused, the racism it generated and particularly the impact it made on three continents is very much under researched.

Colonization and its continuation

The literature on colonialism is vast compared to the literature on slave trade and particularly its impact and a number of aspects of colonialism have been mentioned in previous chapters. Colonialism is also widely accepted as one of the root causes of the present rural and urban poverty in Mozambique and the developing world in general. Therefore, only a few additional aspects should be mentioned here.

While colonialism in its various forms occurred world-wide for millennia, European colonialism can be dated back to the 15th century, shortly before the slave trade started, but it reached its peak, particularly in Africa, after the slave trade had ended (at least officially). Although colonies had existed in different forms for centuries, during the well known Berlin-Kongo Conference (from November 1884 to February 1885) the division of Africa among the European colonial powers was completed without any regard on local conditions. Indigenous peoples were divided, commercial routes interrupted and already existing economic units torn apart. Now the looting of Africa's natural resources became even more systematic and intensified under the supervision of imperialist states although private companies still had their share. Whether it was minerals, ivory or cash crops, all was transported from Africa to Europe to develop her industry and with it mainly the urban areas. Not only had Africa lost probably one fifth of its young, healthy women and men, it also suffered and still suffers from severe material losses. In addition, forced labour was introduced after the slave trade had ended and later this was changed to indirect forced labour via the poll and hut tax, as mentioned in chapter 2.

Peasants had to produce for the world market either in mines or on commercial farms or even had to sell the products of their family fields. They were often driven away from fertile soils to give way to commercial farms. Producing mainly for export, soon led to food shortages, a phenomenon which still has sad actuality. A new era of urbanization began in Africa, after the indigenous urbanization was to a large extent destroyed by the slave trade. This was also the time when rural-urban migration started, lasting until today and subject of this research.

Along with the unimaginable cruelty of colonial exploitation went the colonization of the mind of Africans and other peoples. This problem cannot be dealt with here, however, a few remarks should show, what was in the underdeveloped minds of politicians, philosophers or other influential people of the imperialist states, which made colonization possible and even justified it. To colonize people, it was not necessary to deprive them of the predicate 'human', it was 'sufficient' to consider them as inferior. Social Darwinism and racism were the widely accepted and hardly questioned doctrines. The influential people and large parts of the population of the colonial states supported their policies, and racism has by far not been overcome since then.

Two of the influential, classical German philosophers of the 18th and 19th century, Krammer (1998, 235-42) deals with, were Herder and Hegel. Herder (1744 – 1803), who was not only a philosopher but also a very influential writer, admitted that little was known at that time about Africa: 'hardly the coasts of the countries and these often not further than the bullets of the European cannons could reach' (Bollacher 1989, 231; quoted in Krammer 1998, 237). He makes, nevertheless, far reaching statements about Africans: their bodies are made for animal like lust and their chests are full of passion. Even though all this is to a large extent due to the hot climate, Africans are, nevertheless, not capable of a higher spirituality. As nature has made Africans as they are, we should only pity but not despise them[6] (Bollacher 1989, 236; quoted in Krammer 1998, 238) – which is an implicit justification to colonize them.

According to Hegel (1770 – 1831), Africans do not have any idea of objectivity such as God or objective laws. They put themselves into the highest position, therefore, nothing is human like in their character, because, according to Hegel, only when human beings are conscious of a higher being, they can respect each other. As Africans do not have this consciousness they despise each other. This becomes apparent in tyranny and slavery (which, according to Hegel, was worse within Africa than was the transatlantic slave trade, sic!) and cannibalism. The latter is according to Hegel directly related to an African principle according to which the very physical Africans see only voluptuousness in the human flesh. In Hegel's opinion Africans are unrestrained and this cannot be changed. They are not capable of any development.

In the opinion of Hegel Africa has no history. In his philosophy of history he stresses that the world is dominated by reason. In the world history the human mind is developing through self-knowledge. The essence of the human mind is freedom and the world history is determined by progress in the consciousness of freedom. Having no history is, therefore, necessarily connected with the lack of freedom and the ability for self-reflection.

Hegel not only depreciates Africans severely but justifies at the same time a European claim to govern the world, an attitude which necessarily leads to imperialism and would even justify the extinction of all African cultures as they have no chance to survive anyway (Krammer 1998, 241-2). There exists a direct link from the slave trade via colonialism to today's debt crisis, a modern form of slavery.

The debt crisis

The debt crisis is so serious for many African and also other developing countries, that the years from 1980 to 1990 are often called the 'lost development decade'. But also the current decade has brought little progress. In many developing countries the prices of staple exports have collapsed, import and investment levels were diminishing, growth rates were falling, there was widespread inability, especially in sSA, to service debts and arrears built-up. The debt burden of many of the low income countries of sSA, (34 of the 62 low income countries are in sSA and Mozambique is one of them) has become unsustainable (O'Neill 1990). For the low income countries the ratio of outstanding debts to exports of goods rose from 149 per cent in 1980 to 438 per cent by 1988. Outstanding debt for several countries in sSA was equivalent to the GDP, for others it was between 125 and 165 per cent, while it was 2.5 times the GDP for Zambia (Taylor 1990) it was 3.2 times the GDP in 1991 for Mozambique (Wellmer 1992). The debt problem in Africa must be seen in the context of drastic decline in export earnings and very sharp drops in net capital inflows. The growth of medium and long term debts grew fastest in sSA compared to any other region. These debts grew from US$ 16 billion in 1974 to US$ 126 billion by the end of 1987 (Taylor 1990).

The indebtedness of the Third World in general is a symptom of the power of a few industrialized countries over many developing countries. It is the modern form of colonialism or even slavery. After 500 years of general exploitation, the debt crisis constitutes a new particular form of exploitation which prevents sustainable development for many countries and means absolute poverty with all its concomitants (as they were shown for Mozambique in the empirical part of this research) for more than a billion of people in the developing world (Hartwig and Jungfer 1990, 7; Nohlen and Nuscheler 1993, 23).

From 1980 to 1990 the flow of financial resources from the South to the North, to governments, private banks or international organizations amounted to US$ 1,528 billion but the flow of financial resources from the North to the South was only US$ 1,195, which leaves a net payment from the South to the North of US$ 333 billion (Kraemer 1994, 146), in other words the South was developing the North. Even though this flow of financial resources from the South to the North ended in 1993, debt repayment remains an extremely heavy burden for the South.

Both parties involved in the current debt crisis, the creditors, i.e. the industrialized countries, their governments, their private banks, and 'their' international organizations (as the IMF and World Bank are completely dominated by the North), as well as the debtors, the developing countries, could be made responsible for it as the former failed by careless lending and the latter by careless borrowing.

However, it was not only carelessness on both sides. After the first oil crisis in the 1970s oil producing countries deposited their additional financial resources in Western banks and by doing so endangered the banking system. It was feared the system would suffer from a similar collapse as it occurred in the 1930s. The West was desperately looking for borrowers and what is now called careless borrowing of the developing countries was actually the rescue of the Western banking system. Neither the United States nor the IMF, but the developing countries saved the West. The IMF and Western governments advised the developing countries to borrow because interest rates were low. They also assured the latter that they would be able to pay back their loans because prices for raw material would remain stable or even rise as, for instance, the copper prices of Zambia. Nobody foresaw any rise of interest rates. Developing countries needed capital badly either to industrialize – as, for example, the Latin

American countries – or start to build an economy from scratch – as, for example, a number of countries in Southern Africa as they were left with, so to speak, no economy at their political independence (Kaunda in Sauer et al. 1998). Therefore, a burden sharing approach between creditors and debtors in this debt crisis would not be appropriate as the failures of the industrialized countries are much more serious and the South has been forced long enough to develop the North.

At a meeting of the Western Allies still during the Second World War in 1944 in Bretton Woods the IMF and the World Bank were created (therefore often also called the two Bretton Woods Institutions) in order to create a new economic world order and prevent a new recession similar to the one in the 1930s. At that time nobody knew what role they would be playing for the Third World from the 1970s onwards. Their role became a powerful one, particularly since 1982 when Mexico declared her insolvency, which was the starting point of the current severe debt crisis. This does not mean that many states had foreign debts before and Latin American and other states had declared their insolvency several times from the first half of the nineteenth century to the beginning of the Second World War (Firlus 1988). However, the current crisis is more severe and of a different nature and affects incomparably more people. Its origin, as mentioned above, dates back to 1973 when OPEC increased the price for oil, it was the first time that Third World countries showed their power over the industrialized world, but, unfortunately, they deposited their profits in the banks of the West. The companies and entrepreneurs of the West did the same. Because of the recession in the industrialized countries, they did not engage in new investments. Therefore, the banks were desperate to look for borrowers and developing countries were all too willing to borrow. The capital was needed to start the process of industrialization and to create a new infrastructure. From export earnings, it was reasoned, the debts could be repaid. However, hardly any country managed to do so. Most became highly indebted within a decade. Apart from the high oil prices, which constituted a heavy burden for all non-OPEC developing countries, it was the rising interest rates which made repayment more and more difficult. The above mentioned drop of the prices for raw material and the deteriorating terms of trade did the rest. In 1985 Tanzania, for instance, had to export the double amount of any crop, compared to 1975, in order to import one tractor (Hartwig and Jungfer 1990, 29). If prices for exports of African countries had risen to the same level as the prices for imports, then Africa would have been able to pay for all her imports without taking further loans and she would have been able to pay a considerable part of her debts and interests. Africa lost in terms of trade between 45 and 50 billion English Pounds from 1980 to 1992. For this loss of purchasing power incompetent, or even corrupt African leaders cannot be blamed. It had much more to do with developments in the North (Kaunda in Sauer et. al. 1998).

While Mozambique's debts were 3.2 times the GDP in 1991, they increased to 4.2 times the GDP in 1993 amounting to a total of US$ 5.3 billion. However, due to frequent rescheduling of debts, long term repayment, and low interest rates the debt service was at that time relatively low compared to other countries, at 20.6 per cent of export earnings, but much to high considering a GDP per capita of merely US$ 75 (Langthaler 1995, 3).

Mozambique's bilateral debts to countries belonging to the Paris Club make up for 35 per cent and those to other countries also 35 per cent. Debts to the World Bank were about 16 per cent and 12 per cent of the debts were owed to the IMF. As there is a general tendency of decline of bilateral and an increase of multilateral debts it was estimated that the percentage of debts which Mozambique owes to the IMF would be about 18 per cent in 1998 amounting to US$ 200 million (Kaiser and Mueller 1997).

At last the IMF, the World Bank and other regional development banks started to recognize the insustainability of the debt crisis particularly for the poorest countries and, therefore, the HIPC (Heavily Indebted Poor Countries) Initiative was launched in 1995 aiming at lowering the multilateral in accord with the bilateral debt burden for the first time. Unfortunately, it is intended to lower this burden not so much for the purpose of enabling the respective countries to achieve an independent, sustainable development but mainly for the purpose to re-install their ability to pay. Although it looks like a positive step forward to plan to relieve 90 per cent of Mozambique's debts, it is, on the other hand, still questionable, when a debt service/GDP ratio of 20 – 25 per cent and a stock of debt of 150 per cent of export earnings is considered acceptable for a war torn country like Mozambique suffering in addition from droughts and floods (Kaiser and Mueller 1997).

On 7 April 1998 the substantial amount of Mozambique's debt of US$ 1.4 billion was cancelled under the Heavily Indebted Poor Countries (HIPC) initiative debt relief programme of the IMF and the World Bank. However, this is, unfortunately, not at all a reason to rejoice. According to the Mozambique – and debt – expert, Hanlon, only those debts were cancelled which could never ever have been paid back anyway. The rest of the debts and interests have to be paid back under the same inhuman conditions as during the last years. Mozambique had to spend more money on debt and interest repayment ($ 7.45 per person, per year) than she spent on health and education ($ 6.76 per person, per year). According to IMF figures, which have been released only after a long struggle fought by the Mozambican debt initiative, Jubilee 2000 Coalition, Mozambique gains merely 80 US *cents* per person, per year. According to British Treasury figures Mozambique gains nothing at all. And this deal took one year of intensive negotiations, was bitterly opposed by the then conservative German government and could only be reached when Brazil and Britain where ready to put in an extra US$ 10 million each.

Germany objected that Mozambique's debt service payment would be brought down to four times the level Germany paid after the London Agreement in 1953, when it was granted to her to pay 3.5 per cent of export earnings only. Mozambique is also a post war country, which suffered $ 20 billion damage in the war, backed mainly by apartheid South Africa but also by certain circles of the West including Germany (Hanlon in Sauer 1998, 218-21).

Mozambique shows clearly that the debt relief programme on offer now is totally insufficient. Debts for the poorest, most indebted countries must simply be cancelled.

'A 1 percentage point increase in average share of GDP invested in health and education is estimated to reduce ... the child mortality rate by 24 percentage points' (Human Development Report 1996, 113). So, increasing spending on health and education by 2.5 per cent of GDP would halve child mortality. A similar fall in maternal mortality can be assumed. As Mozambique's debt service is over 6 per cent of GDP, 3 additional percentage points for health and education, would surely halve child and maternal mortality. Each year it would save the lives of 115,000 children and 6,000 mothers giving birth (Hanlon in Sauer 1998, 219).

The HIPC initiative is based on a concept of sustainability meaning the amount a country can pay back without defaulting. Mozambique is supposed to pay the same debt service in the future as it has been paying in the past on the costs of hundreds of thousands of lives and incredible poverty and misery.

The structural adjustment programmes

As many other developing countries during the last two decades, Mozambique had to agree to the introduction of SAPs in 1987. These programmes were and are similar for most Third World countries but Mozambique is probably the only one, where it was introduced during wartime. In Mozambique as in many other developing countries the IMF and the World Bank ignored external factors which were and are just as much or even more responsible for the enormous economic problems, such as the unfavourable terms of trade, the low prices for raw material or the debt crisis.

Between 1970 and 1980 the debt crisis was one of the reasons why developing countries became particularly vulnerable for the demands of their powerful creditors, especially the United States and the United Kingdom, where exactly at that time influential neo-liberal politicians were in power. Both these facts led to the domination of neo-liberal ideas in the development debate of the 1980s and thereafter so that structural adjustment could be equated with the forcible inclusion into neo-liberalism. Without the long political tenure of the Reagan and Thatcher governments the debt crisis would probably have been approached in a much less recessionary way. But the neo-liberal ideas were spreading far beyond the USA and the UK and gave the international aid donors an unprecedented influence to shape both, the macro economy and the social policy in the developing countries (UNRISD 1995, 37).

Today the macro economy as well as the social policy are dominated by inhuman competition as the highest principle of the world market is economic efficiency. According to this principle industrialized countries are awarded and developing countries rigorously punished. Countries with a labour productivity above the world's average make profits, those with a labour productivity below that level constantly lose. Unless one is of the opinion that it is the fault of the developing countries themselves when they have a labour productivity far below the world's average, one must see that the competition is extremely unfair as the poorest countries with a productivity level hundred times below the world's average have to compete openly with the industrialized countries who have a productivity of labour many times above the average (Golansky 1996). SAPs must also be seen against this background. Nobody denies that most economies of the Third World must be restructured and made more efficient, but this could also be done in a much more just and human way.

The forerunners of SAPs in the first post war decades were often called stabilization programmes. Government saving schemes were worked out between developing countries and their creditors. They included amongst others:
- the reduction of state expenditures which often resulted in the cancelling of unproductive projects and reduced the budget deficit;
- they included incentives to increase traditional exports and the development of new export activities in order to gain more foreign exchange and improve the balance of trade;
- the freezing of wages and salaries, the devaluation of the currency, and the limiting of the amount of money in circulation in order to fight inflation;
- a general restructuring and increase of taxes so that also those with higher income could not evade them (Kraemer 1994, 150-1; UNRISD 1995, 37).

However, in the following decades these earlier stabilization measures were accompanied by ever more rigid loan conditions. SAPs were forced upon the debtor countries as without adhering to the demands of the IMF and the World Bank neither any new private nor any new state nor any new international credits would be granted.

The debtor countries were forced to lower the trade barriers drastically, exposing local producers to foreign competition. They had to reduce or eliminate subsidies and price controls in order to remove 'distortions' in local prices for goods and services. Controls on capital movements had to be abolished and state owned enterprises privatized. The debtor countries were forced to remove controls on private foreign investment and adhere to a completely open door policy. In the management of the economy as well as in the provision of social services state intervention had to be minimized (UNRISD 1995, 38).

It was expected to carry out these reforms quickly and simultaneously, because they would reinforce each other. It was feared that gradualism could lead to organized dissent.

> Neo-liberal advisors had a vision of the ideal: its economy would be largely self-regulating through open competition between private firms; and its public sector would be relatively passive – providing the minimum services necessary to conduct private business efficiently and to protect societies weakest members. *This picture unfortunately corresponded to no known place on earth – not to any of the industrial countries of the North, and*

certainly not to any of the developing countries (UNRISD 1995, 38; emphasis by the author).

As criticism increased (Aldermann 1990, Prendergast 1991, Adepoju 1991, Scott 1992) the IMF and World Bank themselves had to react with a number of programmes to protect the poor during the period of adjustment; however, these measures were by far not sufficient. While it must be acknowledged that a number of elements of SAPs were and are necessary to improve the economic performance of the Third World countries, too many measures had and still have negative, often disastrous effects. The most negative feature is the fact that they hit the poorest strata of society hardest, as was shown for Mozambique in chapter 3 and chapter 10.

Trying to increase and exploit existing national resources, another element of SAPs, can and often does lead to the destruction of the environment if economic growth is to be achieved at all costs without putting the main concern on sustainable development. SAPs indirectly also worsen the ecological problem as the richest as well as the poorest in this world harm the environment most, the former knowingly, the latter because of lack of any other alternative, and neo-liberal policies increase income disparities within and between nations world-wide. Weak but not completely unimportant examples are the firewood problem and the burning of waste by the poor, discussed in the empirical part.

Freezing wages and salaries often lowers inflation drastically and increases the ability of the economies to compete internationally. However, this means at the same time also a lowering in real terms of the already extremely low wages of the lower strata in the urban areas and of those who are engaged in wage labour in the rural areas. How low these wages are in Mozambique, we saw in chapter 3. According to an ILO study in the 1980s in 28 African countries, the real minimum wage fell by 20 per cent. In LA the real minimum wages fell by 50 per cent (ILO/JASPA 1990). As a result, in recent years salaries and wages have formed a much lower proportion of income. Wages are so low in many countries that an annual income is only sufficient to support one or two months of subsistence. Meanwhile the formal working class is shrinking – in Sierra Leone, Tanzania and Zambia, for example, waged employees now constitute in average only 16 per cent of the urban labour force (UNRISD 1995, 45). In this regard, Mozambique could well be an exception, because of its socialist legacy, where formal employment is extraordinary high. About three fifths of the household heads are formally employed. Even though this proportion is not comparable with the entire labour force, it gives at least a hint of a probably considerable difference. Yet, as wages are so low that in most families of the lower income group two or three people have to work in order to survive and malnourishment is widespread, just a higher degree of formal employment does not solve any problem and the SAP measure of freezing extremely low wages is even more painful. The answer can only be: freezing the higher and constantly raising the minimum wages.

Reduction of state expenditures hits the poorest hardest, and they are the majority in the countryside. When school fees are introduced and medical care is no longer free for the poor, no human security and not even a minimum of quality of life is guaranteed. The answer can only be: collect fees from those who are able to pay and not from the poor (Braunmuehl 1988). 'Hundreds of thousands of the developing world's children have given their lives to pay their countries' debts, and many millions more are still paying the interest with their malnourished minds and bodies.' (UNICEF 1989, 30).

The cancelling of state subsidies results in a higher state income from transport, electric currency and other public services, however, particularly where transport for going to work is concerned, it hits the poorest hardest and here exceptions are absolutely necessary. Several riots occurred in Maputo in the mid 1990s, when bus fares and particular mini-bus fares were raised.

A general increase of taxes constitutes additional burdens for the poor and this must not only be rejected from an ethical point of view but it also keeps the country poor as in this way the majority is neither able to partake in any substantial consumption nor in saving.

Liberalization of food prices gives incentives for the farmers to increase their food production (but hardly to the peasants whose produce has often been subsidized); however, this makes it impossible for the urban poor to buy enough food, not even enough of their staple food (Kreamer 1994, 150-1).

As is well known, this measure has led to food riots in several developing countries. And as was shown in the empirical part, food is one of the main problems in all three investigated areas in Mozambique.

In spite of all these serious problems, SAPs can not be completely condemned, but also not accepted without criticism at least concerning the way they were implemented. In future it must be possible to combine the objective of increasing the economic efficiency of anyone country with the objective of increasing social security of the poorer strata, of implementing

SAPs with a human face (Jolly and Haven 1991), and the IMF, World Bank, and international donors for the ailing economies must consider the external factors more seriously than internal economic inefficiency, even though nobody will doubt that the latter must be corrected as well. However, as SAPs were implemented so far, they constitute a root cause for poverty and the sufferings of the lower strata – in Mozambique the majority of the population. However, SAPs are a root cause for poverty also in many other developing countries.

The failure of rural development programmes

'Why poor people stay poor: urban bias in world development' was the title of Michael Liptons publication of 1977, 'poor people' meaning the rural population of the developing countries. Its main thesis, presented in a very simplified manner, was: the rural classes stay poor because they are exploited by the urban classes. Later (1984) Lipton differentiated his oversimplified view as he had to respond to a wide range of criticism. Then he mentions the large farmers or the rural elites in general who align with urban interests (Gugler 1988, 34). Although exploitation is possible even amongst the poor in some cases, it is hardly imaginable, how the poor urban population as a whole can substantially exploit the poor rural population. Not even the people living in the fully urbanized areas do directly exploit the rural areas, at least not in their function as city dwellers. Exploitative is the capitalist system and its structure as such. Crehan hits the point, when she writes:

> Just as developing countries do not represent some prior stage of historical development but have been subject to a process of underdevelopment which distorted their economies and created patterns of dependence, so rural areas do not represent the original economy out of which urbanization, industrialization and the rest evolved, but are the residue left when whole sections of production – and production in the full sense of reproduction of a whole social, economic and political system – have been extracted so that what was a more or less autonomous socio-economic unit is reduced to a subordinate part dominated by a more powerful and dynamic capitalist industrial sector (Crehan 1981).

Therefore, rural poverty persists, unfortunately, throughout the Third World in-spite of more than four decades of different strategies of rural development programmes. Following mainly Benterbusch 1988 it should be shown briefly how these programmes themselves, their misconception and their shortcomings in implementation constitute also a root cause for the persistence of rural poverty.

In the 1950s Community Development was much propagated. However, it was wrong already in its concept: the consideration of traditional behaviour as the main cause for poverty overlooked the unequal structures and with it the differential disposition over resources as determinants of poverty. Several implementation blockades contributed to the failure as, for instance, the attempt of decentralization to bring about more political influence to the lower strata which was never really put into practice (Benterbusch 1988, 38).

After the 'green revolution' in the 1960s a new multi-sector concept was started at the end of the 1970s and the beginning of the 1980s, now called 'integrated rural development' which tried to expand the 'green revolution' to the peasants and even marginal peasants.

However, only recently the necessity of active participation of the target groups of rural development, the rural poor themselves, was recognized as well as the importance of the role of international and national Non-Governmental Organizations (NGOs). Apart from some isolated success stories, in general we can observe that the frequent change of strategies did not bring any victory in the struggle against rural poverty, mainly because national as well as international economic, political, and social structural problems were hardly taken into account (Benterbusch 1988, 2).

In addition to the inadequacy of the strategies and the technical deficits of implementation, Benterbusch distinguishes three blockades of implementation. First, the complete lack of influence of the rural poor on the allocation of resources on the national level and the very limited influence on the local level. Second, the dependency of the rural poor on the local elites, who are patronized by the powerful of the state also in the distribution of development aid. Third, the autonomous position of the local administration, which is not obliged to allocate the resources for the benefit of the poor.

Peil & Sada have analyzed this problem in a similar way. They see a problem in the stationing of bureaucrats in large villages to supervise tax collection and services:

These civil servants seldom have ties to the village and are often from another part of the country. Their major orientation is toward the city, and most hope for eventual promotion for an urban position. The officers, clerks, and teachers represent urban power structures, and their dominance in many village situations demonstrates to the villagers the triumph of urban ways (Peil and Sada 1984, 42).

According to Benterbusch, these structural blockades can only be overcome if those in power, on the national as well as on the local level, show interest in getting rid of them. This interest exists mainly then when there is a direct connection between the decision makers and the majority of the rural poor, the rural lower strata, and if the decision makers can be democratically controlled via elections.

The situation of the rural lower strata in developing countries is characterized, as already mentioned, by having no political influence, of being socially weak compared to other social strata, and of not being able to increase the income by their own efforts. Successful development is not possible without the state. Here again SAPs exercise a negative influence by weakening the state.

Notes

1. In spite of the ostracism of slavery by the human rights convention of the UN in 1948, too many slavery-like dependencies of people on other people exist. There is the enormous problem of forced child labour, there are still traders who trade with human beings and enterprises in Europe and North America, who capture unemployed men of the peri-urban areas of the mega cities of Brazil and sell them to the commercial farmers (Brockhaus 1998, 294). There is also the well-known trade with women who are supposed to work as prostitutes, and labour conditions in the capitalist system are sometimes not far away from slavery. According to a German newspaper, *Die Zeit,* in more than 40 states around the globe slavery still exists. The victims are always poor, politically weak, uneducated, mainly women and children (Die Zeit, 26 April 1996, 11).
2. The main source areas of the Atlantic slave trade were: Guinea-Bissao, Guinea, Sierra Leone, Liberia, Ivory Coast, Ghana, Togo, Benin Nigeria, Cameroon, Equatorial Guinea, Gabon, Congo, the Democratic Republic of Congo, Angola, Mozambique, Madagascar (Loth, 1981, 30).
3. Ki-Zerbo (1979, 228-9) mentions seven authors of which only two remain below 60 million in their estimates of human beings Africa has lost during the slave trade. His own estimate is also 50 to 100 million.

4

year	population in millions	year	population in millions
1000	50	1800	90-100
1200	61	1850	95-100
1400	74	1900	120-150
1600	90	1920	140
1650	100	1930	164
1750	95-100	1940	191

Sources: Hance 1970,16; table and source adopted from Krammer 1998, 86, who used additional sources.

5 One of the most important slave uprisings was in Bois Calman on the then French colony of Santo Domingo in the night of August 22/23 1791. Therefore, August 23 was chosen as international day for the remembrance of the slave trade and its abolition.

6 On the other hand, Herder could also be considered a cultural relativist when he states that basically all cultures have the same value and just as we (he apparently means himself and many of his contemporaries) consider Africans as the decendants of the cursed son of Chams, as monsters, so Africans could consider their cruel robbers (the Europeans) as Albinos and white Satans, who have only out of weakness of nature become so degenerated like animals near the North Pole (Bollacher 1989, 228; quoted in Krammer 1998, 236).

12 Aspects of an alternative development and an alternative globalization

> What will replace the capitalist world-economy eventually may be better, but it could be worse. Thus we have reason neither for despair nor for celebration. Nonetheless, there is one fundamentally encouraging element. The outcome will be the result of our collective effort, largely as expressed by the work of the new anti-systemic movements. Whereas before large fluctuations resulted in small changes (hence the determinism, hence the disillusionment with the outcomes of reformism, even when called 'revolution') now small fluctuations will result in big changes (hence the opening for true 'agency', hence the responsibility we all bear) (Wallerstein 1992, 15).

The following themes are only a selection of many other possible themes, they were to some extent chosen arbitrarily and are in themselves only sketches. To some of them a lot of literature exists already, others are completely or to a large extent under-researched, as the reparation for the slave trade or urban agriculture. Nevertheless, each theme – even if only a sketch – does claim to show alternatives to the status quo, a development and globalization process in favour of the marginalized. The topics are supposed to give an answer – however imperfect – to the issues raised in the last chapter and in the empirical part. The proposed solutions are not revolutionary, unfortunately not, as the development of only a blueprint of a real revolutionary global alternative to the existing capitalist world system would be a huge, separate project altogether, which one person could hardly complete. Social scientists of various fields should be encouraged to engage in such an endeavour. We urgently need a real alternative. Many socialist thinkers, particularly the classics, would have to be re-written and the enormous societal changes that have occurred since, would have to be taken into account.

Wallerstein's observation, that we have entered an era where small fluctuations can result in big changes allow the interpretation, that some of the following suggested solutions could result in big changes, no matter how deeply reformist they are. It is a question of interpretation, whether they are even anti-systemic or not. They are not anti-systemic in the sense that a real reparation for the slave trade, the total cancellation of the Third World's debts, a different implementation of SAP, the end of protectionism, a different approach to rural development, flourishing greenbelts around all Third World cities and agriculture on all open spaces within the cities, the development of secondary urban centres, functioning regional unions of states, and even the eradication of poverty would not necessarily endanger the capitalist system. It is unfortunate, that the powerful of this system have not started to understand yet, that their system would function even better, if all these measures would be taken. This lack of understanding bears as its consequence the lack of a political will for constructive changes. On the other hand, could a system without poverty, with equality and social justice, where people are self-determined and liberated, still be called a capitalist system? A capitalist system with a human face? Is this possible or would such a system already have surpassed itself and be a different system, a socialist system with a human face or could it be given any other name? The questions must be left unanswered here.

Reparations for the slave trade

The crime of the slave trade can never be repaired, but it would only be a minimum of fairness to do something for the descendants of those who have survived the tragedy, in this case it would mean to Africa as a whole.

Reparation in the sense of making amends or giving satisfaction for a wrong doing or injury is a standard practice in international law, the UN negotiates it and the international court of justice orders it. Some nations wilfully grant reparations; they are paying damages for injuries and wrong doings with land and money.

Germany helped Israel after the Second World War, although she was not obliged to do so. She also could not make undone the crime against the Jewish people during the Nazi-regime but the Germans felt their moral obligation (Soglo 1992). In addition, the UN granted a homeland to the Jews and the money paid to Jewish victims and their families will amount to about 200 billion DM in the year 2000 (Trudy, internet text 1998). More than 50 years after World War II the Austrian mass media are still full of reports about negotiations and court cases concerning compensation of Nazi-regime victims, as for instance, giving back their art objects, compensation for forced labour etc. Why should we not start an even more intensive discussion about the possibilities of a reparation for the slave trade?

Trudy lists numerous other examples of reparations: Native Americans have received more than 1 billion US Dollars for stolen land and broken treaties, Japanese who have survived the internment camps during World War II have also received 1 billion US Dollars of compensation and a formal apology. Who has ever apologized to Africa for the crime of the slave trade? In 1976 Australia gave its Aborigines more than 96.000 square miles of land after appropriating it during European settlements in the 18th and 19th centuries. Alaskans were also compensated with nearly 1 billion US Dollars and 44 million acres of land through the Alaska Native Claim Settlement Act. The Canadian government was more or less forced by the United Nations to return 260,000 square miles of land to certain native people and to give them the right to an autonomous government and Iraq pays millions on oil revenue to Kuwait (Trudy, internet text 1998).

The columnist Trudy writes mainly in favour of a reparation/compensation to 40-50 million African Americans for the enslavement of their ancestors. He demands a modest 5 billion of the 200 billion US Dollars of surplus which President Clinton expected in 1998. This is certainly justified, but the reparation, which Africa should receive, is just as urgent.

The African World Reparation and Repatriation Truth Commission is – according to its Accra declaration – planning to set up an international team of lawyers from Africa and the diaspora to collect no less than 777 *trillion* US Dollars from Europe and the Americas in reparation for enslaving Africans while colonizing the continent. The money would be collected from all those nations and institutions of Western Europe and the Americas which participated and benefited from the slave trade and colonialism. At least some justice should be done through monetary compensation with the help of the UN and the OAU. Interest should be paid on the money due. A world-wide monitoring and networking system should be instituted to ensure that reparation and repatriation will be achieved by 2004. All those in the diaspora, who wanted to return and settle in Africa, should be allowed to do so and those who enslaved and colonized Africa should provide seaworthy vessels and aircraft for such repatriation (Hipolito and Soeiro, August 24, 1999).

The amount of 777 trillion US Dollars might not be reached, but a reparation of 7 trillion US Dollars would already help Africa a great deal, if the money is used for poverty eradication and proper development. The attempts to reach compensation for the slave trade should be combined with the demand for an end to the debt crisis. In fact, according to the Accra declaration there is no African debt and the so-called international debt owed by Africa must be unconditionally cancelled.

Resolving the debt crisis

The literature on the debt crises has grown to the unmanageable, but all the analyses, proposals and models – be it the Brady-plan, the Debt-Equity-Swap, the Debt-for-Nature and Debt-for-Development-Swap or the Conditions of Naples,[1] all these attempts have until recently only led to the cancellation of a ridiculous half per cent of the entire debt load (Becker 1996). However, in the last two years a number of positive developments were observed. Under the pressure of a number of movements, particularly the Jubilee 2000 Coalition, the issue is on the programme on each G-7 (Group of seven industrial countries) economic summit and substantial amounts of debts have been cancelled, unfortunately so far mainly those debts which could never ever have been paid back anyway. This is insufficient. It is therefore essential to support initiatives, such as the Jubilee 2000 of the South and the North, the European network on debt and development (Eurodad) or Action Aid,[2] which also support Jubilee 2000 and demand the cancellation of the unpayable dept.

The aim of debt cancellation for the 41 HIPC (heavily indebted poor countries) as well as for the 21 HIMC (heavily indebted middle income countries) is ambitious, but not unrealistic. According to the HDR of 1997 the debt burden of the HIPC could be lifted for the cost of one Stealth bomber or the cost of the amusement park, Eurodisney, in France. The costs would only be around 15 billion US Dollar. These costs appear really low also when set into relation to the 13 billion US Dollar loan which the European Development Bank granted very quickly to the Eastern European problems.

In order to reach the goal of complete debt cancellation, it is crucial that the citizens of the creditor countries support the demand, because they must bear the cancellation with their taxes. So, it is equally crucial, that the people get enlightened about the small amount involved. The amount each

Austrian, for example, would have to pay per month for the next 10 years, after all debts having been cancelled, is a ridiculously little sum of about two US Dollars, the price of a soft drink (Neuwirth in Amon and Liebmann 1998).

To lift the debt burden for Africa would cost less than 1 billion US Dollars per year over the next few years. This very small sum in global terms the IMF and the donor countries do not even need. The countries of the North would not even notice debt cancellation. But Africa would notice. Life would change for everyone. SAPs are often the cause for additional problems and mass poverty. SAPs will not work as long as countries are burdened by an overhang with debt. Debt is a modern form of slavery, in fact it is the most potent form of it. Just as the slave trade was not abolished or political independence not brought about by technical experts, economists or financiers, so the technically insoluble debt crisis, the unpayable debts, will not be solved without an appropriate public opinion, a social outrage of ordinary people which will compel politicians to end the crisis (Kaunda in Sauer et al. 1998). This is exactly the aim of Eurodad and Action Aid. They demand from the EU (European Union)[3] to play a co-ordinated leading role in developing a comprehensive strategy for long term debt management with debtor governments. The EU must push for a more flexible swift and substantial debt relief, as substantial debt relief is a prerequisite for a successful debt management. The EU must give a good example for other creditors and publish annual creditor tables in order to allow for greater transparency in debt relief negotiations.

> In the new global market place, development will only be sustainable if it is built on strong foundations-policies for economic reform that are based on transparency, openness, good corporate governance and a concentration of resources on what matters – education, health and poverty reduction (Brown 1998, 107-8).

The debt management process should be opened up to greater scrutiny and information sharing. While outstanding repayments are reported publicly on an annual basis by the World Bank in its *Global development financial tables* (formerly known as the *World debt tables*), it is difficult to obtain information from the creditor side.

Greater institutional and financial support is needed to debtor governments and appropriate civil society organizations to built their debt management capacity. With a weak debt management capacity debtor governments are at a considerable disadvantage when negotiating. It is not possible to make fully informed decisions without being fully aware of the amount of debt owed, the debt to export ratios and the consequences of the terms of agreement with creditors. Also civil society organisations are at a disadvantage without full information about debt management techniques. Soft ware programmes used to calculate essential base-line debt statistics need to be made more user friendly particularly for the debtor countries. Debt swaps for debt management capacity building would be a possibility.

It is necessary to establish an international debt management commission (IDC) to monitor lending, borrowing, and debt management practices. This commission would have to promote transparency in debt relief negotiations and debt management, support debt management capacity building, and stimulate constructive policy discussions on key debt management issues. The commission would have to determine amongst others, whether borrowed resources are invested efficiently to support social development, income generation, and productive economic capacity as well as whether debtor countries have the human resources and technical capacity to effectively manage debt accumulation and debt repayment. The IDC should publicly release an annual report with key statistics on international lending and borrowing and debt accumulation and serve as a think tank and consultative mechanism on key policy issues related to debt management (Eurodad and Action Aid in Sauer et al. 1998).

Alternatives to SAP

According to Macamo, alternatives to SAP in Mozambique (and some of his approaches are certainly applicable to other developing countries) would mean the 'reinvention of politics'. This reinvention of politics is necessary, because the IMF, the World Bank and the 'development bureaucracy' of the numerous aid agencies (180 of these agencies were present in 1990; Hanlon 1991, 60) have deprived the Mozambican state of its sovereignty and have trivialized its politics. On the one hand, it is so much in the grip of the 'development bureaucracy' that actually all political parties are required to believe in the same economic wisdom of the dominant financial institutions and the political class cannot respond to its electorate on issues which really matter to the people. On the other hand, there are loopholes in this system and, according to Macamo, it is absolutely necessary to identify and exploit these loopholes, so that the Government can enjoy – at least there – a relatively full scope for its own action. While Macamo acknowledges that Mozambique needs the IMF, the World Bank, and the aid agencies because many people more would have died without them, there would not have been another shot of development and there would not have been hope for further foreign investment and economic credibility abroad, he, on the other hand, points out that those institutions also need Mozambique. SAP cannot be abandoned because for many institutions the only raison d'etre is SAP. Bureaucracies are not only concerned with a means-end rationality, they must also legitimate themselves, they must reproduce themselves. Letting SAP appear with a 'human face' (Cornia et al. eds 1990), giving the impression that one is doing something against the inequities produced by adjustment – by introducing school meals, for instance, – has only given more life to these institutions and has been rightly labelled 'charity approach'. Macamo sees one way out of all these dilemmas, apart from identifying and exploiting loopholes of the system for appropriate political actions, in finding a relevant concept of citizenship which might be used to define the nature of politics under adjustment or alternatives to it. Such a concept would overcome any charity approach. It would include apart from legal and political rights also a bundle of social rights, so that the Mozambican people – or any people of developing countries – could organize themselves and have, for instance, reasoned debates at their disposal instead of riots (which are only crushed down by the police anyway) after each devaluation of the currency and each price rise (Macamo 1996). This argument will be resumed below when discussing rural development.

Abolition of protectionism

Protectionism of the North is one of the most unfair, inhuman and cruel forms of oppressing the Third World, preventing development and maintaining poverty. It must be abolished to give way to an alternative globalization. Countries in the North do not only protect their markets, particularly their agricultural markets, they also heavily subsidize them. However, the governments of the North and the IMF tell the African countries to take away subsidies from their peasants who depend on them. Developing countries are forced via the SAPs to open their markets for foreign imports but the markets of the North remain closed for imports of manufactured goods from the South.

Through the forced opening of their economies for subsidized agricultural products from industrial countries, the peasants of poor countries are exposed to an overwhelming, extremely unfair competition. An example should illustrate the point. After the Uruguay Round the Philippines were forced to halve the import tax and allow a higher quantity of maize from the United States to be imported. The price of maize will be 30 per cent below the current prices in the Philippines. This will deprive a large proportion of peasants on the island Mindanao – where half the population already lives below the poverty line – of the rest of their livelihood. In the US maize farmers receive a subsidy of $ 29,000 per capita per year. The per capita income in Mindanao is $ 300 per year. So, a US maize farmer receives about one hundred times more on subsidies than a person in Mindanao on income. Those who are convinced that the liberalization of trade will in the long run raise the average income should also think of the human costs. For the people in Mindanao the words of Keynes: 'in the long run we will all be dead', have a very real meaning (HDR 1997, 104).

Agriculture is the only section of international trade in which export dumping is accepted.[4] On numerous commodities from developing countries anti-dumping measures were imposed. There are only vague regulations which can hardly justify the anti-dumping measures. Just as complete debt cancellation would harm the North not at all, commodity imports from the South would not ruin their economies. A study of the OECD found that in 90 per cent of the anti-dumping measures the national industries of the US and the EU would not have been threatened if the commodities from the developing countries would have been allowed to be imported (HDR 1997, 105).

According to the HDR of 1992 *developing countries lose about 500 billion US Dollars per year because of unequal access to trade, labour markets and financial resources; this is ten times more than they receive in development aid per year.* The argument that the benefits of globalization will in any case trickle down to the poorest countries is very questionable, as long as we do not move towards an alternative globalization.

For many states, particularly for sSA, the disadvantages of globalization outweigh the benefits by far. This applies to an even greater extent to the poor of a state and here particularly to the poor of the rural areas, as we have been able to show for Mozambique in the empirical investigation.

From a trade, development, and co-operation agreement between the EU and South Africa also the rest of the countries of the Southern African

Development Community (SADC; see paragraph on development regionalism in this chapter) would benefit. Free trade agreement between the SADC states is supposed to be reached in the year 2004. If an agreement between the EU and South Africa could be achieved the latter would lower the customs faster than the other countries so that within a few years SADC would be a free trade area. Unfortunately, even the 21st round of negotiations in 1998 did still not yield final results. The main reason is European protectionism. The EU is heavily subsidising her agriculture and unwilling to include South Africa's agricultural products into the free trade agreement. However, trade with these products is very important for South Africa and the European market would not at all be threatened by them. In 1994 a factory for tinned fruits had to be closed in South Africa because the products could not compete against the heavily subsidised ones of the EU and customs were too high (Leonhard citing Hanekom, 1998).

Less rural disadvantages and less urban problems

The level of urbanization as such is not a cause for rural poverty but the stagnation of rural development. The way out of this stagnation would only lead via a change in the global economic structure which would have to include a loosening of the constrains SAP is imposing on the states of the Third World.

If the states would not be hampered so much by SAP, they would have the proper instruments to its disposal leading to an integration of the rural lower strata into the development process. Not free market forces, but proper state intervention to organize a market beneficial to both the rural and the urban poor would be part of the solution. The question is not so much, market or state, but rather which role each one of them has to play. The state could intervene bureaucratically and it could carry the relevant laws into effect. By allowing social and political opposition the rural poor could also gain a voice in the development process (Benterbusch 1988, 12).

One necessary measure the state has to carry out in the process of rural development, is the decentralization of power and resources, on the one hand, while maintaining a central role in many aspects, on the other hand. Decentralization is possible in different political systems. In Zambia, for instance, in the late 1970s and early 1980s under Kaunda's one party system and his state philosophy of humanism a country-wide educational reform was discussed even in the remotest rural areas. During the same time period communist China launched successful campaigns mobilizing the peasants who obtained in this way more power and more resources. It is fruitless to carry out merely organizational decentralization without any financial support. However, distributing grants only to rural districts and municipalities without strengthening the institutions there, without educational measures and capacity building would also not achieve real development. It must also be possible in rural areas not only in urban regions, to organize citizenship forums and to develop consensus agreements on programmes to combat poverty and marginalization and to balance local interests with regional interests (compare Thorns 1999).

One of the many possibilities of mobilization and political education in the rural areas was introduced in Mozambique shortly after independence and is being re-assumed now: mobile cinemas. They are supposed to bring information and entertainment to 'places God forgot', areas were there are no televisions or video sets, let alone conventional cinemas. Only 22 per cent of the households in the rural areas have a radio (Triebkorn 1999, 77). However, since private operators are encouraged to run the mobile cinemas, one can be afraid that the films might not be too educational. President Chissano complained recently that the main part of the Mozambican TV-programme is filled with football and Brazilian soap operas (Hypolito de Jesus and Soeiro, ibonews, No. 439).

Of course, in order to combat poverty in the countryside, it needs more vigorous, comprehensive efforts, especially since too many of the powerful within the Third World and on the global level are not really interested in a radical change of the situation. Poverty and underdevelopment are still with us and organized efforts become ever more important, to increase control over resources and regulative institutions in given social situations, on the part of groups and movements of those hitherto excluded from such control (Pearce and Stiefel in Nebeleung 1986, 82).

In order to integrate the lower strata into the state, a long and comprehensive struggle is necessary, a struggle which goes beyond formal political participation. Unjust structures of power can only be changed by strengthening the opposition and the ability to carry out conflicts of the lower strata (Jessen and Nebelung 1987, 38).

> The so-called self-help projects – which can be useful in some cases – cannot bring any advantage to the country as a whole as long as the basic problems of the unjust distribution of income and the lack of self-determination in the economic and political sector of national life remain unresolved. This means

that all income generating projects must include education and organisational training, which can bring more power to the people (Mananzan 1988, 3).

One hope for an improvement of the rural situation in Mozambique is the planned co-operation with the movement of the landless (MST – movimento sem terra) of Brazil. The MST, a non-violent grassroots movement, was very successful in the last few years and could serve as a model for other nations in the southern hemisphere. More than three hundred thousand families have gained land through this movement. It provides the people with medical, agricultural and administrative training and helps establish schools and leadership classes. In spite of this remarkable success, it could not solve the huge problem of the landless in Brazil, where 1 per cent of the population owns 50 per cent of the land, while one fourth of the people live in conditions of the most abject poverty. Even though so many families gained land through the movement, more than four hundred thousand other small farmers have lost their plots and have nowhere to go but the streets. Although MST is a peaceful movement it is persecuted by the land owners and the government. Recently in one province alone 41 leaders have been thrown into jail on trumped up charges, and 6 have been tortured. In addition, the World Bank is now threatening the MST with extinction, because it does apparently not at all like such a successful alternative development[5] (Harbury in ibonews, 8th September 1999). One can only hope that the movement will, nevertheless, survive and the Mozambican peasants will learn a lot from their Brazilian counterparts.

Urban agriculture

However, organization and training would also be necessary among the urban poor. One of the essential actions towards a short term solution for the big problem of malnutrition, not only of Mozambique's but also of many other countries' peri-urban areas, would be urban agriculture. Here not only the people but also the city administrations have yet to start the process of learning how to overcome negative attitudes towards urban agriculture and how to support cultivators.

> Science and development work could not close the eyes towards the enormous gain on importance of urban agriculture, especially in Africa in the eighties, so that now there exists some literature on urban agriculture at least for most African capitals which confirms its continental spread and

importance. Nevertheless, the promotion of urban agriculture by local and international agencies is still in its beginnings (Streiffeler 1993).

In Mozambique like in many other African countries this initiative was started long ago by the people themselves out of necessity. Forty-five per cent of the households in the peri-urban areas of the two investigated cities have a field (38 per cent in Maputo and 66 per cent in Beira).[6] However, this field produces the major part of the food only for 9 per cent of the households and half of the food for another 12 per cent; for the remaining 24 per cent less than half or even only very little is supplemented by urban agriculture.

It is likely that malnutrition is more widespread amongst the families who do not have a field. A research project carried out in Kenya from October 1984 to July 1985 found out that 65 per cent of the inhabitants of Nairobi produced food in rural or urban areas (Mazingira Institute 1987, quoted by Streiffeler 1993). However, this same Institute also found out that 55 per cent of the households had no household garden near the house and these were generally the poorest not living in the periphery who were thus forced to cultivate at the insecure 'open spaces' of the town and/or in the periphery (Streiffeler 1993). On the other hand, it has also been observed that the worse the economic situation of a city the more people have to resort to cultivation. This seems to receive support from the data of this research as Beira has a lower household income than Maputo and a much higher percentage do have a family field there. However, we must also bear in mind that Beira is surrounded by fertile soil and since the city is much smaller than Maputo, it is a lot easier to reach the fields.

In Lusaka it was found that more than half of the households in some low income areas cultivate plots near their shelter or elsewhere during the rainy season and this constitutes a vital food supplement. Also in Dar es Salaam many families cultivate plots within the city or in the surrounding rural areas (Hardoy and Satterthwaite 1989, 256).

We saw the crucial role which family fields can play in increasing the household budget in chapter 8 when discussing the situation of the female headed households.

> (Unfortunately) African urban agriculture is largely underdeveloped, despite its enormous social and ecological significance. This fact contrasts sharply with the situation in many Asian cities which can even entirely feed themselves as Yue (1985) has shown for Shanghai. It is a challenge for municipalities and national governments to proceed from 'indulgence' of

informal urban agriculture to its active promotion as also for international agencies to venture in this field. Since the rise of urban agriculture in the eighties is related to the structural adjustment programmes, it would be logical that the later added buffering programmes would have a special interest in urban agriculture (Streiffeler 1993).

Already fifteen years ago Jose Forjaz, the former Secretary of State for Physical Planning of Mozambique and now Dean of the School of Architecture and Physical Planning in Maputo, saw the need for urban agriculture when he wrote: 'we need urban planners who know how to plan a city of a million people that has to live on agriculture and still be the capital of the country' (Forjaz 1984).

It is a fallacy to think that urban space applies solely to habitation, public buildings, commercial areas and industries. This is also not the case in the European cities with numerous large parks and particularly it is not the case in some Asian cities as, for instance, the two Chinese cities of 'paradise', Suzhou and Hangzhou, where huge trees dominate the view in most parts over the hidden houses and buildings in most parts. In Ottawa a huge field for agricultural experiments has been established in the middle of the city.

As African cities cannot yet afford numerous parks, urban agriculture could make a contribution to the greening of cities and in this way help to overcome some of the environmental problems. Plants would filter the dust from the air, lower the temperature at noon and in the hot season, increase the humidity of the air without creating sultriness, and contribute to a better circulation of the air (Fellenberg 1991). Urban agriculture could also make use of waste water, even though the danger of pollution must be taken into account.

Besides the useful contribution to the environmental problems and the above mentioned alleviation of the nutrition problem, urban agriculture could also help to solve some of the hygiene problems by collecting organic waste, composting it and using it as fertilizer. This kind of fertilization would in addition strengthen the plants against diseases. Almost one third of the respondents in a survey in Kisangani mentioned plant pests and diseases as one of their main problems in urban agriculture (Streiffeler 1998).

Already in the 19th century the cities of Europe and their immediate hinterland were seen as cycles of nutrition, digestion, secretion and fertilization. It was proposed to collect human waste from every dwelling, carry it to a processing plant and turn it into manure, which could then be used to fertilize the soil of the surrounding farmlands, which in turn would produce the crops to feed the urban citizens (De Swaan 1999).

Because of the pollution of air, water, and soil, the heat stress, the decline of soil fertility and the lack of systematic plant rotation, plants in an urban area are particularly vulnerable towards diseases and it is in addition a specific feature of globalization, actually a negative side effect that, because of the higher degree of integration of urban areas into interregional and international areas, new diseases spread here more rapidly than in remote rural areas.

As mentioned above a lot of consciousness raising among urban administrators is still necessary so they will act in favour of urban agriculture. The lower the administrators in the hierarchy the more positive their attitude is already. Persons in charge of poor quarters know the urgent needs of their people and know the conditions to obtain votes. Urban planners should be aware of urban agriculture too and provide green zones and open spaces far away from polluting industries.

Secondary and intermediate towns and cities

Under the pressure of a globalizing world economy the policies of slowing down urban growth were more or less abandoned during the 1980s and the urban policies reformulated. The emphasis shifted from a policy of urban growth control to a policy of urban diffusion (Rondinelli 1991).

One aspect of this urban diffusion is the development of secondary and intermediate towns and cities. They could have a crucial function as economic, commercial and administrative centres. Through these regional power centres the needs and priorities of the local and regional population could be channelled to influence national policies (Hardoy and Satterthwaite 1986).

Secondary towns and cities could bridge the rural – urban gap and foster a more equal distribution of income within a developing country. Even the entire economic performance could improve via an appropriate development of this middle segment of the urban hierarchy. They would contribute to an environmentally more sustainable development and could smooth the process of socio-cultural transformation for migrants (Schneider and Vorlaufer 1990, 2). Secondary towns and cities could also be focal points of bottom-up and participatory forms of planning and development practice. They could contribute in achieving more balanced patterns as far as settlement structures, economic activities, incomes, and living conditions are concerned (Potter 1990). Secondary towns and cities could play a role as relief centres for the large urban agglomerations and serve as supply and development centres for the surrounding regions. Economic activities could thus be decentralized and local and regional markets developed which would stimulate rural development. Through such intermediate centres urban-rural linkages and social networks between them and their hinterland could be intensified. It is necessary to strengthen the administrative, financial and planning capacities of secondary cities, if they are to become real potentials for regional growth and development (Schneider and Vorlaufer 1998, 7-8).

There still are great differences between the developing countries in the implementation of 'urban diffusion' instead of the 'urban control' policy. In order to implement the former, more knowledge is needed about secondary towns and cities. They have often been neglected in empirical research in the past. Therefore, little is known about their real and potential role (Schneider and Vorlaufer 1998, 8). So, the comprehensive data on Beira of this research may be seen as a contribution to the facilitating of an urban diffusion policy in Mozambique.

However, also intensified efforts would be needed to develop all the other provincial capitals. A particular potential for such intermediate centres exists in Mozambique in its 68 small towns, called 'vilas' – mentioned in chapter 5 – which are already partly urban, partly rural and cannot be placed into one or the other category without difficulties. But exactly because of their already existing intermediate position, their development to viable socio-economic centres would be a real alternative development.

Development regionalism

Following the dependency theory, Hettne (1996) argues that the emerging world order is regionalized and constituted by core, intermediate regions and periphery. The new regional order further generates the disorder created on the sub-national level in the wake of globalization. Thus integration and disintegration are simultaneous processes, order and disorder paradoxically related. The structural gap between core and periphery could be reduced via security and development regionalism, which implies a substantial degree of interventionism in contrast to the neo-liberal hegemony established by the core. According to Hettne, the only way to become less peripheral is to become more regionalized.

Alternative development, defined as development for the excluded and marginalized, can not easily be reconciled with the strategy of development regionalism, since this strategy implies a considerable degree of transnational co-ordination and the development of supra state institutions. It could, nevertheless, be argued that the counterpoint initiatives are more easily carried out under the protective shield of development regionalism than if exposed to the 'chilly winds' of globalization (Hettne 1996).

> The actors behind regionalist projects are no longer states only, but a larger number of different institutions, organisations and movements. Furthermore, today's regionalism is extroverted rather than introverted, which reflects the deeper interdependence of today's global economy. The 'new regionalism' is thus one way of coping with global transformation, as an increasing number of states are realizing that they lack the capability and the means to manage such a task on the national level. One of the defining characteristics of the new regionalism is finally that it takes place in a multi-polar global order. The decline of US hegemony and the breakdown of the communist 'subsystem' created a room for manoeuvre in which the new regionalism could develop (Hettne 1996).

Economic globalization is often seen as a world-wide disorder which would require the return of the political. (Compare Macamo's 'reinvention of politics' above). For Hettne one form of the return of the political would be regionalism and the other, new social movements. Both would finally lead to redistribution and reciprocity (Hettne 1996).

It is easier for a single national state to pursue certain political objectives within a community of states with free trade agreement. Within regional co-operation trade can be expanded, financial flows facilitated and transport connections improved. Such co-operation protects poor states at least to a certain extent from harsh global competition and leads to a cost saving distribution and specialization of specific tasks amongst such state unions.

One such example of development regionalism and state unions is the Southern African Development Community (SADC). Her primary goal is, to raise the economic capacity of the entire region through sector specific co-operation and in this way facilitate coping with global transformation.

The SADC of today has its roots in a union of five Front-line States, Angola, Mozambique, Botswana, Zambia, and Tanzania which strongly supported the liberation movements of Zimbabwe and South Africa. After the liberation of Zimbabwe in 1980, the latter became the economically strongest of the then nine states, which in the same year founded the SADCC (Southern African Development Co-operation Conference). In addition to the above mentioned states, Lesotho, Swaziland, and Malawi joined the newly born union. It was the primary objective of SADCC to diminish the economic dependency on the then apartheid South Africa but also the dependency on the North, in particular the EU, although the latter financed 80 per cent of SADCC's development projects – also with the objective to minimize communist influence in the region. Through the military and economic aggression of the apartheid South Africa from 1980 to 1989 SADCC lost 60 billion US Dollars which constituted more than twice her GDP and more than twice she received on development aid during that period (Rabitsch in OEFSE 1998). Apart from Angola, Mozambique was the main target of aggression. The two seashore states were of particular importance to SADCC in order to lessen dependency on South Africa on the transport sector. For apartheid South Africa it was also unbearable to have a successful socialist model on her door steps (see chapter 1).

After Namibia won her independence in 1990, she immediately joined SADCC and the now 10 States founded SADC in 1992. This was a big step forward in the regional integration, from a not very binding co-operation to a legalized union of states with international status.

After – mainly – the African National Congress (ANC), supported by a world-wide anti-apartheid movement, won the struggle, apartheid came – at least officially – to an end in South Africa. In 1990 the ANC was recognized by the State, Nelson Mandela was released, after 26 years of imprisonment and the first democratic elections were held in South Africa in 1994 (Sauer in OEFSE 1998). In the same year South Africa, with Mandela as president, joined SADC as by far the largest and richest country of the region, with almost one third of the population of SADC and three times the GDP compared to all other SADC states of 1995.[7] In 1997 the Democratic Republic of Congo joined the union under the pressure of South Africa. In addition, Mauritius and the Seychelles became members, so that SADC comprises now almost as many countries, namely fourteen, as the European Union (EU) with fifteen states.

The objectives of SADC are ambitious and socially-minded and would constitute a real alternative to the status quo. It is the aim of SADC to raise the living standard and the quality of life of the peoples of southern Africa.

The socially disadvantaged should be supported through regional integration. Development must be self-sustaining and sustainable and the use of natural resources must consider the protection of the environment. It is another aim of SADC to promote economic, social and cultural co-operation among the peoples of southern Africa and to alleviate poverty.

The principle of consensus should guarantee that all member states benefit equally from commonly planned projects and programmes, not only the economically strongest. Responsibility is decentralized in a threefold way. Firstly, during the annual summit of the heads of states decisions are made concerning SADC as a whole. Secondly, each member state is responsible for one or more particular sectors of the union. Mozambique, for instance, is in charge of culture and information, transport and communication, Zimbabwe for food, agricultural and natural resources, and South Africa for finance, investment and health. (for the rest of the sector responsibility of states see Rabitsch in OEFSE 1998). Thirdly, if an industrialized country, or any other state or the EU wants to support a specific project, it has to consult that particular government responsible for that particular sector.

The highest decision making body is the annual summit of the heads of states of SADC. This summit is crucial for the political and economic direction the union is supposed to take. The chairmanship rotates. Nelson Mandela was chairman in the years after 1996. During the recent summit in Maputo in August 1999, Joaquim Chissano, the president of Mozambique was elected new Chairman of SADC.

The region faced severe economic difficulties in 1998 with a growth rate of only 1.7 per cent, while this rate was 2.7 per cent in 1997 and 4 per cent in 1996. While economically weak countries, like Mozambique, had arround 10 per cent growth, the economically strongest South Africa had a growth rate of 0.2 per cent only (Hypolito de Jesus and Soeira, 12th August 1999). It was the only economy in the region directly affected by the world financial crisis. This shows that the 'chilly winds of globalization' cannot yet be eased off by regionalism.

SADC, like many other regional state unions within the Third World, would also have the potential for co-ordinated negotiations concerning the debt crisis. Although, so far the most important debtors insist on negotiations with single states to prevent the developing countries from having more power collectively.

Eradication of rural and urban poverty – a real possibility

It is a scandal that one quarter of mankind still lives in great poverty, particularly if we consider the affluence of the North. It is a failure of national, but mainly international politics, a false direction of globalization, as we have shown and analyzed all along in a manifold way.

In the world of today there are sufficient material and natural resources as well as know-how to overcome poverty within less than thirty years. Poverty must no longer be endured by the masses in silence, and those in power to eradicate poverty are urged not to tolerate it any longer (HDR 1997, iii). However, it is also the responsibility of every ordinary citizen to get organized, join forces and campaign against poverty. One hundred and sixty years ago there was a world-wide campaign against slavery, and slavery was abolished. For decades we had a world-wide anti-apartheid movement and apartheid was abolished in South Africa. Why should we not succeed this time and eradicate poverty in the first half of the new century? But, just as slavery was not only abolished for humanitarian reasons only and because of the campaign, but rather because it became more profitable to trade with commodities than with human beings, so our campaign for moral and ethical reasons would be only part – an essential part though – of the solution. Important for the time being might well be, the discovery by the powerful of this globe that a world without poverty would also bring great economic advantages for them. However, they would also have to acknowledge that it must be a world with limited affluence, 'prosperity-light', for the sake of the environment.

Poverty is, of course, always a relative concept and there are different aspects of poverty. The HDR 1997 (which we will mainly follow in this paragraph) distinguishes between income poverty and human poverty. The latter we would prefer to call poor living conditions (see below). Poor living conditions are measured by the Human Poverty Index (HPI) and the absence of poor living conditions by the Human Development Index (HDI). In order to define income poverty, poverty lines have to be set, and through these, the relativity of the concept becomes particularly visible. It is, nevertheless, necessary to set poverty lines, so that one can at least roughly grasp the situation and it is also necessary for reasons of comparison. According to the HDR of 1997 (and the definition is maintained in the HDR of 1998 and 1999) in the developing countries all those are considered as poor who have to live on less than US$ 30 per month (calculated in international prices of 1985) and this is one third of the population there, or

1.3 billion people. Of these 1.3 billion 950 million live in South-, East-, Southeast Asia, and the Pacific region. In sSA the proportion of those living in poverty is even about half of the population or 220 million. This proportion is less than 30 per cent in Latin America, but still, even there, 110 million have to live on less than US$ 30 per month.

In the former communist Eastern Block the poverty line is a very different one. It is set at about US$ 120 per capita per month. If calculated in this way, then one third of that population, or 120 million are considered as poor.

In the industrialized countries 100 million, about 8 per cent live under the income poverty line. Here income poverty means having less than half of the average net income at one's disposal. Those considered as poor in the industrialized North, would belong to the well-off in developing countries. So the economic crisis here is of a very different nature. Yet still, one can speak of a crisis, when 37 million, 9.6 per cent of the work force are unemployed in the EU (European Commission 1999) and the level is as high as in the 1930s.

In the developing countries poverty is closely related to the prices for raw materials. In the 1990s these prices were 45 per cent lower than in the 1980s and even 10 per cent lower than the lowest level in the 1930s.

As mentioned above, the HDR of 1997 considers, apart from income poverty, also 'human' poverty which is not a very fortunate expression. The term indicates other aspects of poverty apart from low income, such as insufficient sanitary facilities, poor water supply, poor health facilities, high illiteracy and child mortality rates, low life expectation, etc., it means lack of possibilities and chances for an endurable life. However, it would be much more appropriate to call additional aspects of poverty poor living conditions. With 'human' poverty one automatically associates lack of ethical, moral, cultural or social values. Yet, since the term has been established, with a completely different meaning, one just has to refrain from such associations.

The Indian economist and Nobel price winner in economic science of 1998, Amartya Sen, for whom developing countries constituted the most important realm of research, found a way to measure this lack of possibilities and chances which is inherent in poor living conditions, by developing the Human Poverty Index (HPI). This index – in a very simplified way – uses three social indicators – also reflected in the Human Development Index (HDI) – to measure poverty and marginalization: low life expectation, lack of basic education, and lack of access to official and private resources or in other words: lack of longevity, lack of knowledge and lack of a decent standard of living. The latter is composed again of three indicators: access to safe water, access to health services and underweight children under five.[8] According to this index, in Cuba, Chile, Costa Rica, Singapore, and Trinidad and Tobago only 10 per cent of the population were poor in 1995. However, in Niger, Sierra Leone, Burkina Faso, Ethiopia, Mali, Cambodia, and Mozambique more than half of the population lived in poor conditions. The HPI for China was only 17 in 1995 and 19 in 1997, while it was 39 or 36 respectively in the same years for India. In a number of countries the high HPI is due to a very unequal distribution of resources and income.

Amartya Sen repeatedly stressed the importance of the distribution of income. He was able to combine philosophy with economy and even brought in an ethical dimension in the theory of economy. Therefore, movements for the eradication of poverty have a strong supporter in him. He was not only brilliant in his theoretical work, noticeable his social-choice theory, which opened up fields for future generations of researchers, also his empirical investigations were essential for his Nobel price. As it is often the case with famous discoveries, after they have been made, one is surprised, why dozens of researchers had not seen it before, so it is with Sen's findings that famine is often not a consequence of food shortage, but a consequence of unequal distribution and wrong policies. When food is exported while people are starving in a country and/or the government is not democratically elected and good governance is lacking, one cannot be surprised about such catastrophes as famine (Neue Zuercher Zeitung, 15th October 1998).

With such Nobel price winners, all the winners of the alternative Nobel price founded in 1980 by Jacob von Uexkuell with his Right Livelihood Foundation and so many new social movements there is justified hope for poverty alleviation with the final goal of eradicating it.[9] Another essential element for optimism are the not very well known successes of the last fifty years. In the last fifty years poverty was reduced to a much larger extent than in the 500 years before.

This rapid diminishing of poverty in the 20th century started already in the 19th century with the industrial revolution. Incomes rose, health and educational facilities improved, and a social security net was developed. After 1950 the welfare state and full employment was developed, particularly in Western Europe.

In the 1950s the second big departure in poverty alleviation took place in the developing countries. In almost each state poverty was diminished at least in some aspects. This process intensified after 1960: *child mortality was halved, malnourishment lowered by a third, the proportion of children not attending school sank from one half to a quarter, and the proportion of families not having access to clean water in the countryside sank from 90 per cent to a quarter.* In the face of this progress, eradication of poverty is no longer a distant ideal but a real possibility (HDR 1997, 1-2).

The extent of poverty is still frightening. There are also set backs in the process of development. There was a decline of the HDI in more than 30 countries in 1996. However, the above mentioned successes should encourage further actions without delay. Strategies will be different from country to country but certain measures are necessary everywhere. Appendix 5 shows the complexity of interventions necessary for the eradication of poverty and proper development. All these must be achieved within one generation and not be postponed to the next.

The abilities of the poor themselves must be developed, which means empowerment of the people. Their political, economic, social, and civil rights must be protected. Equality and empowerment of women must be achieved. This is a prerequisite for the eradication of poverty. The declaration of the fourth world conference on women in Beijing must be put into practice in all its points.

Another prerequisite for the eradication of poverty is economic growth. In the poorest countries, growth must be at least 3 per cent per annum. With the right kind of growth and its just distribution incomes could be doubled within one generation. With the right politics income poverty could be halved within a decade. Full employment must be re-established and income inequalities drastically reduced. Those states which let the income gap widen unhampered, like the USA, should be sanctioned,[10] but then the entire North would have to be sanctioned for alowing the gap to widen between the North and the South.

The rural poor need attention most. A favourable framework for smallholders, small entrepreneurs and the informal sector must be created. In the successful campaign in China between 1978 and 1985 small peasants received the highest support. Technical progress must be promoted. While the first Green Revolution drastically changed the conditions of peasants producing wheat, maize, and rice, we now need a second Green Revolution for poor peasants producing millet or manioc.

Aspects of an alternative development and an alternative globalization 267

Basic education and basic health care are the strongest driving forces for economic growth. However, progress in these two aspects is possible even in times of stagnation or even recession as several countries have shown, which in this way created a basis for growth (see HDR 1997, 8 – 9).

Globalization would offer great chances but only if it is headed in the right direction and global balance receives more attention. All states must invest more generously in human development, but particularly the North in its relations to the South in order to face the challenges of globalization.

> The world-system is in mutation now. This is no longer a moment of the minor, constant cumulating of cycles and trends. ... We have perhaps arrived now in the true realm of uncertainty. The world system will continue, of course, to function, even function 'well'. It is precisely because it will continue to function as it has been functioning for 500 years, in search of the ceaseless accumulation of capital, that it will soon no longer be able to function in this manner. Historical capitalism, like all historical systems, will perish from its successes not from its failures (Wallerstein 1992, 15).

Notes

1 The Brady-plan, named after the then foreign minister of the USA, was first applied to Mexico and a few other states as, for instance, Nigeria. It did not solve the problem as it maintained all the mechanisms which led to the crisis in the early 1980s and Mexico had serious financial problems again in 1995. The Debt-Equity-Swaps were mainly applied to Argentina and Chile, again without solving their problems, as it allowed the creditors a higher participation in any surplus and constituted a further denationalization of the weak economies. The Debt for Nature and Debt for Development-Swap has maybe some merit in its concept, but has so far not reached any significant extent. From 1984 to 1992 only 177.4 billions of debts were redirected that way. The conditions of Naples remained equally insufficient. Although it was planned to cancel two thirds of particular debts, the creditor states did not apply the plan fully (Becker 1996).

2 Eurodad: European network on debt and development was established in 1990 and is a network of European NGOs in sixteen European countries with a secretariat in Brussels, working on issues related to debt, structural adjustment, the accountability of the Bretton Woods Institutions and financial markets. The networks objectives are to achieve greater co-ordination, coherence and impact of NGOs and civil society work on this fields. It also endeavours to bring the views of Southern governments and civil society to bear on decision making in Europe.
Action Aid is an international development agency which works with poor communities to overcome poverty and secure lasting improvements in the quality of their lives. Action Aid programmes reach over 5 million poor people in 24 countries in Africa, Asia, and Latin America. Fifteen of these are classified as 'heavily indebted' (Eurodad and Action Aid in Sauer et al. 1998).

3   As a group of sixteen creditors (15 states and the European Commission) the EU represents the largest block of creditors of developing country debt. Four of the EU member states are members of the G-8 (Group of eight industrial nations). According to Eurodad the EU member states hold 25 per cent of all bilateral developing country debts (not including the Commission's multilateral claims). The developing countries owed to the EU an estimated $132.4 billion in 1996. All bilateral claims totalled $550.9 billion. The EU has therefore an enormous responsibility in the problem of debt relief (Eurodad and Action Aid in Sauer et al. 1998).
4   Dumping means the selling of commodities at prices below production costs in order to win the competition in the country of import. After the domination of a large proportion of the market the prices can be raised (HDR 1997, 103).
5   The MST was – amongst other reasons – so successful, because the Brazilian constitution requires all land to serve a social function. Unused or empty lands may be forcibly purchased by the government and resold to the landless poor at low interest rates and flexible payment schedules. Now the World Bank is forcing the Brazilian government to go back to market principles and ignore the constitution. By setting up a 'land bank' the landless will get loans to buy the land. But firstly, no landowner will be forced to sell unused land, secondly, the five years grace period before repayment begins will be cancelled, and thirdly, instead of 6 per cent interest rate they will have to pay 18 per cent. This would mean the extinction of MST.
6   The 'Inquerito Nutricional' of the Ministerio de Comercio, Departamento para a Seguranca Alimentar of 1989 found out that 33 per cent of the families had a field in Maputo, while according to the UNDP (1996, 55) 37 per cent of urban households surveyed in Maputo produce food and 29 per cent raise livestock. The proportion of households engaging in urban agricultural is similar in the capitals of Burkina Faso, Cameroon, and Uganda but it is higher in Zambia (45 percent), much higher in Tanzania where more than two thirds of the families of the capital city produce food and this proportion is even 80 per cent in Gabun.
7   The importance of South Africa (SA) within SADC in 1995

	SA	SADC without SA
inhabitants	41 million	92 million
GDP	US$ 130 billion	US$ 38 billion
export into SADC/SA	US$ 1.9 billion	US$ 0.43 billion

Source: Rabitsch in OEFSE 1998.
8   For the appropriate, complicated procedure of calculating the Human Poverty Indices (HPI) for developing as well as for industrialized countries see HDR 1997, 110 and HDR 1999, 163.
9   See the recent initiative of the 40 members of the European Council; 'Globalization without Poverty:' which is learning from Thailand's experience. The message of the campaign: 'Europe is not a planet but part of one world, and that creates both opportunities and responsibilities' (HDR 1999, 101).
10 According to an investigation of the Centre on Budget and Policy Priorities in the USA, the income of the richest fifth increased by 38 per cent, while the wages and salaries of the poorest fifth diminished by 12 per cent in the last 20 years. One of the reasons is the booming stock market in the last decades, to which only the rich have access. The other one is the tax policy. Under the Reagan administration a tax reform was introduced through which those in the highest income category gained about US$ 40,000 per year. Two thirds of the US citizens earn less than what the richest fifth save in taxes (Neue Kronen Zeitung, 8th September 1999).

Bibliography

Abel, Wilhelm, *Massenarmut und Hungerkrisen im vorindustriellen Deutschland,* Vandenhoeck and Ruprecht, Goettingen 1972

Abu-Lughod, Janet, 'Migrant adjustment to city life: the Egyptian case', in Gerald Breese (ed), *The city in newly developing countries – Readings on urbanism and urbanization,* Prentice Hall Inc., Englewood Cliffs, N. J. 1972

Adepoju, Aderanti (ed), *The impact of structural adjustment on the population of Africa. The implication for education health and employment,* James Currey, London 1993

Altman, Irwin, 'Homes, housing, and the 21st century: Prospects and challenges' in Arias, Ernesto G. (ed), *The meaning and use of housing – International perspectives, approaches and their applications,* Ashgate Publishing Ltd., Aldershot 1993

Altmann, Joern, 'Ueberleben im Schatten. Was versteht man unter dem Begriff informeller Sektor' in *Der Ueberblick,* 3/1991

Arias, Ernesto G. (ed), *The meaning and use of housing – International perspectives, approaches and their applications,* Ashgate Publishing Ltd., Aldershot 1993

Atkinson, A., 'Are Third World megacities sustainable? Jabotabek as an example', *Journal of International Development,* Vol. 5, 6/1993

Austin, Kathi and Minter, William, *Invisible crimes – U.S. private intervention in the war in Mozambique,* Africa Policy Information Centre, Washington 1994

Austrian Social Survey 1993, unpublished statistical material at the Institute of Advanced Studies, Vienna

Bachofen, Johann Jackob, *Das Mutterrecht. Eine Untersuchung ueber die Gynaikokratie der alten Welt nach ihrer religioesen und rechtlichen Natur. Eine Auswahl,* Heinrichs, Hans J. (ed), Suhrkamp Verlag, Frankfurt am Main 1975

Baiculescu, Michael and Becker, Joachim (eds), *Kap der kleinen Hoffnung – Das suedliche Afrika nach der Apartheid,* Promedia, Vienna 1993

Baiculescu, Michael, St. Josef in der Delagoa Bucht, *Mosambik Rundbrief,* Vienna, 3/1995

Bairoch, Paul and Kozul-Wright, Richard, 'Globalization myth: some historical reflections on integration, industrialization and growth in the world economy', in *UNCTAD Discussion papers*, No. 113, March 1996

Beck, Ulrich, *Was ist Globalisierung?* Suhrkamp, Frankfurt am Main 1997

Becker, Charles M. et al., *Beyond urban bias in Africa. Urbanization in an era of structural adjustment*, Heinemann, London 1994

Becker, Joachim, 'Von der De- zur Restabilisierung – Die westliche Politik gegenueber dem suedlichen Afrika', Baiculescu, M. and Becker, J., *Kap der kleinen Hoffnung – Das suedliche Afrika nach der Apartheid*, Promedia, Vienna 1993

Becker, Joachim, 'Verschuldungskrise und Strukturanpassung – ein Ueberblick', in *Mosambik Rundbrief,* Vienna, 41/1996

Becker Joachim, 'Krise ohne Ende – Afrikas Aussenverschuldung und internationale Entschuldungsmodelle', in *Mosambik Rundbrief,* Vienna, 41/1996

Behrendt, R. F., *Soziale Strategie fuer Entwicklungslaender,* Fankfurt am Main 1968

Benterbusch, Ulrich, *Laendliche Armut trotz Entwicklungsprogrammen,* Verlag Breitenbach Publishers, Saarbruecken, Germany – Fort Lauderdale, USA 1988

Bolaji, Idowu E., *African traditional religion,* SCM Press Ltd., London 1973

Bollacher, Martin (ed), *Johann Gottfried Herder: Werke* (in 10 volumes) volume 6, Deutscher Klassiker Verlag, Frankfurt am Main 1989

Bolte, Martin, Kappe, Dieter and Schmid, Josef, *Bevoelkerung. – Statistik, Theorie, Geschichte und Politik des Bevoelkerungsprozesses,* Leske und Budrich, Opladen 1980

Bottomore, T. B., *Karl Marx. Selected writings in Sociology and Social Philosphy – with an introduction and notes by T.B. Bottomore and Maximilien Rubel*, McGraw-Hill, New York 1964

Bradburn, Norman M., 'On psychological well being' in *The structure of psychological well being,* Aldine Publishing Company, Chicago 1969

Bradshaw, York W., 'Urbanization and underdevelopment: a global study of modernization, urban bias, and economic dependency', *American Sociological Review*, 52/1987

Bradshaw, York. W and Noonan, Rita, 'Urbanization, economic growth, and women's labour force participation: a theoretical and empirical reassessment', in Gugler, Josef (ed), *Cities in the developing world: issues, theory and policy,* Oxford University Press, Oxford 1997

Brauen, Martin, *Irgendwo in Bhutan. Wo die Frauen (fast immer) das Sagen haben,* Frauenfeld, Waldgut (Germany) 1994

Braunmuehl, Claudia von, 'Strukturanpassung mit Frauenaugen gesehen. Was die Politik des Internationalen Waehrungsfonds (IWF) und der Weltbank fuer die Frauen in Jamaika bedeutet', in *beitraege zur feministischen theorie und praxis, modernisierung der ungleichheit – weltweit,* Koeln, 23/1988

Brochmann, Grete and Arve Ofstad, *Mozambique – Norwegian assistance in a context of crisis,* Chr. Michelson Institute, Department of Social Science and Development, Fantoft 1990

Brockhaus, F. A., *Die Enzyklopaedie,* Leipzig – Mannheim 1998

Bronger, D., 'Megastaedte', in *Geographische Rundschau,* 48/2, 1996

Brown, Gordon, 'Commentary' in *The Economist,* February 21, 1998

Busia, Kofi, *The Challenge of Africa,* Praeger, New York 1962

Caldwell, J. C., *Population growth and family change in Africa,* Columbia University Press, New York 1968b; reprinted, C. Hurst, London 1977

Castells, Manuel, 'Die zweigeteilte Stadt – Arm und Reich in den Staedten Lateinamerikas, der USA und Europas', in Schabert, Tilo (ed), *Die Welt der Stadt,* Piper, Muenchen 1991

Central Statistical Office of Zambia, *1980 – population and housing census,* Analytical Report, Lusaka 1982

Centro de Estudos Africanos. *Direito a sucessao e heranca,* Maputo 1994

Chossudovsky, Michel, *The globalization of poverty. The impact of IMF and World Bank reforms,* Pluto Press, Australia et al. 1998

Cline, William R., *International debt and the stability of the world economy,* Institute for International Economics, Washington D.C. 1983

Crehan, Kate, 'Mukunashi – an exploration of some effects of the penetration of capital in North-Western Zambia', paper presented at the School of Humanities and Social Sciences at the University of Zambia, January 1981

Davidson, J. and Dankelmann, I., *Frauen und Umwelt in den suedlichen Kontinenten,* Wuppertal 1990

Davis, Kingsley and Golden, Hilda H., 'Urbanization and the development of pre-industrial areas,' *Economic Development and Cultural Change,* Chicago Vol. 3, 1/1954

De Swaan, Abram, 'Keynote speech' in Proceedings of the international conference: 'Research community for the habitat agenda: linking research and policy for the sustainability of human settlements', Geneva 1999

Departamento de Segurança Alimentar de Ministério de Comercio, *Inquérito nutricional,* Maputo 1988

Dibaja, Zuhair, 'Globalization: the last sky', paper presented at the 8th General EADI-Conference 11–14 September, Vienna 1996

Direcção Nacional de Estatistica (Central Statistical Office), *Inquérito às famílias, 1° modulo,* Maputo 1992

Direcção Nacional de Estatistica (Central Statistical Office), *Relatorio sobre os resuldados finais do inquérito às famílias na cidade de Maputo,* Maputo, Setembro 1993

Direcção Nacional de Estatistica e Departamento de Segurança Alimentar de Ministério de Comercio, *Estudo sobre as condições actuais de produção e consumo de alimentos em cinco provincias,* Maputo 1990

Direcção Nacional de Estatística, Departamento de Demografia, *Inquérito demográfico nacional (IDN): Composição por sexo e idade da população abrangida,* Documento 1, Maputo, Maio 1993

Direcção Nacional de Estatística, Departamento de Demografia, *Projecções anuais de população províncias: 1990 – 2000,* Documento 3, Maputo, Junho 1994

Direcção Nacional de Estatística, Gabinete Central de Recenseamento (GCR), *Força de trabalho e a sua utilização em Moçambique 1991,* Maputo, Julho 1994

Direcção Nacional de Estatística, *Relatório sobre os resultados do 1° módulo do inquérito às famílias (IAF) nas capitais provinciais,* Maputo, Janeiro 1994

Direcção Nacional de Estatística, *Relatório sobre os resultados finais do inquérito às famílias nas capitais provinciais,* Maputo, Outubro 1994

Dow, Susan, *Urban settlement strategies in Mozambique – A case study of Maputo,* School of Social Sciences, Flinders University of South Australia 1989

Drakakis-Smith, David, *The Third World City,* Methuen and Co. Ltd., London 1987

Drakakis-Smith, David, *Urban and regional change in Southern Africa,* Routledge, London 1992

Dullemen van, C. E. and Hommes, E. W., 'Globalization of the economic system calls for the development of a global human security package', paper presented at the 8th General EADI-Conference 11–14 September, Vienna 1996

Dunning, John H., *The globalization of business,* Routledge, London 1993

Elwert, Georg and Fett, Roland (eds), *Africa zwischen Subsistenzoekonomie und Imperialismus,* Campus-Verlag, Frankfurt am Main 1982
Emmerij, Louis, 'Paradoxes of Globalization and what can be done to diffuse them', paper presented at the 8th General EADI-Conference 11-14 September, Vienna 1996
Engels, Friedrich, *The conditions of the working class in England,* Blackwell, Oxford 1958; Original 1844
Entwicklungsprogramm der Vereinten Nationen (UNDP), *Bericht ueber die menschliche Entwicklung 1997,* Deutsche Gesellschaft fuer die Vereinten Nationen e. V., Bonn 1997
European Commission, Directorate-General for Economic and Financial Affairs, 'European Economy', Supplement A, Economic trends, No. 4 - April 1999
European Network on Debt and Development (EURODAD), 'Recommendation to the European Union Council of Ministers', in Sauer, Walter et al., *European Southern African cooperation in a globalising world – conference reader,* Vienna, 12 – 14 October 1998, SADOCC, Vienna 1998
Fandrych, Sabine, 'Mosambik hat gewaehlt', in *Mosambik Rundbrief,* Vienna 4/1994
Feldbauer, P. et al. (eds), *Megastaedte – Zur Rolle von Metropolen in der Weltgesellschaft,* Boehlau, Vienna 1993
Feldbauer, Peter and Parnreiter, Christof, 'Einleitung: Megastaedte – Weltstaedte – Global Cities', in Feldbauer, Peter et. al. (eds), *Mega-Cities. Die Metropolen des Suedens zwischen Globalisierung und Fragmentierung,* Brandes and Apsel/Suedwind, Frankfurt am Main 1997
Feldbauer, Peter et al. (eds), *Mega-Cities. Die Metropolen des Suedens zwischen Globalisierung und Fragmentierung,* Brandes and Apsel/ Suedwind, Frankfurt am Main 1997
Fellenberg, G., *Lebensraum Stadt: Zuerich,* Verlag der Fachvereine, Teubner, Stuttgart 1991
Firlus, Leonhard, *Zwischen Schock und Kalkuel – Die permanenten Probleme der Entwicklungslaender,* Verlag Weltarchiv, Hamburg 1988
Forjaz, José, 'Research needs and priorities in housing and construction in Mozambique', in *Habitat International,* 2/1985
Fouquin, M., Chevallier, A. and Pisani-Ferry, J., 'The new international competition: effects on employment', in Simai, Mihaly, *Global employment. An international investigation into the future of work,* Zed Books, London 1995

Francescato, Guido, 'Meaning and use: a conceptual basis' in Arias, Ernesto G. (ed), *The meaning and use of housing – International perspectives, approaches and their applications,* Ashgate Publishing Ltd., Aldershot 1993

Fromm, Erich, 'Foreword' in Bottomore T. B., *Karl Marx. Selected writings in Sociology and Social Philosophy – with an introduction and notes by T.B. Bottomore and Maximilien Rubel,* McGraw-Hill, New York 1964

Furtado, C., 'Elements of a theory of underdevelopment – The underdeveloped structures', in Bernstein, Henry (ed), *Underdevelopment and Development. The Third World today,* Penguin Books, London 1964

Garcia-Chafardet, 'Sexism as an obstacle to development', in Lozoya, J. and Birgin, H. (eds), *Social and cultural issues of the new international economic order,* New York 1981

Gehmacher, Ernst, *Erwarte das Schlimmste und freue dich darauf – Vorbereitungen auf das Zeitalter der Illusionslosigkeit,* Orac, Vienna 1994

Ghai, Dharam, 'Economic globalization, institutional change and human security', paper presented at the 8th General EADI-Conference 11–14 September, Vienna 1996

Gilbert, Alen and Gugler, Josef, *Cities poverty and development. Urbanization in the Third World,* Oxford University Press, Oxford 1982

Glyn, A. and Sutcliffe, B., 'Global but leaderless? The new capitalist order', in *The Socialist Register,* Merlin, London 1992

Golansky, Mark, 'Rise and fall of the global economy (world totalitarianism)', paper presented at the 8th General EADI-Conference 11–14 September, Vienna 1996

Green, Reginald, *Direito de uso da terra das mulheres na Africa Subsahariana. Modernização como marginalização – o que ha para facer,* Faculdade de Direito da Universidade de Windson, 1991

Griffin, Keith and Khan, Azizur Rahman, *Globalization and the developing world: an essay on the international dimension of development in the post-cold war era,* UNRISD, Geneva 1992

Grossboetzl, Gertrud, 'Abschaffung der Sklaverei – Sieg der Moral ueber ein wirtschaftliches Kalkuel?' Diplomarbeit, Universitaet Innsbruck, Innsbruck 1995

Gugler, Josef, 'Minimale Verstaedterung und maximale Verlaendlichung: Kubanische Erfahrungen', in *Die Dritte Welt,* Neustadt, 3-4/1980

Gugler, Josef, 'Overurbanization reconsidered', in *Economic Development and Cultural Change,* Chicago Vol. 31, 1/1982

Gugler, Josef (ed), *The urbanization of the Third World,* Oxford University Press, Oxford 1988

Gugler, Josef, 'Third world urbanization re-examined', Revised version of the seminar paper presented in the seminar series: The New Development Debate of the 1990s at Indiana University, Fall 1991

Gugler, Josef (ed), *Cities in the developing world. Issues, theory and policy,* Oxford University Press, Oxford 1997

Gugler, Josef, 'Overurbanization reconsidered', in Gugler, Josef (ed), *Cities in the developing world. Issues, theory and policy,* Oxford University Press, Oxford 1997

Hance, William A., *Population, migration and urbanization in Africa,* Columbia University Press, New York 1970

Hanlon, Joseph, *Mosambik – Revolution im Kreuzfeuer,* Edition Suedliches Afrika, Bonn 1986

Hanlon, Joseph, *Who calls the shots,* London 1991

Hanlon, Joseph and Jubilee 2000 Coalition, 'Mozambique gains little or nothing from debt relief', in Sauer, Walter et al., *European Southern African co-operation in a globalising world – conference reader,* Vienna, 12 – 14 October 1998, SADOCC, Vienna 1998

Harbury, Jennifer, 'World Bank's 'Land Bank' puts land back into the hands of the rich', in ibonews, No. 424, 8th September 1999

Hardoy, Jorge E. and Satterthwaite, David (eds), *Small and intermediate urban centres. Their role in national and regional development in the Third World,* London 1986

Hardoy, Jorge E. and Satterthwaite, David, *Squatter citizen. Life in the urban Third World,* Earthscan, London 1989

Hartwig, Uwe and Jungfer, Uwe, *Zum Beispiel Verschuldung,* Lamuv Verlag, Goettingen 1992

Harvey, David, *Social Justice and the City,* Edward Arnold, London 1973

Hedman, Brigitta, Perucci, Francesca and Sundström, Pehr, *Engendering statistics – A tool for change,* Gender Statistics Programme, Statistics Sweden, Stockholm 1997

Heisler, H., *Urbanization and the government of migration: The interrelation of rural and urban life in Zambia,* C. Hurst, London 1974

Henderson, Charloner, 'Editor's Introduction', in Engels, Friedrich, *The conditions of the working class in England,* Blackwell, Oxford 1958; Original 1844

Hettne, Björn, 'Development and world order: a regionalist approach', paper presented at the 8th General EADI-Conference 11–14 September, Vienna 1996

Hirst, Paul and Thomson, Graham, *Globalization in question,* Polity Press Cambridge 1996

Ho, K. C., 'The global economy and urban society in Pacific Asia', in *International Sociology,* Vol.12, 3/1997

Hopkins, Terence K., Wallerstein, Immanuel et al., *The age of transition. Trajectory of the world-system 1945 – 2025,* Zed Books, London 1996

Hoselitz, Bert F., 'Urbanization and economic growth in Asia', *Economic Development and Cultural Change,* Chicago, 1/1957

Instituto Nacional de Estatística, *Inquérito nacional aos agregados familiares sobre condiçes de vida – 1996-1997. Relatorio final,* Maputo, December 1998

International Labour Organisation, *Why labor leaves the land. A comparative study of the movement of labor out of agriculture,* Studies and Reports, New Series, Geneva, 59/1960

International Labour Organization (ILO), *World labour report,* Geneva 1995

International Labour Organisation / Jobs and Skills Programme for Africa (ILO/JASPA), *Narrowing the gaps – Planning for basic needs and productive employment in Zambia,* Addis Ababa 1977

International Labour Organisation / Jobs and Skills Programme for Africa (ILO/JASPA) *Zambia – basic needs in an economy under pressure,* Addis Ababa 1981

International Organization for Migration, *Migration indicators in SADC countries,* Pretoria 1998

International Social Survey – ISS 1991

Jackson, J. A., *Migration,* Cambridge University Press, London 1969

Jamal, Vali and Weeks, John, *Africa misunderstood or whatever happened to the rural-urban gap,* McMillan, London 1993

Jellinek, L., *Wheel of fortune: the history of a poor community in Jakarta,* University of Hawaii Press, Honolulu 1991

Jenkins, Paul, Study of a framework for a national housing policy – analysis of resedential area characteristics, U.N.C.H.S. – Habitat project, Moz/86/005

Jenkins, Paul, 'Mozambique', in Kosta Mathey (ed), *Housing policy in the socialist Third World,* Mansell, London 1990

Jenkins, Paul, 'Urban development and housing in Mozambique: a current analysis and bibliography', research paper No. 50, Edinburgh College of Art, Hariot Watt University, Centre for Environment and Human Settlements, 1993

Jessen, Brigitte and Nebelung, Michael, *Hilfe muss nicht toedlich sein*, Express Edition, Berlin 1987

Jolly, Richard and Hoeven, Ralph van der, 'Adjustment with a human face – record and relevance', *World Development*, Oxford, 12/1991

Jubilee 2000 Coalition, 'World Bank Senior Vice President admits HIPC conditions wrong' in Sauer, Walter et al., *European Southern African co-operation in a globalising world – conference reader*, Vienna, October 12 – 14, 1998, SADOCC, Vienna 1998

Kapstein, Ethan B., 'Workers and the world economy', *Foreign Affairs*, Vol. 75, 3/1996

Kaunda, Kenneth, *Humanism in Zambia and a guide to its implementation*, Part II, Lusaka 1974

Kaunda, Kenneth, 'Africa's crisis and the external debt', in Sauer, Walter et al., *European Southern African co-operation in a globalising world – conference reader*, Vienna, 12 – 14 October 1998, SADOCC, Vienna 1998

Kay, George, *A social geography of Zambia*, London 1967

Ki-Zerbo, Joseph, *Die Geschichte Schwarz-Afrikas*, Peter Hammer Verlag, Wuppertal 1979

Kiely, Ray, 'Globalization, post-Fordism and the contemporary context of globalization', in *International Sociology*, Vol. 13, 1/1998

Kiess, Walter, Urbanismus im Industriezeitalter. Von der klassischen Stadt zur Garden City, Ernst und Sohn, Berlin 1991

Knauder, Stefanie, The West African new elite – Value systems old and new, Brooklyn College, New York 1975

Knauder, Stefanie, *Shacks and mansions – An analysis of the integrated housing policy in Zambia*, Multimedia Publications, Lusaka 1982

Knauder, Stefanie, 'Aspekte sozialen Wandels in Zambia', *Oesterreichische Zeitschrift fuer Soziologie*, 4/1984

Knauder, Stefanie, *The consequences of imprisonment – The social situation of ex-convicts in Austria and Zambia – An inter-cultural comparison*, African University Studies, Munich – Kinshasa 1994

Knox, P. L. and Taylor, P. J. (eds), *World cities in a world-system*, Cambridge University Press, Cambridge 1995

Komlosy, Andrea et al. (eds), *Ungeregelt und unterbezahlt. Der informelle Sektor in der Weltwirtschaft,* Brandes and Apsel/Suedwind, Frankfurt am Main 1997

Kossman, E. H., 'The Low Countries' in Cooper J. B. (ed), *New Cambridge modern history,* Vol. 4, *The decline of Spain and the thirty years war, 1909–48/59,* Cambridge University Press, Cambridge 1970

Kraemer, Georg, *Atlas der Weltverwicklungen,* Dritte Welt Haus Bielefeld, Peter Hammer, Wuppertal 1992

Krahl, András, 'Globalization and trends in development studies', paper presented at the 8th General EADI-Conference 11 – 14 September, Vienna 1996

Krammer, Alois, *Ueber die Verstaedterung im tropischen Afrika und ihre kulturellen Grundlagen – Eine soziologische, kultur- und ideengeschichtliche Untersuchung vor dem Hintergrund des Kolonialismus,* Verlag fuer Entwicklungspolitik, Breitenbach 1998

Kriedte, P., *Spaetfeudalismus und Handelskapital. Grundlinien der europaeischen Wirtschaftsgeschichte vom Anfang des 16. bis zum Ausgang des 18. Jahrhunderts,* Goettingen 1980

Kuper, Hilda, *Urbanization and migration in West Africa,* Berkeley and Los Angeles 1965

Kuznets, S., 'Quantitative aspects of the economic growth of nations II: industrial distribution of national product and labour force', *Economic Development and Cultural Change,* Part II, Chicago, 4/1957

Lamadé, Rebecca, 'Der Krieg ist noch nicht vorbei', in *Mosambik Rundbrief,* Vienna, 1/1997

Langthaler, Richard (OEFSE), *Laenderprofil: Mosambik – Politik, Gesellschaft, Wirtschaft,* Oesterreichische Forschungsstiftung fuer Entwicklungshilfe, Vienna 1995

Lee, H., Kim, K. D. and Shin, D. C., Perception of quality of life in an industrializing country; the case of the Republic of Korea, *Social Indicators Research,* 10/1982

Lenin, W. I., *Der Imperialismus als hoechste Stufe des Kapitalismus,* Dietz, Berlin 1979; Original 1917

Leonhard, N., Weltnachrichten - Zeitschrift der Oesterreichischen Entwicklungszusammenarbeit im Aussenministerium, 3/1998

Lipton, Michael, *Why poor people stay poor: Urban bias in world development,* Maurice Temple Smith, London 1977

Lipton, Michael, 'Urban bias revisited', in *Journal of Development Studies,* 3/1984

Loth, Heinrich, *Sklaverei,* Wuppertal 1981
Loth, Heinrich, *Die Frau im alten Afrika,* Fourier 1986
Luczak, Hania and Ernsting, Thomas, 'Das Reich der Frauen' in *Geo,* 9/1996
Lundin de Coloane, Iraê Baptista, 'An analysis of the relationship between social organization and the strategies for survival', paper presented at the Seminar: Rural Transformation, Social Movements and Non-Governmental Organisations, Kadoma, Zimbabwe 1989
Mabogunje, A. L., *Urbanization in Nigeria,* University of London Press, London 1968
Macamo, Elísio, 'Alternative structural adjustment or the reinvention of politics; some notes on the experience of Mozambique', University of Bayreuth 1996
Macamo, Elísio, 'Die Lokalisierung des Globalen am Beispiel von Mosambik', paper presented at the Graduiertenkolleg, interkulturelle Beziehungen in Afrika - Afrika und Globalisierung, Bayreuth 11 February 1999
MacIver, Robert, 'Social causation', in Marvin E. Wolfgang et al., *The Sociology of Crime and Delinquency,* second edition, John Wiley, New York 1970
Madeiros, Eduardo, *As etapas da escravatura na norte de Moçambique,* Arquivo historico de Moçambique - Estudos 4, Universidade Eduardo Mondlane, Maputo 1988
Maged-Scherney, Ingrid, 'Die Entwicklung der Matriarchatsdebatte im deutschsprachigen Raum', in *Oesterreichische Zeitschrift fuer Geschichtswissenschaften,* Vienna, Vol. 6, 2/1995
Malinowski, Bronislaw, *The dynamics of culture change,* Yale University Press, New Haven 1961
Mamdani, Mahmood and Oloka-Onyango, Joe (eds), *Uganda – Studies in living conditions, popular movements, and constitutionalism,* Austrian Journal of Development Studies, Vienna 1994
Mananzan, Mary John (OSB), 'Schriftliche Stellungnahme zum Fragenkatalog des Ausschusses fuer wirtschaftliche Zusammenarbeit des deutschen Bundestages: Materialien zum Hearing: Armutsbekaempfung durch Selbsthilfe', Bonn 1988
Marshall, Judith, 'Economic recovery for whom?' The social cost of the structural adjustment programme in Mozambique, A paper presented to SAP, Multilateral Imperialism and African Strategies for

Development', A conference organised by the Institute of African Studies, Columbia University, New York 1990

Martin, Hans Peter and Schuhmann, Harald, *Die Globalisierungsfalle. Der Angriff auf Demokratie und Wohlstand*, Rowohlt, Hamburg 1996

Martin, R., 'Urbanization, squatter settlements and upgrading', in National Housing Authority, *Human Settlements in Zambia*, Lusaka 1975

Maslow, A., *Motivation and Personality*, New York 1954

Mbikusita-Lewanika, Inonge M., *Learning to live in pre-colonial Bulozi (Zambia)*, Ph.D. Thesis, New York University, New York 1979

Mead, Margaret, *Cooperation and competition among primitive peoples*, New York 1937; reprinted 1961

Menon, Bhaskar, 'Why the poverty gap is growing' in *Choices - The Human Development Magazine*, UNDP, July 1992

Merton, R. K., 'Social structure and anomie', in *American Sociological Review*, 3/1938

Meyns, Peter (ed), *Demokratie und Strukturreform im portugiesisch-sprachigen Afrika – Die Suche nach einem Neuanfang*, Arnold Bergstraesser Institut, Freiburg 1992

Michalos, Alex C., 'Satisfaction and happiness', in *Social Indicators Research*, 8/1980

Midgley, J., *Social development: the development perspective in social welfare*, Sage Publications, London 1995

Miner, Horace, 'The city and modernization: an introduction', in Horace Miner (ed), *The city in modern Africa*, Pall Mall Press, London 1967

Mingione, Enzione, 'The urban question in socialist developing countries', in Forbes, Dean and Thrift, Nigel (eds), *The socialist Third World – Urban development and territorial planning*, Basil Blackwell Inc., New York 1987

Ministério de Construção e Águas, UNCHS – Habitat, Project MOZ 86/005, Urban rehabilitation and employment generating projects – Site and Service Scheme component. Project proposal report, Maputo 1988

Ministry of Local Government and Housing, Local authorities returns and estimates, Lusaka 1974

Mitchell, R. E., 'Some social implications of high density housing', *American Journal of Sociology*, 36/1971

Morris, R., *Urban Sociology*, 1968

Mozambique News Agency (Agência de Informação Moçambicano AIM), 155/1999

Nader, Ralph et. al., *The case against free trade, GATT, NAFTA, and the globalization of corporate power*, Earth Island Press 1993

Naksoon, C., 'Occupation and income in a Bangkok slum', in *Southeast Asian Journal of Social Science*, Vol. 20, 2/1992

National Housing Authority, *Human Settlements in Zambia*, Lusaka 1975

Nebelung, Michael, *Politische Partizipation und Entwicklung: Basisorientierte Projekte in Bangladesh*, Peter Lang, Frankfurt 1986

Nederveen, Pieters Jan N., 'Growth and equity revisited. A supply side approach to social development', paper presented at the 8th General EADI-Conference 11 – 14 September, Vienna 1996

Nelson, Nici, 'How women and men get by: the sexual division of labour in the informal sector of a Nairobi squatter settlement', in Gugler, Josef (ed), *The urbanization in the Third World*, Oxford University Press, Oxford 1988

Neuwirth, Martina, 'Die Schuldenkrise der Entwicklungsländer' in: Liebmann, A. and Amon, W., Dimensionen 2000, Vienna 1997

Newitt, Malyn, *The history of Mozambique*, Hurst, London 1995

Nohlen, Dieter and Nuscheler, Franz (eds), *Handbuch der Dritten Welt. Grundprobleme, Theorien Strategien*, Band 1, 3. Aufl., Dietz, Bonn 1993

Nussbaumer, Josef, *Tragoedien. Katastrophen in Industrie, Verkehr und Zivilleben*, Sandkorn Science, Gruenbach 1999

Nyerere, Julius, *Ujamaa, essays on socialism*, Oxford University Press, Oxford 1968

O'Neill, Helen, 'Globalization, competitiveness and human security: challenges for development policy and institutional change' in Petitat-Côté (ed), *Proceedings of the 8th EADI General Conference, Vienna 11 – 14 September 1996*, Geneva 1998

O'Neill, Helen (ed), *Third world debt: how sustainable are current strategies and solutions*, Frank Cass, London 1990

OECD, *Report on the Helsinki conference on women and structural change – A mirror on the future*, OECD, Paris 1994

Oesterreichische Forschungsstiftung fuer Entwicklungshilfe (OEFSE), *Oesterreich und die Entwicklungsgemeinschaft suedliches Africa (SADC)*, Suedwind-Verlag, Vienna 1998

Ottenberg, Simon and Phoebe, *Cultures and societies in Africa*, Random House, New York 1965

Parnreiter, Christof, 'Entwurzelung, Globalisierung und Migration; ausgewaehlte Fragestellungen', *Journal fuer Entwicklungspolitik*, 3/1995

Parsons, Talcot, *The social system,* Free Press, Glencoe, IL 1951

Peil, Margaret and Sada, Pius O., *African urban societies,* John Wiley and Sons Ltd., New York 1984

Peil, Margaret, 'African urban life: components of satisfaction in Sierra Leone towns', in *Social Indicators Research,* Vol. 14, 3/1984

Peil, Margaret, *Cities and suburbs. Urban life in West Africa,* Holmes and Meier, New York 1981

Peil, Margaret, *Consensus and conflict in African societies,* Longman, London 1977

Peil, Margaret, *Lagos – The city is the people,* Belhaven Press, London 1991

Pélissier, René, 'Mozambique – physical and social geography', *Africa South of the Sahara 1989,* Europa Publications Ltd., London 1988

Perlmann, I., *The myth of marginality,* University of California Press, Berkeley 1976

Petitat-Côté (ed), *Proceedings of the 8th EADI General Conference, Vienna 11 – 14 September 1996,* Geneva 1998

Pfeiffer, Dietmar K. and Scheerer, Sebastian, *Kriminalsoziologie,* Kohlhammer, Berlin 1979

Pfeil, Elisabeth, *Groszstadtforschung,* 2. Auflage, Hannover 1972

Pinches, M., 'Modernization and the quest for modernity: architectural form, squatter settlements and the new society in Manila' in Askew, M. and Logan, W. S. (eds), *Cultural identity and urban change in Southeast Asia,* Deakin University Press, Geelong 1994

Pinsky, Perry, 'The urban problems in Mozambique; initial post-independence responses 1975 – 1980', Major Report No.21, Centre for Urban and Community Studies, University of Toronto, December 1984

Pinsky, Perry, 'Territorial dilemmas: Changing urban life', in John S. Saul, *A difficult road: the transition to socialism in Mozambique,* Monthly Review Press, New York 1985

Portes, A., 'The urban slum in Chile – types and correlates', in *Land Economics,* 1971

Potter, R. B., 'Cities, convergence, divergence and Third World development', in Potter, R. B. and Salau, A. T. (eds), *Cities and development in the Third World,* Mansell Publishing Ltd., London 1990

Prendergast, Renee et al. (eds), *Development perspectives for the 1990s,* Macmillan, Basingstoke 1991

Preston, Samuel H., 'Urban growth in developing countries: a demographic reapprisal', in Gugler, Josef, *The urbanization of the Third World*, Oxford University Press, Oxford 1988

Proceedings of the international conference: 'Research community for the habitat agenda: linking research and policy for the sustainability of human settlements', Geneva 1999

Rabitsch, Armin, 'Ein SADC-Ueberblick', in Oesterreichische Forschungsstiftung fuer Entwicklungshilfe (OEFSE), *Oesterreich und die Entwicklungsgemeinschaft suedliches Africa (SADC)*, Suedwind-Verlag, Vienna 1998

Rapoport, A., 'Towards a cross-culturally valid definition of housing', presented at the 11th Environmental Design Research Association Conference, 1980

Ringel, Erwin, *Die oesterreichische Seele*, Hermann Boehlhaus, Vienna 1984

Ripken, Peter, 'Mozambique', in Hofmeier, Rolf and Schoenborn, Mathias (eds), *Politisches Lexikon – Afrika*, Muenchen 1987

Robertson, Ronald, *Globalization, social theory and global culture*, Sage Publications, London 1994

Robertson, Ronald and Khondker, Habib Haque, 'Discourses of globalization – Preliminary considerations', in *International Sociology*, Vol. 13, 1/1998

Rodney, Walter, *How Europe underdeveloped Africa*, Tanzania Publishing House, Dar-es-Salaam 1972

Rondinelli, D. A., 'Asian urban development policies in the 1990s: from growth control to urban diffusion', in *World Development*, 19/7, 1991

Sachs, Jeffrey and Warner, A., 'Economic reform and the process of global integration', *Brookings papers on economic activity*, 1/1995

Sachs, Wolfgang (ed), *Wie im Westen so auf Erden. Ein polemisches Handbuch zur Entwicklungspolitik*, Rowohlt, Hamburg 1993

Saevfors, Ingemar, *Maxaquene – A comprehensive upgrading account of the first upgrading experience in new Mozambique*, UNESCO 1986

Sauer, Walter, 'Von der Schwierigkeit auf Entwicklung zu reagieren - Oesterreichs Beziehungen zum suedlichen Afrika seit 1980', in Oesterreichische Forschungsstiftung fuer Entwicklungshilfe (OEFSE), *Oesterreich und die Entwicklungsgemeinschaft suedliches Africa (SADC)*, Suedwind-Verlag, Vienna 1998

Sauer, Walter, Ehrenreich, Gerlinde and Pekny, Elfriede, *European Southern African co-operation in a globalising world. – Conference reader,* 12-14 October, Vienna 1998

Schlyter, Ann, *Twenty years of development in George, Zambia,* Swedish Council for Building Research, Stockholm 1991

Schneider, Helmut, 'Social networks and access to employment and accommodation – an intercultural comparison', in Schneider, Helmut and Vorlaufer, Karl (eds), *Employment and housing – Central aspects of urbanization in secondary cities in cross-cultural perspective,* Ashgate Publishing Ltd., Aldershot 1997

Schneider, Helmut and Vorlaufer, Karl (eds), *Employment and housing – Central aspects of urbanization in secondary cities in cross-cultural perspective,* Ashgate Publishing Ltd., Aldershot 1997

Schoeller, Wolfgang, 'Mosambik in der 'strukturellen Anpassung'', in Peter Meyns (ed), *Demokratie und Strukturreform im portugiesischsprachigen Afrika – Die Suche nach einem Neuanfang,* Arnold Bergstraesser Institut, Freiburg 1992

Schulz, Wolfgang et al., *Lebensqualitaet in Oesterreich,* Institut fuer Soziologie, Sozial- und Wirtschaftswissenschaftliche Fakultaet, University of Vienna, 1985

Seymour, T., 'Squatter settlements and class relations in Zambia', in *Review of African Political Economy,* 3/1975

Simmel, Georg, 'The metropolis and mental life' in Wolf, Kurt H. (ed), *The sociology of Georg Simmel,* Free Press, Glencoe Ill. 1964

Simon, D., 'The world city hypothesis: reflections from the periphery', in Knox, P. L. and Taylor, P. J. (eds), *World cities in a world-system,* Cambridge University Press, Cambridge 1995

Simons, H. J., 'Zambias urban situation', in Turok, Ben (ed), *Development in Zambia,* Zed Press, London 1979

Sippel, Harald, 'Die Konkurrenz der 'Indolenten' – Konflikte zwischen marktorientierten afrikanischen Bauern und europaeischen Pflanzern in der ehemaligen Kolonie Deutsch-Ostafrika', Papier präsentiert auf der Jahrestagung der Vereinigung von Afrikanisten in Deutschland, 'Afrika hilft sich selbst', Mainz 1993

Sjoberg, Gideon, 'The pre-industrial city', *American Journal of Sociology,* 60/1955

Soglo, Nicephore, 'Wir sind keine Bettler', in *Der Spiegel,* 51/1992

Sovani, N. V., 'The analysis of 'over-urbanization'', in Breese, G., *The city in newly developing countries. Readings in urbanism and urbanization*, Prentice Hall Inc., London 1969

Stacher, Irene, 'Nairobi: eine afrikanische Metropole', in Feldbauer et al. (eds), *Megastaedte – Zur Rolle von Metropolen in der Weltgesellschaft*, Boehlau, Vienna 1993

Stacher, Irene, 'Afrika suedlich der Sahara. Erzwungene Abkoppelung und Informalisierung', in Komlosy, Andrea et al. (eds), *Ungeregelt und unterbezahlt. Der informelle Sektor in der Weltwirtschaft*, Brandes and Apsel – Suedwind, Frankfurt am Main 1997b

Stekl, H., *Österreichische Zucht- und Arbeitshäuser 1671 – 1920*, Verlag fuer Geschichte und Politik, Vienna 1978

Streiffeler, Friedhelm, *General principles and approaches for sustainable urban greenbelts with special reference to Africa*, Berlin 1993

Streiffeler, Friedhelm, 'The importance of urban agriculture', paper presented at the international conference: Research community for the Habitat Agenda. Linking research and policy for the sustainability of human settlements, 6 – 8 July, Geneva 1998

Studer, Raymond G., 'Meaning and use: a basis of understanding', in Arias, Ernesto G. (ed), *The meaning and use of housing – International perspectives, approaches and their applications*, Ashgate Publishing Ltd., Aldershot 1993

Swedish International Development Authorities (SIDA), *Country report Mozambique – Studies from the Research Division*, Stockholm 1988

Swindell, Kenneth, 'Accumulation, uncertainty and survival; households in North-Western Nigeria', paper presented at the international workshop on migration and the uprooting of people, Internationales Forschungszentrum Kulturwissenschaften, Vienna. German version in *Journal fuer Entwicklungspolitik*, 3/1995

Taylor, Alwyn B., 'The debt problem in sub-Saharan Africa' in O'Neill, Helen, *Third world debt: how sustainable are current strategies and solutions*, Frank Cass, London 1990.

Taylor, Ian, Walton, Paul and Young, Jock (eds), *Critical criminology*, Routledge and Kegan Paul, London 1975

Taylor, Ian, Walton, Paul and Young, Jock, *The new criminology – for a social theory of deviance*, Routledge and Kegan Paul, London 1979

The Ohio State University, Peri-urban baseline research results, Maputo, 1991

Thorns, David C., *Fragmenting societies – A comparative analysis of regional and uban development*, Routledge, London 1992

Thorns, David, 'Report on the working group C: social integration', in Proceedings of the international conference: 'Research community for the habitat agenda: linking research and policy for the sustainability of human settlements', Geneva 1999

Tomich, Thomas P., Kilby, Peter and Johnston, Bruce F., *Transforming agrarian economies: opportunities seized, opportunities missed*, Cornell University Press, Ithaca, NY 1995

Triebkorn, Erwin, *Inquérito nacional aos agregados familiares sobre condições de vida – 1996-1997, quadros gerais*, Maputo 1999

Tschirley, David L. and Weber, Michael T., 'Food security strategies under extremely adverse conditions: the determinants of household income and consumption in rural Mozambique', *World Development*, Vol. 22, 2/1994

Turner, A. H., *Wage trends, wage policies and collective bargaining. Problems of underdeveloped countries*, Cambridge University Press, Cambridge 1966

Turok, Ben (ed), *Development in Zambia*, Zed Press, London 1979

UN Department of Public Information, *Advancement of women 1945 – 1996*, The UN Blue Books Series, Volume 6, New York 1996

UN/UNESCO, *Urbanization in Asia and the Far East*, Proceedings of the joint UN/UNESCO Seminar, Bankok, 8 – 18 August 1956, Calcutta, UNESCO Research centre on the social implications of industrialization in Southern Asia, 1957

UNCTAD, 'Promoting growth and sustainable development in a globalizing and liberalizing world economy', Pre-conference text TD/367, 3 April 1996

UNESCO, *Statistical Yearbook 1993*

UNICEF (United Nation's Children's Fund), *The state of the world's children, 1989*, Oxford University Press, Oxford 1989

United Nations, *Growth of the world's urban and rural population 1920-2000*, New York 1969

United Nations, *World urbanization prospects: The 1994 revision*, New York 1995

United Nations, Department for Economic and Social Information and Policy Analysis, Population Division, *Living arrangments of women and their children in developing countries – a demographic profile*, New York 1995

United Nations, Low cost sanitation programme, Moz/91/014
United Nations Development Programme, *Human Development Report 1990*, New York 1990
United Nations Development Programme, Government of Mozambique, INDER, *Project terminal report: Environment, health and sanitation III*, Maputo 1991
United Nations Development Programme, *Human Development Report 1994*, New York 1994
United Nations Development Programme, *Food, jobs and sustainable cities. Urban Agriculture*, New York 1996
United Nations Development Programme, *Human Development Report 1996*, New York 1996
United Nations Development Programme (UNDP), Human Development Report 1999, Oxford University Press, Oxford 1999
United Nations Fund for Population Assessment (UNFPA), *Weltbevoelkerungsbericht 1996 – Welt im Wandel: Bevoelkerung, Entwicklung und Zukunft der Stadt*, Deutsche Gesellschaft fuer die Vereinten Nationen, Bonn 1996
Universidade Eduardo Mondlane, Faculdade de Arquitectura e Planeamento Físico, *Inquérito às 694 Fogos da A.P.I.E. em quatro Zonas da Cidade de Maputo*, Inquérito solicidado por Direcção Nacional de Economia de Construção, Ministerio da Construção e Água, Maputo 1989
UNRISD (United Nations Research Institute for Social Development) *States of disarray: the social effects of globalization*, United Nations, Geneva 1995
Veenhoven, Ruut and co-workers, *Correlates of happiness – 7838 findings from 603 studies in 69 nations 1911 – 1994*, World data base of happiness, Studies in socio-cultural transformation, Erasmus University, Rotterdam 1995
Wallace, P., 'Mixed blessings in the two way flows of foreign investments', in *Independent*, 22 February, 24/1996
Wallerstein, Immanuel, *Das moderne Weltsystem – die Anfaenge kapitalistischer Landwirtschaft und die europaeische Weltoekonomie im 16. Jahrhundert*, Koenigstein 1986
Wallerstein, Immanuel, *The modern world-system II – Mercantilism and the consolidation of the European world-economy, 1600 – 1750*, San Diego 1992

Wallerstein, Immanuel, *Geopolitics and geoculture. Essays on the changing world system*, The Press Syndicate of the University of Cambridge, Cambridge 1991; reprinted 1992

Wallerstein, Immanuel, 'Die Grenzen des Weltsystems. Das suedliche Afrika in der neuen Weltordnung', in Baiculescu, M. and Becker, J. (eds), *Kap der kleinen Hoffnung – Das suedliche Afrika nach der Apartheid*, Promedia, Vienna 1993

Waters, Malcolm, *Globalization*, Routledge, London 1995

Weber, A., *The growth of cities in the nineteenth century. A study in statistics*, Columbia University, New York 1899

Wellmer, Gottfried, 'Frieden beginnt mit der Streichung der Schulden', in *Mosambik Rundbrief*, Vienna, 3/1992

Wellmer, Gottfried, 'Entschuldung als Erpressungsmittel', *Informationsbrief Weltwirtschaft und Entwicklung*, 5/1995

White, Rodney R., 'The influence of environment factors in the urban crisis', in Stren, E. and White, R. R., *African cities in crisis – Managing rapid urban growth*, Westview Press, London 1989

Wichterich, Christa, *Wir sind das Wunder, durch das wir überleben. 4. Weltfrauenkonferenz in Peking*, Heinrich Böll Stiftung, Köln 1996

Wirasinha, Ransjit, 'The water and sanitation situation in the Third World', paper presented at the international conference 'Research community for the Habitat agenda. Linking research and policy for the sustainability of human settlements', 6 – 8 July, Geneva 1998

Wirth, Louis, 'Urbanism as a way of life', *American Journal of Sociology*, 44/1938

Wirz, A., *Sklaverei und das kapitalistische Weltsystem*, Frankfurt am Main 1984

Wolf, Kurt H. (ed), *The sociology of Georg Simmel*, Free Press, Glencoe Ill. 1964

Wolf, Martin, 'The global economy myth', Financial Times, 13 February, 1996, p.22

World Bank, *Mozambique – An introductory economic survey*, 1985

World Bank, *World development report*, 1986b

World Bank, *The East Asian miracle*, Oxford University Press, Oxford 1993

World Bank, *World debt tables 94 – 95*, Washington D.C. 1994

World Bank, 'Country assistance strategy', Maputo 1995

World Economic Forum, *The global competitiveness report 1996*, World Economic Forum, Geneva 1996

Yachan, Antonio, *Habitação vernacular,* Centro de Formação Agrária e de Desenvolvimento Rural, Maputo 1990

Yue-Man, Yueng, *Urban agriculture in Asia,* United Nations University/ Food Energie Nexus Program, Paris 1985

Newspapers

Neue Kronen Zeitung, Vienna, 8th September 1999
Neue Zuercher Zeitung, Zuerich, Switzerland, 15th October 1999

Internet and e-mails as sources

Trudy, Goodwin, columnist at http://www.afronet.com/COLUMN/10.98.1trudy.html

Hypolito de Jesus, Etevaldo and Soeiro, Maria Clara, editors of ibonews - daily top news published by multimedia Ltda. Mozambique, e-mail: ibonews@zebra.uem.mz

Appendices

Appendix 1: Questionnaire on the housing problem, the infrastructure and the social facilities in the peri-urban areas of Maputo and Beira

Explanation to the interviewee

This investigation is carried out by a sociologist from the National Institute for Physical Planning in order to obtain more information about the problems of housing, the infrastructure and the social facilities in the peri-urban areas of Maputo and Beira as well as the personal situation of the people living in these areas and some villages. This information should assist those in responsible positions for urbanization and housing in their attempt to improve the current situation. You can be critical in your answers, because you will remain anonymous.

Number of questionnaire. .... Date of interview ....

1. Name of interviewer .... 1. ____

2. Province
   1 Maputo   2 Sofala.................................. 2. ____

3. Name of bairro/village .... 3. ____

4. Category
   1 urbanized area   3 non-urbanized area
   2 semi-urbanized area   4 communal village
                                       5 traditional village .... 4. ____

Number of the house...

Number of quarterao...

5. Language used for the interview
   1 Portuguese   4 Ndau/Sena
   2 Changana / Ronga   5 Ndau/Sena with translation
   3 Changana / Ronga with translation 6 other languages .... 5. ____

6. A couple was interviewed
   1 yes   2 no .... 6. ____

I. Information about the family

7. Sex of interviewee
   1 female
   2 male .... 7. ____

8. In what year were you born? _____
   1 16 - 20   5 41 - 50
   2 21 - 25   6 51 - 60
   3 26 - 30   7 61 - 70
   4 31 - 40   8 71 - 80
                    9 over 80 .... 8. ____

9. What is your marital status?
   1 single   4 married informally
   2 married formally   5 separated
   3 married traditionally   6 divorced
                               7 widow/er .... 9. ____

10. How many wives/husbands do you have? .... 10. ____

What is the age of your first born child?
(fill in all daughters, sons, and relatives who live with this family)

	sex			goes to a school			doesn't	employment		
sons and daughters	m	f	age	kinder garten	escol- inha	school		yes	occasi onally	no
1										
2										
3										
4										
5										
6										
7										
8										
9										
relatives relationship										
1										
2										
3										
4										
5										
6										

11. Total number of persons living in the household
    1 1   5 11 - 13
    2 2 - 4   6 14 - 16
    3 5 - 7   7 17 - 19
    4 8 - 10   8 20 and more .... 11. ____

Level of formal education

12. What is your level of education?
    1 without formal education   6 pre-university/college
    2 between first and third class   7 elementary technical school
    3 primary school 1 (4th class)   8 basic technical school
    4 primary school 2 (6th class)   9 medium level technical school
    5 secondary school (9th class) 10 higher education .... 12. ____

13. Are you satisfied with your level of education?
    1 very satisfied   3 neither satisfied nor dissatisfied
    2 satisfied   4 dissatisfied
                                     5 very dissatisfied .... 13. ____

14. If you currently go to school what class are you attending? .... 14. ____

15. What kind of school do you attend?
    1 primary school   3 technical school
    2 secondary school   4 higher education .... 15. ____

16. Are you going to school?
    1 during the day   2 in the evening .... 16. ____

17. Do you have any training in your workplace?
    1 yes   2 no .... 17. ____

If yes: What kind of training or course did or do you attend? ....

If the interviewee is discontent with her/his level of education, but does not attend any school

18. What are the main reasons?
    1 lack of money   3 you think you are too old
    2 not having the opportunity to do so 4 other reasons .... 18. ____

Occupation

What is your occupation? ....

For housewives

19. You are a housewife, but are you doing other things as well?
    1 working in your field
    2 producing beverages
    3 selling things
    4 others
    5 I am just a housewife .... 19.____

20. Use the above mentioned codes for the second answer .... 20. ____

21. Use the above mentioned codes for the third answer .... 21. ____

22. Are you looking for employment?
    1 yes
    2 no .... 22. ____

23. What kind of job do you have presently?
    1 working for the government
    2 working in the private sector
    3 working for a co-operative
    4 house servant
    5 trader
    6 business woman/man
    7 working mainly in the field
    8 working in the informal sector (very small enterprises without license; e.g. repairing shoes)
    9 working occasionally
    10 unemployed
    11 retired
    12 housewife .... 23. ____

24. Are you content with the atmosphere at work?
    1 very content
    2 content
    3 neither content nor discontent
    4 discontent
    5 very discontent .... 24. ____

25. Are you content with your job conditions?
    1 very content
    2 content
    3 neither content nor discontent
    4 discontent
    5 very discontent .... 25. ____

26. How many of your sons, daughters and relatives over 14 years who live with you neither go to school nor have a job? .... 26. ____

Income

27. What is your monthly income?
    1 nothing
    2 less than 24 contos
    3 25 - 50
    4 51 - 100
    5 101 - 200
    6 201 - 500
    7 more than 500 .... 27. ____

28. Do some members of your family work in South Africa or Swaziland?
    1 yes   2 no .... 28. ____

29. Do they support your family regularly
    1 with money   3 with both
    2 with goods   4 they don't support .... 29. ____

If 1: 30. What is the approximate quantity per month?
       (use codes of question 27) .... 30. ____

31. Do some of your other relatives work in South Africa or Swaziland?
    1 yes   2 no .... 31. ____

32. Do they support your family regularly?
    1 with money   3 with both
    2 with goods   4 they don't support you .... 32. ____

If 1: 33. What is the approximate quantity per month?
       (use codes of question 27) .... 33. ____

34. How many other people who live with you have a job? .... 34. ____

35. What is the approximate total income of all of them per month?
    (use codes of question 27) .... 35. ____

36. What is the total income of your household per month?
    (use codes of question 27) .... 36. ____

37. Are you content with the income of your household?
    1 very content   3 neither content nor discontent
    2 content   4 discontent
                                    5 very discontent .... 37. ____

38. Do you have a field?
    1 yes   2 no .... 38. ____

If no: 39. Would you like to have one?
    1 yes   2 no .... 39. ____

If interviewee has a field

40. Where is your field situated?
    1 on the Costa do Sol   2 on infertile soil .... 40. ____

41. How many kilometres from here is it? .... 41. ____

42. Your field is producing
    1 the major part of your food 3 less than half
    2 about half   4 very little .... 42. ____

Migration

43. Did you live in this bairro before independence?
    1 yes
    2 no .... 43. ____

44. In which year did you arrive here?
    1 less than six months ago
    2 about six months ago
    3 about one year ago
    4 about one and a half years ago
    5 two years ago
    6 3 - 5 years ago
    7 6 - 10 years ago
    8 11 - 16 years ago .... 44. ____

45. Where did you live before?
    _____
    (fill in name of locality, village, district, town, city, bairro)
    1 locality / village
    2 communal village
    3 small town (vila)
    4 other city
    5 other bairro
    6 always lived in this bairro .... 45. ____

46. In which province did you live before?
    1 Maputo
    2 Gaza
    3 Inhambane
    4 other
    5 Sofala .... 46. ____

47. When did you emigrate from the countryside (from a village) to the city to another village (year)......................
    1 less than six months ago
    2 app. 6 months ago
    3 app. one year ago
    4 app. one and a half years ago
    5 more than two years ago
    6 3 - 5 years ago
    7 6 - 10 years ago
    8 11 - 16 years ago
    9 17 years and more .... 47. ____

48. Where were you born? (locality, village, district, town/city, province)
    1 locality/village
    2 communal village
    3 small town (vila)
    4 other city
    5 other bairro .... 48. ____

49. Which province were you born in?
    1 Maputo
    2 Gaza
    3 Inhambane
    4 other
    5 Sofala .... 49. ____

50. What was your main reason for emigrating from the countryside?
    1 because of my marriage
    2 searching for employment
    3 wanting to go to school
    4 looking for better conditions of life
    5 part of my family already lived in the city
    6 because of the war
    7 because of droughts/floods
    8 other reasons .... 50. ____

Appendix 1   297

51. What kind of relationship do you have with your relatives
    in the countryside (in the city)?
    1   I often help my relatives in the countryside (in the city)
    2   I visit them frequently
    3   I visit them sometimes
    4   I have no contact to my relatives in the countryside (in the city)
    5   I have no family members in the countryside (in the city)............ 51. ____

52. What kind of relationship do your relatives in the countryside
    (in the city) have to you?
    1   they frequently help me
    2   they frequently visit me
    3   they sometimes visit me.. 52. ____

53. After the end of the war, would you like to return to the countryside?
    1   yes   2   no .... 53. ____

If yes: 54. Why?
    1   I want to work on my field to feed my family
    2   my family is still there and I want to live with them
    3   I have my property there
    4   (for wives) only myself and the children will go there,
        my husband will continue to work in town
        (for husbands) I will only send my family there
    5   I have my land and the ancestral graves (holy trees) there
    6   other.. 54. ____

If no: 55. Why?
    1   we have work here   4   we have already established
                                         our lives here
    2   we have a safe house   5   we have no family there
                                         anymore
    3   our children go to school   6   other .... 55. ____

II. Information about the house

56. This house is:
    1   your private property   3   rented from others without
                                         payment
    2   rented from APIE   4   rented from others with
                                         payment .... 56. ____

If 1 57. In which year did you start with the construction of your house?
    1   less than a year ago   3   3 - 6 years ago
    2   1 - 2 years ago   4   7 - 16 years ago................ 57. ____

58. Who built your house?
    1. myself
    2. myself with the help of family members
    3. myself with the help of neighbours
    4. a bricklayer
    5. other .... 58. ____

59. How many times did you already repair your house substantially?
    1. never
    2. once
    3. 2 - 3 times
    4. more than 3 times .... 59. ____

60. What type of improvements did you make?
    1. repair of the roof
    2. the walls
    3. the floor
    4. doors/windows
    5. other .... 60. ____

61. Improvements (for second answer use codes as above) .... 61. ____

62. Improvements (for third answer use codes as above) .... 62. ____

63. Material used for the walls of your house
    1. reed
    2. corrugated iron sheets
    3. pau-a-pique
    4. mud
    5. concrete blocks
    6. bricks
    7. other.................. .... 63. ____

64. Material used for the floor
    1. soil
    2. mud
    3. tiles
    4. cement
    5. wood
    6. stone / granulit .... 64. ____

65. Material of the roof
    1. grass
    2. corrugated iron sheets
    3. tiles
    4. fibre cement (lusalite)
    5. plastic sheets .... 65. ____

66. Is the kitchen within the house?
    1. yes
    2. no .... 66. ____

67. How many rooms (not counting the kitchen) does your house have? .... 67. ____

68. Approximate size of house in m^2
    1. less than 10m^2
    2. 10 to approximately 25m^2
    3. 25 to approximately 70m^2
    4. more than 70m^2 .... 68. ____

69. Does the house have windows?
    1. no
    2. yes, but without glass
    3. yes, glazed .... 69. ____

70. This house is:
 1 better than the previous one
 2 similar to the previous one
 3 worse than the previous one. .... 70. _____

71. Which aspects of your house do you like most?
 1 the roof
 2 the living room
 3 like all of it
 4 like everything, because it is a product of my own effort
 5 like my house because I never had another one before
 6 like its masonry
 7 other   .... 71. _____

72. Which aspects of your house do you like least?
 1 it's tiny   4 it's not finished
 2 it's made of reed   5 it's old
 3 rain enters through the roof   6 it's about to collapse
                                           7 other .... 72. _____

73. Which changes should have priority in order to improve your house?
 1 the roof   3 the floor
 2 the walls   4 other................. .... 73. _____

74. Are you going to make these changes in the near future?
 1 yes   2 no ......:............................... 74. _____

If no: 75. Why?
 1 no money   4 I want to return to South Africa
 2 lack of material   5 I intend to return to the countryside
 3 responsibility of APIE   6 other .... 75. _____

76. What do you use for illumination?
 1 candle   3 petromax
 2 petroleum lamp   4 electricity .... 76. _____

77. What do you use for cooking?
 1 firewood   3 petroleum
 2 charcoal   4 gas
                                           5. electricity .... 77. _____

78. For second reply use codes above .... 78. _____

79. Are you pleased with your house?
    1   very satisfied
    2   satisfied
    3   neither satisfied nor dissatisfied
    4   dissatisfied
    5   very dissatisfied .... 79. ____

80. Do you suffer a lot because you don't have a good house?
    1   yes, a lot
    2   I suffer, but not a lot
    3   I don't suffer .... 80. ____

81. Which type of house would you prefer most?
    1   my present house is good
    2   a big house of the same type
    3   a maison house with two rooms
    4   a maison house with three rooms
    5   a maison house with four rooms
    6   other .... 81. ____

Land rights

82. What size is the plot around your house (in m^2) approximately?
    1   less than 10 x 16 (160m^2)
    2   10 x 16 (160m^2)
    3   10 x 26 (260m^2)
    4   8 x 50 (400m^2)
    5   more than 400m^2 .... 82. ____

83. Who allocated the plot to you?
    1   the grupos dinamazadores
    2   the City Council
    3   we bought the plot
    4   other .... 83. ____

84. Do you have a document concerning the land use right for your house and your plot?
    1   yes
    2   no............ .... 84. ____

If no: 85. Would you like to have such a document?
    1   yes
    2   no..................... .... 85. ____

If yes: 86. Why?
    1   I would feel safer
    2   I am afraid that one day the authorities might destroy my house
    3   If I had that document I would invest more in my house
    4   other .... 86. ____

If no: 87. Why?
    1   I don't intend to stay here
    2   I would like to go back to the rural areas
    3   I intend to build another house in another bairro
    4   other .... 87. ____

III. Infrastructure

88. What is your situation in terms of sanitation, the situation of the *toilet* or the *latrine?*
    1. we have no latrine, we go to the bushes
    2. we use one latrine together with two or more other families
    3. we use one latrine together with one other family
    4. we have our own latrine
    5. our latrine is an improved one/we bought the lid in the workshop
    6. we have a toilet within our house
    7. we have a sewer
    8. we have septic tanks .... 88. ____

89. Is the sanitary situation a problem for you?
    1. a serious problem
    2. a problem, but not a very serious one
    3. no problem .... 89. ____

90. What do you use for your *water supply:*
    1. we use rivers or lakes
    2. we have to carry the water from a distant well
    3. we use a well nearby our house
    4. we have to carry water from a distant public water outlet
    5. we use a public water outlet nearby
    6. we have a water tap in our yard
    7. we have piped water within our house.................................... 90. ____

91. Do you have to buy water?
    1. yes   2. no .... 91. ____

If yes: 92. What is the price per bucket of water?
    1. 15 - 30 meticais   3. more than 60 meticais
    2. 30 - 60 meticais   4. we are billed monthly
                                  5. other .... 92. ____

93. How many buckets of water does your family approximately use per day?
    1. 1 - 4 buckets
    2. 6 - 10 buckets
    3. more than 10 buckets... 93. ____

94. Is the supply of water a problem for you?
    1. a serious problem
    2. a problem but not a very serious one
    3. no problem .... 94. ____

95. Which means of transport do you use normally when going to work?
    1   I walk
    2   chapa cem (private minibus)
    3   bus service
    4   the train
    5   hitch hiking
    6   my bicycle
    7   my motorbike
    8   my own car
    9   transport is supplied by the employer
    10 other .... 95. ____

96. How many times each month do you go down town?
    to Maputo/to Beira? .... 96. ____

97. What other places do you have to go to frequently?
    1   to other bairros
    2   to other districts
    3   other places
    4   I don't go anywhere .... 97. ____

98. Which means of transport do you use most frequently to deal with other errands? (use codes as above) 98. ....

99. Transport is
    1   a serious problem for you
    2   a problem but not a very serious one
    3   no problem .... 99. ____

100. How close is your house to the nearest *street*
    1   it is situated directly on a road
    2   100 meters
    3   200 - 300 meters
    4   1 km
    5   more .... 100. ____

101. The road closest to your house is:
    1   of sand
    2   compressed soil
    3   tarred .... 101. ____

102. What do you do with *waste*?
    1   we bury it
    3   we burn it
    3   we throw it onto a public gound
    4   it is collected by the City Council
    5   other .... 102. ____

103. The waste is:
    1   a serious problem for you
    2   a problem but not a very serious one
    3   no problem .... 103. ____

104. Is there a *telephone*
    1 in your neighbourhood
    2 there is a telephone in the centre of this bairro
    3 there is a telephone in other places of this bairro
    4 I make calls at my workplace only
    5 I never use a telephone
    6 I have a telephone in my house
    7 other .... 104. ____

105. Do you have a radio set?
    1 yes   2 no .... 105. ____

106. Do you have a television set?
    1 yes   2 no .... 106. ____

IV. Social facilities

Schools

107. How many children between 2 and 6 years do you have?
    (Fill in using the table and the help of the interviewee) .... 107. ____

108. How many of these children go to a nursery school? .... 108. ____

109. How many of your own children and of those of your relatives who live with you go to a escolinha? .... 109. ____

110. How many of your *daughters and female relatives* are between 6 and 14 years?
    (Fill in using the table and the help of the interviewee) .... 110. ____

111. How many of these go to school? .... 111. ____

If not all: 112: Why?
    1 there are not sufficient places
    2 I don't have enough money for school fees and/or school books
    3 other reasons .... 112. ____

113. How many of your girls (daughters and female relatives) in this age group go to school in this bairro?................................ 113. ____

114. How many of your girls (daughters and female relatives) in this age group go to school in another bairro?............................. 114. ____

115. How many of your *sons and male relatives* are between 6 and 14 years?
    (Fill in using the table and the help of the interviewee................... 115. ____

116. How many of these go to school?.. 116. ____

If not all: 117. Why?
   1   there are not sufficient places
   2   I don't have enough money for schoolfees and/or school books
   3   other reasons .... 117. _____

118. How many of your boys (sons and male relatives) in this age group
     go to school in this bairro?... 118. _____

119. How many of your boys (sons and male relatives) in this age group
     go to school in another bairro?................... .... 119. _____

120. The primary schools are:
   1   a serious problem for you
   2   a problem, but not a very serious one
   3   no problem .... 120. _____

121. How many of your *daughters and female relatives* are between
     14 and 20 years?
     (Fill in using the table and the help of the interviewee)......... .... 121. _____

122. How many of them go to a school? .... 122. _____

123. The school they go to is a
   1   primary school   4   higher institute
   2   secondary school   5   the university
   3   technical institute   6   other .... 123. _____

124. Use the above codes for the second answer... 124. _____

125. How many of your *sons and male relatives* are between
     14 and 20 years?
     (Fill in using the table and the help of the interviewee)........ .... 125. _____

126. How many of them go to school? .... 126. _____

127. The school they go to is a
   1   primary school   4   higher institute
   2   secondary school   5   the university
   3   technical institute   6   other .... 127. _____

128. Use the above codes for the second answer .... 128. _____

Religion

129. Are you religious?
   1   yes   2   no .... 129. _____

130. To which church/denomination do you belong to?
    1 I am religious in the traditional way
    2 protestant
    3 catholic
    4 muslim
    5 mazione
    6 baptist
    7 assembly of god
    8 old catholic
    9 church of 12 apostels
    10 other .... 130. ____

131. Is there a church of your denomination in this bairro?
    1 yes
    2 no .... 131. ____

132. You go to church:
    1 almost every day
    2 more than once a week
    3 each weekend
    4 sometimes
    5 never
    6 we go to the beach for our ceremony .... 132. ____

133. Do you have contacts with other members of your church?
    1 the members of our church help each other
    2 we have many contacts
    3 I have contact with them sometimes
    4 I never have contact with them. .... 133. ____

Social and political centres

134. Do you visit the 'circulo' of this bairro?
    1 more than once a week
    2 once a week
    3 sometimes
    4 never .... 134. ____

135. Do you like the multi-party system:
    1 yes
    2 no
    3 I am not interested in it
    4 I don't know what it is...... 135. ____

If yes: 136. Why?
    1 more parties could improve the situation of the country
    2 having more parties, we can see who is competent and who is not
    3 when having more parties, errors committed by one could be corrected by others
    4 other .... 136. ____

If no: 137. Why?
    1 I only know FRELIMO
    2 I only want FRELIMO
    3 all party leaders have the same tendency: they all only want to improve their own life
    4 other .... 137. ____

138. How often do you go to the barracks of this or another bairro?
    1 several times per week   3 sometimes
    2 once a week   4 never .... 138. ____

139. And the youths who live with you, how often do they go
     to the barracks in this or another bairro?
    1 several times per week   3 sometimes
    2 once a week   4 never .... 139. ____

140. Do you go to the sports center in this bairro to watch a game?
    1 several times per week   3 sometimes
    2 once a week   4 never .... 140. ____

141. Do you use the sports center in this bairro to play in a game?
    1 several times per week   3 sometimes
    2 once a week   4 never .... 141. ____

Shops and markets

142. Where do you do your shopping most frequently in this bairro?
    1 at the market
    2 at the black market   3 in the shops
       (dumba nengues/chunga moios)   4 other .... 142. ____

143. Use the above codes for the second answer .... 143. ____

144. Which other places outside this bairro, do you use to shop most frequently?
    1 central market   3 other markets
    2 shops down town   4 other shops outside of this bairro
                                       5 other .... 144. ____

Health facilities

145. If you or one of your family members is ill, where do you go
     most frequently in the first place?
    1 to a mazione   6 to the health centre in this bairro
    2 to a person of my church   7 to the health centre in another bairro
    3 to the traditional healer   8 to the hospital in this bairro
    4 to the health post in this bairro   9 to the hospital in another bairro
    5 to the health post in another bairro 10 to the central hospital
                                       11 other .... 145. ____

146. Where do you go in the second place?
     (use codes as above) .... 146. ____

147. Do you think it is necessary to have:
    1 more traditional healers in this bairro
    2 more health posts
    3 more health centres
    4 a hospital
    5 we are sufficiently supplied .... 147. ____

148. Do these health services normally have sufficient medicines?
    1 yes   2 no .... 148. ____

149. The health services are:
    1 a serious problem for you
    2 a problem but not a very serious one
    3 no problem .... 149. ____

V. Social Integration

183. Do you feel isolated/or lonesome?
    1 frequently
    2 sometimes
    3 never .... 183. ____

184. If you work on your field or do other things, do you normally work only with your family or do you often work with other families?
    1 normally only with my family   3 sometimes with other families
    2 frequently with other families   4 never with other families .. 184. ____

Could you describe your work
....
....

185. Do you frequently exchange the things you produce with your family, friends or neighbours for other things?
    1 yes frequently
    2 sometimes
    3 never.. 185. ____

186. How many of your relatives live in this bairro/village?
    1 all of them   3 app. half of them
    2 the majority   4 only a few
                          5 none................... 186. ____

187. And the relatives of your wife/husband?
    1 all of them   3 app. half of them
    2 the majority   4 only a few
                          5 nobody .... 187. ____

188. How often do you visit one or some of your relatives?
    1 every day
    2 two or three times per week
    3 once a week
    4 once each month
    5 hardly ever
    6 never .... 188. ____

189. How often do they visit you?
    1 every day
    2 two or three times per week
    3 once a week
    4 once each month
    5 hardly ever
    6 never .... 189. ____

If the interviewee does have relatives in the bairro:

190. In which way do your relatives in this bairro/village help you most frequently?
    1 they help us with food
    2 they bring food stuff for us from the province
    3 they help us with money
    4 we exchange what each of us can spare
    5 they help us whenever someone is ill
    6 they help us whenever we have a ceremony
    7 they do not help us, because they do not have anything
    8 there is no mutual help
    9 other .... 190. ____

191. Use the above codes for the second answer .... 191. ____

192. Use the above codes for the third answer .... 192. ____

193. In which way do you most frequently help your relatives in this bairro/village?
    1 we help them with food
    2 we bring food stuff for them from the province
    3 we help them with money
    4 we exchange what each of us can spare
    5 we help them whenever someone is ill
    6 we help them whenever they have a ceremony
    7 we do not help them because we do not have anything
    8 there is no mutual help
    9 other .... 193. ____

194. Use the above codes for the second answer .... 194. ____

195. Use the above codes for the third answer .... 195. ____

196. Do you have *friends* in this bairro/village?
    1 many
    2 a few
    3 none .... 196. ____

If 1 or 2: 197. How many times do you visit one or more of your friends?
    1 every day   4 once each month
    2 two or three times per week   5 very rarely
    3 once a week   6 never .... 197. ____

198. How many times do they visit you?
    1 every day   4 once each month
    2 two or three times per week   5 very rarely
    3 once a week   6 never .... 198. ____

199. In which way do your friends help you?
    1 they lend me whatever I need
    2 they lend me money
    3 we exchange whatever we can spare
    4 they help me with some work
    5 they give me moral support
    6 they cannot help me because they do not have anything
    7 there is no mutual help
    8 other .... 199. ____

200. Use the above codes for the second answer .... 200. ____

201. Use the above codes for the third answer .... 201. ____

202. In which way do you help your friends?
    1 I lend them whatever they need
    2 I lend them money
    3 we exchange whatever we can spare
    4 I help them with some work
    5 I give them moral support
    6 I cannot help them because I do not have anything
    7 there is no mutual help
    8 other .... 202. ____

203. Use the above codes for the second answer .... 203. ____

204. Use the above codes for the third answer .... 204. ____

205. How many *neighbours* do you have?   205. ....

206. How many of your neighbours do you have contact with?............... 206. ____

If not with all: 207. Why do you not have contact with some of them?
    1   we have not become acquainted yet
    2   they are reserved
    3   we do not trust them
    4   they are proud
    5   one of our neighbours does not like to communicate with us
    6   the house of one of our neighbours has its entrance on the other side
    7   we do not understand the language of one of our neighbours
    8   other .... 207. _____

208. Use codes above for the second answer .... 208. _____

209. Use codes above for the third answer .... 209. _____

210. Do you visit the neighbours with whom you have contact?
    1   frequently
    2   sometimes   3   we always meet outside ... 210. _____

211. Do these neighbours visit you?
    1   frequently
    2   sometimes   3   we always meet outside.... 211. _____

212. In which way do your neighbours help you?
    1   they lend me whatever I need
    2   they lend me money
    3   we exchange whatever we can spare
    4   they help me with some work
    5   they give me moral support
    6   they cannot help me, because they do not have anything
    7   there is no mutual help
    8   other .... 212. _____

213. Use the above codes for the second answer .... 213. _____

214. Use the above codes for the third answer .... 214. _____

215. In which way do you help your neighbours?
    1   I lend them whatever they need
    2   I lend them money
    3   we exchange whatever we can spare
    4   I help them with some work
    5   I give them moral support
    6   I cannot help them, because I do not have anything
    7   there is no mutual help
    8   other .... 215. _____

216. Use the above codes for the second answer .... 216. _____

Appendix 1 311

217. Use the above codes for the third answer .... 217. ____

218. Everybody has conflicts once in a while with family members, neighbours or other persons.
    What are, in your opinion, the main reasons for your conflicts?
    1 misunderstandings
    2 some people envy you
    3 some have inferiority complexes
    4 some are proud
    5 other .... 218. ____

VI. Degree of satisfaction or depression

219. With which of the following statements can you identify yourself most?
    1 life is very difficult for me these days
    2 life is difficult
    3 life is neither easy nor difficult / it is dull
    4 life is easy for me now
    5 life is very easy for me now
    6 other statements about your life........ .... 219. ____

220. Right now:
    1 I suffer a lot
    2 I suffer but not a lot
    3 I do not suffer .... 220. ____

221. With which of the following statements can you identify yourself best?
    1 I am very unhappy - very miserable
    2 I am unhappy - miserable
    3 I am neither happy nor unhappy
    4 I am happy - I am fine
    5 I am very happy - very fine .... 221. ____

222. What is your main problem right now
    1 food   8 the war situation
    2 my house   9 the lack of a field
    3 the low wage   10 water supply
    4 I am afraid of criminals   11 transport
    5 afraid of the armed bandits   12 lack of places in schools
    6 unemployment   13 other problems................. 222. ____

223. Which is the second most difficult problem you have?
    (use codes as above) .... 223. ____

224. Which is the third most difficult problem?
    (use codes as above) .... 224. ____

225. When was life most difficult for you?
   1 before independence
   2 right after independence until approximately 1981
   3 between around 1981 to. 1987
   4 after 1987
   5 now .... 225. _____

226. With which of the following statements can you identify yourself best?
   1 I have not been cheerful for a long time
   2 I am rarely cheerful
   3 I am cheerful sometimes
   4 I am cheerful not every day but frequently
   5 I am cheerful almost every day...................................... .... 226. _____

227. Today you feel:
   1 very depressed, very sad
   2 depressed, sad
   3 somewhat depressed, a little sad
   4 not depressed, not sad .... 227. _____

228. Have you ever heard of PRE
   1 yes   2 no .... 228. _____

If yes: 229. What is PRE in your opinion?
   1 the multi-party system   3 an economic programme
   2 a political programme   4 I don't know
                                      5 other   .... 229. _____

230. During the last 3 years:
   1 life improved in many ways
   2 life improved in some ways
   3 for me life did not change much after 1987
   4 life has become more difficult
   5 life has become much more difficult .... 230. _____

231. The state of your house during the last 3 years:
   1 has become worse
   2 has not changed
   3 has improved .... 231. _____

232. Of the following aspects of your life, which do you like most?
   1 the life in town   5 one of the new parities
   2 your work   6 sports
   3 your church   7 Frelimo
   4 music   8 life in the rural areas .... 232. _____

233. Which of these aspects do you like second best?
   (use codes as above) .... 233. ____

234. Which of these aspects do you like third best?
   (use codes as above).................................... 234. ____

235. Which aspects of your life do you think will improve when the war is over?
   1 I can go back to my home area
   2 I can produce again on my field in the rural areas
   3 I can go to the countryside and buy things cheaper
   4 I can visit my relatives
   5 my personal life will not change much after the end of the war
   6 other .... 235. ____

236. How do you think life will change in the next five years?
   1 it will improve
   2 it will not change much
   3 it will become worse .... 236. ____

314 *Globalization, urban progress, urban problems, rural disadvantages*

Appendix 2: Demographic characteristics, level of urbanization, GDP, HDI, HPI of large Third World countries

Table 1 Demographic characteristics and income of major Third World countries[a] Adapted from Gugler (ed) 1988

Region/country	Population (millions) mid-1985	GNP per capita (dollars) 1985[b]	Urban population as percentage of total population 1985[c]	Urban growth, average annual growth-rate (per cent) 1965–80	Urban growth, average annual growth-rate (per cent) 1980–5	Population growth, average annual growth-rate (per cent) 1980–5
East Asia						
Burma	37	190	24	2.8	2.8	2.0
China[d]	1040	310	22	2.6	3.3	1.2
Indonesia	162	530	25	4.7	2.3	2.1
Korea, North	20	930	63	4.6	3.8	2.5
Korea, South	41	2150	64	5.7	2.5	1.5
Malaysia	16	2000	38	4.5	4.0	2.5
Philippines	55	580	39	4.0	3.2	2.5
Taiwan	19	2670	51	5.4	3.1	1.6
Thailand	52	800	18	4.6	3.2	2.1
Vietnam	62	240	20	4.1	3.4	2.6
South Asia						
Bangladesh	101	150	18	8.0	7.9	2.6
India	765	270	25	3.6	3.9	2.2
Nepal	17	160	7	5.1	5.6	2.4
Pakistan	96	380	29	4.3	4.8	3.1
Sri Lanka	16	380	21	2.3	8.4	1.4
Middle East and North Africa						
Afghanistan[e]	17	230	17	5.6	6.2	2.6
Algeria	22	2550	43	3.8	3.7	3.3
Egypt	49	610	46	2.9	3.4	2.8
Iran	45	1690	54	5.5	4.6	2.9
Iraq	16	1930	70	5.3	6.3	3.6
Morocco	22	560	44	4.2	4.2	2.5
Saudi Arabia	12	8850	72	8.5	6.1	4.2
Syria	11	1570	49	4.5	5.5	3.6
Turkey	50	1080	46	4.3	4.4	2.5

Appendix 2 315

Subsaharan Africa					
Cameroon	10	810	42	8.1	7.0	3.2
Ethiopia	42	110	15	6.6	3.7	2.5
Ghana	13	380	32	3.4	3.9	3.3
Ivory Coast	10	660	45	8.7	6.9	3.8
Kenya	20	290	20	9.0	6.3	4.1
Madagascar	10	240	21	5.7	5.3	3.2
Mozambique	14	160	19	11.8	5.3	2.6
Nigeria	100	800	30	4.8	5.2	3.3
South Africa	32	2010	56	2.6	3.3	2.5
Sudan	22	300	21	5.1	4.8	2.7
Tanzania	22	290	14	8.7	8.3	3.5
Uganda	15	*240*	7	4.1	3.0	3.0
Zaïre	31	170	39	7.2	8.4	3.0
Latin America					
Argentina	31	2130	84	2.2	1.9	1.6
Brazil	136	1640	73	4.5	4.0	2.3
Chile	12	1430	83	2.6	2.1	1.7
Colombia	28	1320	67	3.5	2.8	1.9
Cuba	10	*1180*	71	2.7	0.8	0.8
Mexico	79	2080	69	4.5	3.6	2.6
Peru	19	1010	68	4.1	3.8	2.3
Venezuela	17	3080	85	4.5	3.5	2.9

[a] This table includes all Third World countries with a population over 9.5 million in mid-1985.
[b] GNP per capita figures in italics are for 1982 and from a different source; they are not strictly comparable with the other GNP per capita figures.
[c] Urban percentages are based on different national definitions of what is 'urban', and cross-country comparisons should be interpreted with caution.
[d] The data for China include Hong Kong, Macao, and Taiwan.
[e] The demographic data for Afghanistan are for 1983, the growth figures for 1965–73 and 1973–83.

Sources: All data from World Bank (1987: annex Table 1, 27, and 33), except GNP per capita figures in italics (for 1982) from Sivard (1985: statistical annex Table III), demographic data for Taiwan from China (1986: Table 1 and Supplementary Table 3), demographic data for Afghanistan (for 1983) from World Bank (1985: annex Tables 19 and 22).

316 *Globalization, urban progress, urban problems, rural disadvantages*

Table 2 Demographic, economic and human development indicators of large developing countries[a] Adapted from Gugler (ed) 1997

Country/region	Total population	Annual population growth-rate (%)		Urban population[b] (% of total population)		Urban population annual growth-rate (%)		Real GDP[c] per capita (US$)	Infant mortality (per 1,000 life births)
	1993	1960–93	1993–2000	1960	1993	1960–93	1993–2000	1993	1993
East Asia									
China[d]	1,196.4	1.8	1.0	19	29	3.1	3.8	2,330	44
North Korea	23.0	2.3	1.7	40	61	3.6	2.3	3,000	24
South Korea	44.1	1.7	0.9	28	79	5.0	2.3	9,710	11
Taiwan[e]	20.9	1.8[f]	—	—	94	3.0[f]	—	—	5
South-East Asia									
Burma	44.6	2.2	2.1	19	26	3.1	3.7	650	82
Indonesia	191.7	2.1	1.5	15	34	4.7	4.2	3,270	56
Malaysia	19.2	2.6	2.1	27	52	4.8	3.6	8,360	13
Philippines	64.8	2.6	2.0	30	52	4.3	3.9	2,590	43
Singapore	2.8	1.6	0.9	100	100	1.6	0.9	19,350	6
Thailand	57.6	2.4	1.0	13	20	3.8	2.8	6,350	36
Vietnam	71.3	2.2	2.1	15	20	3.2	3.5	1,040	42
South Asia									
Bangladesh	115.2	2.5	2.2	5	17	6.3	5.4	1,290	106
India	901.5	2.2	1.8	18	26	3.4	3.0	1,240	81
Nepal	20.8	2.4	2.6	3	13	6.8	6.9	1,000	98
Pakistan	132.9	3.0	2.8	22	34	4.3	4.6	2,160	89
Sri Lanka	17.9	1.8	1.2	18	22	2.4	2.7	3,030	17
West Asia									
Afghanistan	17.7	1.5	6.0	8	19	4.3	8.2	800	163
Iran	64.2	3.4	2.2	34	58	5.0	3.1	5,380	34
Iraq	19.5	3.2	2.9	43	74	4.9	3.6	3,413	58
Kazakhstan	17.0	1.6	0.6	45	59	2.5	1.4	3,710	27[a]
Lebanon	2.8	1.3	2.3	40	86	3.7	2.9	2,500	34
Saudi Arabia	17.1	4.4	3.1	30	79	7.6	3.6	12,600	28
Syria	13.7	3.4	3.4	37	51	4.4	4.4	4,196	39
Turkey	59.6	2.4	1.8	30	66	4.9	3.7	4,210	64
Uzbekistan	21.9	2.9	2.2	34	41	3.4	2.8	2,510	28[a]
Yemen	13.2	2.8	3.7	9	32	6.8	6.6	1,600	119

Appendix 2   317

Africa								
Algeria	26.7	2.8	2.2	30	54	4.6	3.6	5,570	54
Angola	10.3	2.3	3.5	10	31	5.7	6.0	674	123
Cameroon	12.5	2.6	2.9	14	43	6.2	4.9	2,220	62
Côte d'Ivoire	13.3	3.9	3.3	19	42	6.4	4.9	1,620	91
Egypt	60.3	2.4	2.0	38	44	2.9	2.6	3,800	66
Ethiopia	51.9	2.5	3.0	6	13	4.7	5.2	420	118
Ghana	16.4	2.7	3.0	23	35	4.0	4.3	2,000	80
Kenya	26.4	3.6	3.1	7	26	7.6	6.0	1,400	69
Madagascar	13.9	2.9	3.2	11	26	5.7	5.8	700	91
Malawi	10.5	3.4	2.1	4	13	6.8	5.0	710	142
Mali	10.1	2.6	3.1	11	26	5.2	5.7	530	158
Morocco	25.9	2.5	1.9	29	47	4.0	3.0	3,270	67
Mozambique	15.1	2.2	3.3	4	31	9.0	7.4	640	147
Nigeria	105.3	2.8	2.9	14	38	5.8	5.0	1,540	84
South Africa	39.7	2.5	2.2	47	50	2.8	3.1	3,127	52
Sudan	26.6	2.7	2.7	10	24	5.3	4.7	1,350	77
Tanzania	28.0	3.1	2.8	5	23	8.2	5.9	630	85
Uganda	19.9	3.4	3.1	5	12	6.2	5.6	910	115
Zaire	41.2	3.0	3.1	22	29	3.8	4.4	300	92
Zimbabwe	10.7	3.2	2.2	13	31	6.0	4.6	2,100	67
Latin America								
Argentina	33.8	1.5	1.2	74	88	2.0	1.5	8,350	24
Brazil	156.5	2.4	1.6	45	77	4.0	2.4	5,500	57
Chile	13.8	1.8	1.5	68	84	2.5	1.6	8,900	15
Colombia	34.0	2.3	1.5	48	72	3.6	2.2	5,790	37
Cuba	10.9	1.4	0.7	55	75	2.3	1.2	3,000	12
Ecuador	11.0	2.8	2.0	34	57	4.4	3.3	4,400	49
Guatemala	10.0	2.9	2.9	32	41	3.6	4.1	3,400	48
Mexico	90.0	2.7	1.9	51	74	3.9	2.5	7,010	35
Peru	22.9	2.6	1.9	46	71	3.9	2.5	3,320	64
Venezuela	20.9	3.1	2.1	67	92	4.1	2.5	8,360	23
Developing countries[b]	4,299	2.2	1.8	22	36	3.8	3.5	2,696	70
Industrial countries	1,209	0.8	0.4	6.1	7.3	1.4	0.7	15,136	13
WORLD	5,508	1.9	1.5	34	44	2.7	2.5	5,428	63

Notes to Table 2

a   This table includes all countries with a population of at least 10 million in mid-1993 (and Lebanon and Singapore each of which are the focus of a chapter).
b   Percentages of the population living in urban areas are based on different national definitions of what is 'urban' and cross-country comparisons should be made with caution. For national definitions of urban areas see United Nations (1995) *1993 Demographic Yearbook* (New York: United Nations), notes to table 6.
c   Real Gross Domestic Product is based on conversion of GDP purchasing power parity.
d   The data of China includes Taiwan.
e   The data for Taiwan is from Republic of China (1995) *Statistical Yearbook of the Republic of China 1995* (Taipei: Directorate General of Budget, Accounting and Statistics).
f   The data is for 1965 - 1993.
g   The data is for 1994, from World Bank (1996), *World Development Report 1996: From Plan to Market* (New York: Oxford University Press).
h   The summary measures for developing countries and the world are appropriately weighted values, except for total population.

Sources: United Nations Development Programme (1996), *Human Development Report 1996* (New York: Oxford University Press), except as noted.

Table 3 Indices of large Third World countries for which not more than one index was missing

country/region	level of urbanization 1995	HDI 1995	HPI 1995	real GDP p. c. 1995 rounded in hundreds US$	country/region	level of urbanization 1995	HDI 1995	HPI 1995	real GDP p. c. 1995 rounded in hundreds US$
East Asia					Ivory Coast	43	37		17
China	30	65	17	29	Egypt	45	61	34	38
North Korea	61	77		41	Ethiopia	15	25	55	4
South Korea	81	89		116	Ghana	36	47	32	20
South-East Asia					Kenya	29	46	27	14
Indonesia	35	68	20	40	Madagascar	26	35	48	7
Malaysia	54	83		96	Malawi	13	33	48	8
Philippines	54	68	17	28	Mali	27	24	53	6
Thailand	20	84	12	27	Marocco	52	56	40	35
Vietnam	19	56	26	12	Mozambique	34	28	49	10
South Asia					Nigeria	40	39	41	13
Bangladesh	18	37	47	14	South Africa	49	72		43
India	27	45	36	14	Sudan	31	34	43	11
Nepal	10	35		11	Tanzania	24	36	40	6
Pakistan	34	45	46	22	Uganda	13	34	42	14
Sri Lanka	22	72	21	34	Kongo Dem. R.	29	38	41	4
West Asia					Zimbabwe	32	51	25	21
Iran		59	76	22	55	**Latin America**				
Iraq	75	54	30	32	Argentina	88	89		85
Lebanon	88	80		50	Brazil	78	81		59
Saudi Arabia	83	78		85	Chile	84	89	4	99
Syria	52	75	21	54	Colombia	73	85	11	54
Turkey	69	78		55	Cuba	76	73		31
Yemen	34	36	49	16	Ecuador	59	77	15	46
Africa					Guatemala	39	62	29	37
Algeria	56	75	27	56	Mexico	73	85	11	68
Angola	31	34		18	Peru	71	73	23	39
Cameroon	45	48	31	24	Venezuela	86	86		80

Sources: *Human Development Report 1998;* published for the United Nations Development Programme, Oxford University Press, Oxford 1998.
Table 2 of this appendix must also be considered as source for the selection and order of countries, for comparative purposes of figures and for consideration of the notes to table 2.

320 Globalization, urban progress, urban problems, rural disadvantages

Appendix 3: Additional tables

The tables in this appendix correspond either to a figure in the respective chapter or to a three column table (areas only). If corresponding to a figure, it serves the purpose of showing more details to readers interested in those details and in addition, the differences between the two investigated provinces are shown in six columns (by areas and by provinces). If corresponding to a three column table, normaly only the additional breakdown by province is shown. To spare the busy reader from looking at too many tables, some of them have been ommitted in the text, but appear in this appendix for particular interests.

Additional tables to chapter 3

The tables 3.1a to 3.1e all relate to income either of the household heads or of the entire household by area only as well as by area and province

Table 3.1a The monthly wage of household heads

	urban	peri-urban	rural
nothing	6	10	43
less than 24 contos	2	14	21
25-50	6	42	25
51-100	42	26	2
101-200	27	5	9
201-500	12	2	--
more than 500	6	--	--
n	(52)	(303)	(44)

Table 3.1b The monthly wage of household heads by province

| | urban | | peri-urban | | rural | |
	M	B	M	B	M	S
nothing	8	4	6	21	18	68
less than 24 contos	--	4	16	8	18	23
25-50	4	8	41	44	41	9
51-100	50	34	27	25	5	--
101-200	23	31	6	3	18	--
201-500	15	8	3	--	--	--
more than 500	--	11	1	--	--	--
n	(26)	(26)	(226)	(77)	(22)	(22)

M = Maputo city or Maputo province; B = Beira; S = Sofala province

100 of 'n' would be	26	32	244	86	30	40
The answer was given by	100%	81%	93%	90%	73%	55%

Table 3.1c The monthly income of households

	urban	peri-urban	rural
nothing	--	--	10
less than 24 contos	2	4	24
25 - 50	8	38	24
51 - 100	25	37	24
101 - 200	42	17	17
201 - 500	15	3	--
more than 500	4	1	--
n	(48)	(252)	(29)

Table 3.1d: The monthly income of households by province

	urban		peri-urban		rural	
	M	B	M	B	M	S
nothing	--	--	--	2	14	--
less than 24 contos	--	5	5	2	10	63
25 - 50	8	10	35	48	24	25
51 - 100	28	24	37	39	29	13
101 - 200	40	48	19	10	24	--
201 - 500	20	9	4	--	--	--
more than 500	4	5	1	--	--	--
n	(25)	(21)	(189)	(62)	(21)	(8)
100% of 'n' would be	26	32	244	86	30	40
the question was answered by	96%	66%	77%	72%	70%	20%

Table 3.1e Comparison of the percentages of the *transformed* total income of households of the cement city and the peri-urban areas of *Maputo* of this study with the percentages of the IAF of entire Maputo

	urban	peri-urban	IAF
less than 100 contos	8	40	29
100 - 200	28	36	40
200 - 400	40	18	16
400 +	24	6	15
n	(25)	(189)	(1112)

Table 3.2a Educational level of household heads

	urban	peri-urban	rural
without formal education	2	19	54
between first and third class	7	26	30
primary school 1	24	33	10
primary school 2	22	15	6
secondary school	24	5	--
pre-university college	5	1	--
elementary technical school	--	--	--
medium level technical school	9	1	--
higher education	7	1	--
n	(58)	(328)	(70)

Table 3.2b Educational level of household heads by province

	urban		peri-urban		rural	
	M	B	M	B	M	S
formal education	--	3	16	28	53	56
1st to 3rd class	8	6	28	21	27	32
primary school 1	15	31	33	32	13	7
primary school 2	27	19	16	11	7	5
secondary school	35	16	5	6	--	--
pre-university college	8	3	1	--	--	--
elementary technical school	--	--	0.4	--	--	--
basic technical school	4	12	0.4	1	--	--
higher education	4	9	0.4	1	--	--
n	(26)	(32)	(242)	(85)	(30)	(41)

322 Globalization, urban progress, urban problems, rural disadvantages

Table 3.3a The participation in the labour force of the household heads

	urban	peri-urban	rural
government	40	38	5
private sector	25	18	10
co-operative	--	1	2
domestic worker	--	1	--
trader	4	1	--
business woman/man	5	1	--
working mainly in the field	2	7	44
informal sector	--	3	3
working occasionally	4	5	11
unemployed	--	3	3
retired	4	3	--
housewife	14	19	21
others	3	1	2
n	(57)	(324)	(63)

Table 3.3b The participation in the labour force of the household heads by province

	urban		peri-urban		rural	
	M	B	M	B	M	S
government	46	36	36	42	4	5
private sector	27	23	18	15	17	5
co-operative	--	--	1	--	--	3
house servant	--	--	1	--	--	--
trader	--	7	1	--	--	--
business woman/man	4	7	2	--	--	--
mainly in the field	--	3	2		71	(33+)28
informal sector	--	--	4	2	--	5
occasionally	4	3	5	4	8	12
unemployed	--	--	2	5	--	5
retired	4	3	3	5	--	--
housewife	15	13	18	21	--	33
others	--	6	2	--	--	2
n	(26)	(31)	(239)	(85)	(24)	(39)

Table 3.4a Household size

	urban	peri-urban	rural
1	3	2	3
2 - 4	24	17	39
5 - 7	47	41	39
8 - 10	14	26	16
11 - 13	7	10	1
14 - 16	2	2	1
17 - 19	2	1	1
20 and more	--	--	--
n	(58)	(329)	(70)

Appendix 3   323

Table 3.4b Household size by province

	urban		peri-urban			rural
	M	B	M	B	M	S
1	8	3	2	1	--	5
2 - 4	23	25	14	25	27	49
5 - 7	50	44	38	51	43	34
8 - 10	8	19	30	18	23	9
11 - 13	8	6	11	6	--	2
14 - 16	--	3	3	--	3	--
17 - 19	4	--	2	--	3	--
20 and more	--	--	1	--	--	--
n	(26)	(32)	(243)	(85)	(30)	(41)

Table 3.5a Age of the household heads by province

	urban		peri-urban			rural
	M	B	M	B	M	S
16 - 20	4	3	1	--	--	--
21 - 25	8	9	5	4	--	11
26 - 30	15	6	14	12	3	18
31 - 40	31	34	26	32	31	16
41 - 50	35	38	26	27	21	40
51 - 60	8	3	20	18	21	13
61 - 70	--	3	5	6	21	--
71 - 80	--	3	1	2	3	3
81 +	--	--	1	--	--	--
n	(26)	(32)	(242)	(85)	(29)	(38)

Table 3.6a Marital status of household heads by province

	urban		peri-urban			rural
	M	B	M	B	M	S
single	23	--	5	1	--	5
married formally	39	66	17	15	7	8
married traditionally	15	13	45	64	73	60
married informally	12	19	19	6	17	3
separated	8	--	4	--	--	5
divorced	--	3	2	2	--	5
widow/er	4	--	9	12	3	15
n	(26)	(32)	(241)	(85)	(30)	(40)

Table 3.7a Wives of household heads

	urban	peri-urban	rural
one wife	93	89	85
two wives	6	10.5	13
three wives	--	--	3
five wives	--	0.5	--
n	(33)	(206)	(39)

Table 3.7b Wives of household heads by province

	urban		peri-urban		rural	
	M	B	M	B	M	S
one wife	87	100	89.3	88	92	73
two wives	13	--	10	12	4	27
three wives	--	--	--	--	4	--
five wives	--	--	0.7	--	--	--
n	(15)	(18)	(150)	(56)	(24)	(15)

Additional tables to chapter 4

Table 4.1 Discontentment with income by province

	urban		peri-urban		rural	
	M	B	M	B	M	S
very contented	--	--	2	--	6	--
contented	27	46	10	11	39	21
neither contented nor discont.	23	15	26	14	28	46
discontented	42	19	45	43	17	21
very discontented	8	19	18	31	11	12
n	(26)	(26)	(189)	(70)	(18)	(33)

Table 4.2 Dissatisfaction with the level of education by province

	urban		peri-urban		rural	
	M	B	M	B	M	S
very contented	23	3	7	8	--	3
contented	4	32	11	25	11	29
neither contented nor discont.	8	13	13	10	7	3
discontented	58	52	49	51	57	61
very discontented	8	--	20	6	25	5
n	(26)	(31)	(227)	(79)	(28)	(38)

Table 4.3 Satisfaction with the participation in the labour force by province

	urban		peri-urban		rural	
	M	B	M	B	M	S
very contented	58	39	26	20	28	13
contented	29	50	43	53	56	62
neither contented nor discont.	4	4	17	16	16	15
discontented	8	8	10	10	--	5
very discontented	--	--	4	1	--	5
n	(24)	(26)	(216)	(70)	(25)	(39)

Table 4.4 Satisfaction with job conditions by province

	urban		peri-urban		rural	
	M	B	M	B	M	S
very contented	63	36	28	16	12	3
contented	33	54	51	63	72	66
neither contented nor discont.	--	7	15	10	12	24
discontented	4	4	4	10	4	8
very discontented	--	--	3	2	--	--
n	(240	(28)	(192)	(62)	(25)	(38)

Appendix 3

Additional tables to chapter 5

Table 5.1a Main reasons for migration by province

	urban		peri-urban		rural	
	M	B	M	B	M	S
marriage	7	9	14	13	18	16
employment	27	17	44	44	27	29
education	20	17	9	11	5	--
better living conditions	20	9	11	13	4	7
joining family members	7	9	7	7	5	3
war	--	13	9	11	32	32
other reasons	20	26	5	1	9	13
n	(15)	(23)	(202)	(72)	(22)	(31)

Table 5.1b Time of arrival in the respective bairro by province

	urban		peri-urban		rural	
	M	B	M	B	M	S
less than 6 months ago	4	6	--	--	--	--
about 6 months ago	--	--	1	--	--	3
about 1 year ago	8	3	2	--	--	3
about 1 1/2 year ago	--	--	2	1	23	--
2 years ago	4	9	5	--	7	--
3 - 5 years ago	12	6	14	7	17	15
6 - 10 years ago	8	22	18	7	43	21
11 - 16 years ago	54	19	18	23	10	8
17 or more years ago	11	34	39	62	--	51
n	(26)	(32)	(228)	(84)	(30)	(39)

Additional tables to chapter 10

Table 10.1a Scale from 'very unhappy' to 'very happy' by province

	urban		peri-urban		rural	
	M	B	M	B	M	S
very unhappy	12	7	21	25	17	36
unhappy	16	13	25	25	27	26
neither happy nor unhappy	28	42	39	34	37	33
happy	40	29	14	15	20	5
very happy	4	10	0.4	1	--	--
n	(25)	(31)	(241)	(83)	(30)	(39)

Table 10.2a Scale of being cheerful from 'very rarely' to 'almost every day' by province

	urban		peri-urban		rural	
	M	B	M	B	M	S
never cheerful since long	4	3	13	21	7	39
I am rarely cheerful	8	9	24	28	17	28
I am sometimes cheerful	40	31	38	28	45	23
frequently cheerful	24	31	20	15	24	8
cheerful almost every day	24	25	5	7	7	3
n	(25)	(32)	(242)	(81)	(29)	(39)

326 Globalization, urban progress, urban problems, rural disadvantages

Table 10.3a Degree of suffering at this time by province

	urban		peri-urban		rural	
	M	B	M	B	M	S
I suffer a lot at this time	52	19	58	60	50	69
I suffer, but not too much	40	69	39	38	40	28
I do not suffer at all	8	12	3	2	10	3
n	(25)	(32)	(243)	(84)	(30)	(39)

Table 10.4a Degree of depression on the day of the interview by province

	urban		peri-urban		rural	
	M	B	M	B	M	S
very depressed	--	6	9	12	3	21
depressed	12	3	18	16	17	13
a little depressed	19	22	24	32	20	36
not depressed	69	69	49	40	60	31
n	(26)	(32)	(238)	(82)	(30)	(39)

Table 10.5a Time periods in which life was or is most difficult by province

	urban		peri-urban		rural	
	M	B	M	B	M	S
before independence	--	3	3	5	3	--
after independence	20	13	11	4	3	5
from about 81 to 87	20	32	13	19	23	37
after 87	8	23	31	41	43	16
now	52	29	42	31	27	42
n	(25)	(31)	(238)	(80)	(30)	(38)

Table 10.6a Overall changes of life since the introduction of PRE by province

	urban		peri-urban		rural	
	M	B	M	B	M	S
improved in many aspects	23	22	9	5	10	--
improved in some aspects	23	25	24	16	10	15
did not change much	12	6	4	16	14	13
life became difficult	27	19	30	31	41	28
life became very difficult	15	28	33	32	24	44
n	(26)	(32)	(242)	(80)	(29)	(39)

Table 10.7a Housing in the last three years by province

	urban		peri-urban		rural	
	M	B	M	B	M	S
conditions worsened	28	16	22	51	20	62
remained the same	24	58	57	42	57	21
improved	48	26	21	7	23	18
n	(25)	(31)	(242)	(83)	(30)	(39)

Appendix 4: Pedido de despensa (Permission to stay home from work on the day of the interview)

REPÚBLICA DE MOÇAMBIQUE

COMISSÃO NACIONAL DO PLANO
INSTITUTO NACIONAL DE PLANEAMENTO FÍSICO

À
DIRECÇÃO DA EMPRESA _____

Sua referência: Sua comunicação: Nossa referência:
Assunto: PEDIDO DE DESPENSA

     A fim de ser inquerido sobre problemas de Habitação Infraestruturas e mento Sociais, solicita-se à Direcção dessa Empresa, despensar o (a) vosso (a) lhador (s) _____
no dia _____/_____/1991.

     Secretaria do Instituto Nacional do Planeamento Físico
Maputo, aos 21 de Junho de 1991.

O CHEFE DE SECRETARIA
VASCO MHATSAVE

VP/lc

REPÚBLICA POPULAR DE MOÇAMBIQUE

COMISSÃO PROVINCIAL DO PLANO

SERVIÇO PROVINCIAL DO PLANEAMENTO FISICO DE SOFALA-BEIRA

Rua Major Serpa 7. Andar
Telef. 25734/26139 — Beira

À
DIRECÇÃO DA EMPRESA _____
_____
_____

Sua Referência   Data   Nossa Referência   Data
      __/__/__   __/__/__

ASSUNTO: PEDIDO DE DISPENSA

      Afim de ser inquerido sobre problemas de Habitação Infraestruturas e Equipamento Sociais, solicita-se à Direcção dessa Empresa, despe o (a) vosso (a) trabalhador (a) _____ no dia _____/_____/1991.-

      Secretaria do Instituto Nacional de Planeamento Físico de So
- Beira, aos 26 de Setembro de 1991.-

Appendix 5: The complexity of necessary interventions for an 'alternative' development

Integrating urban and rural *policies* with macro-economic, global, social, demographic, environmental, and cultural policies;
Decentralizing urban and rural *policies* to sub-national and local levels;
Increasing affordability through *housing assistance for the poor;*
Developing environmentally sound and *affordable building material;*
Promoting shelter renovation, rehabilitation and *upgrading;*
Facilitating *community-based production of housing;*
Ensuring *access to land* and legal security of tenure;
Eradicating legal and social barriers to *access to land for women;*
Reviewing restricting planning systems and *standards;*
Ensuring access to basic infrastructure and services;
Improving planning, construction *and maintenance of infrastructure;*
Reducing vulnerability of vulnerable groups;
Encouraging partnership among public, private and voluntary sectors;
Stimul ating income generating, productive *employment opportunities;*
Promoting *access to credit* and innovative banking alternatives;
Promoting micro- and co-operative enterprises;
Developing the full potential of young people by *education and training;*
Promoting *disabilities-sensitive planning* of human settlements;
Preventing, *reducing* and eliminating violence and *crime;*
Increasing awareness of the importance of *family planning;*
Improving the health and well being of people.
Setting *environmental standards;*
Preventing air, water and soil *pollution;*
Promoting access to c*lean water;*
Promoting disposal of sewage, waste water and solid waste;
Promoting productive and recreational *green belts* around cities;
Promoting efficient and *sustainable energy use.*
Supporting an *integrated transport policy;*
Discouraging the increasing growth of *private motorized traffic;*
Promoting the *conservation of cultural, historical and artistic heritage;*
Improving natural and human-made *disaster prevention;*
Strengthening the capacity of both *central and local government;*
Encouraging and *supporting participation and civic engagement;*

Source: Slightly shortened and changed version of 38 policies identified by the Forum of Researchers on Human Settlements, (The Forum's Project, June 1998) using the Habitat Agenda, the Istanbul Declaration, papers of UNCHS-Habitat, EU Working Documents, UN World Resources and similar documents amounting to 13 in total.